Praise

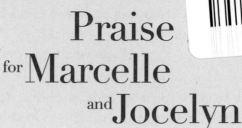

"These two women don't just think outside the box, they think *about* the box and how to keep from getting trapped in it."

—Administrative assistant, Chicago, IL

"From the first time I ever spoke to Jocelyn and Marcelle, they encouraged me to think bigger and be bolder. It has paid off. Following their advice, I finally got noticed and promoted."

—Political consultant, Nashua, NH

"I have an MBA, and let me tell you, the most useful, practical, and powerful business advice for women I've ever heard came from my phone calls with Marcelle and Jocelyn."

—Product manager, Cincinnati, OH

"If you could borrow personalities like library books, I'd take Jocelyn and Marcelle's out for every job interview, every meeting, and probably some dates."

—Managing editor, Hoboken, NJ

"These two are motivated by the pure desire to see good people do better. They are generous, genuine, and the most hilarious mentors ever. I owe them a lot."

—Department store buyer, Washington, DC

"I love this book like a big sister who will never bullshit me, who will set me straight when I'm out of line, will never steer me in the wrong direction, and will think the world of me even when I blow it."

—Public relations director, Philadelphia, PA

"I've been out there in the corporate business world for long enough that I felt like I knew it all. Speaking with Marcelle and Jocelyn made me realize that I didn't know the half of it."

—Magazine researcher, Dallas, TX

"All I have to say is, 'Mysteries Solved.' I didn't know exactly *what* I was doing wrong at work, but something sure as hell felt wrong. Jocelyn and Marcelle made me realize that my problems at work weren't about what others were doing to me, but what I was doing to myself!"

—TV producer, New York, NY

"Marcelle and Jocelyn have been my confessors, personal cheerleaders, shrinks, and career advisors. I don't know what I'd do without them."

—Inventory control manager, Augusta, GA

"They tell me to my face what I need to know to move ahead. It's bottom-line advice."

—VP accounting, advertising agency, Boston, MA

"My new mantra is, 'Don't take it personally.' Marcelle and Jocelyn convinced me to try it for a week. I did. It worked. Now nothing drives me crazy about my boss or coworkers. Stuff just slides off my back."

—Investment banker, San Francisco, CA

"Jocelyn and Marcelle give me answers to questions that I didn't even know I had."

—IT director, San Francisco, CA

"I finally got all the *easy* answers about how to handle the *insane* politics at work."

—Insurance broker, Stamford, CT

"Marcelle and Jocelyn are so candid, and their take on the whole work scene is like nothing I've ever read before, and ten times as useful."

—Talent agent, New York, NY

the Big Sister's Guide to the World of Work

The Inside Rules Every Working Girl Must Know

Marcelle Langan DiFalco and
Jocelyn Greenky Herz

A Fireside Book
Published by Simon & Schuster
New York   London   Toronto   Sydney

FIRESIDE
Rockefeller Center
1230 Avenue of the Americas
New York, NY 10020

Girl icon graphic by Eric Stoll

FIRESIDE and colophon are registered trademarks of Simon & Schuster, Inc.

For information regarding special discounts for bulk purchases,
please contact Simon & Schuster Special Sales
at 1-800-456-6798 or business@simonandschuster.com

Designed by Ruth Lee-Mui

Manufactured in the United States of America

10   9   8   7   6   5   4   3   2   1

Library of Congress Cataloging-in-Publication Data is available.

ISBN 0-7432-4710-8

To my first two bosses
Maureen H. Langan (aka Mom) and William J. Langan
(aka The Geezer). Thanks for teaching me the
meaning of the word R-E-S-P-E-C-T.

—M.L.D.

To my husband, Erik, and son, Ethan.
Erik has lovingly supported me in no uncertain
terms to follow my dreams.

—J.G.H.

Acknowledgments

**If It Were Not for These Amazing People,
You'd Be Doing Something Else Right Now.**

To The Girls Who Call Us: thanks for all the laughs, the candor, for entrusting us with your stories, and especially for encouraging us to get off the phone and get our ideas onto the pages of this book.

To our amazing agent Alička Pistek: thanks for finding such a magnificent home for our book at Simon & Schuster. Thanks, too, girlfriend, for holding our hand when we needed it and for your relentless optimism and support.

To our brilliant editor, Doris Cooper, at Simon & Schuster: thanks for being our patient publishing mentor and for championing our concept and breathing life into our vision for it.

To Sara Schapiro (Doris Cooper's right-hand gal), and to every woman in entry-level administrative positions: the work you do is terrifically important and you'll never know just how much we appreciate it.

To our genius marketing guru at Simon & Schuster Sue Fleming: thanks millions and millions (and more millions we hope).

To John Reedy: thanks for the killer website design. You rule. (big sisterguide.com). To designer Eric Stoll, thanks for defining our attitude with a sassy icon. You rule too.

To our benefactors, those who made an indelible impact on our lives and careers by giving us a chance, by restoring our faith, by sharing their knowledge, by picking us up and brushing us off when we stumbled, and by making us laugh when we needed it most: *mille gracie.* You made it all worth the price of admission.

To our detractors, those who ignored us, misunderstood us, misinformed us, misdirected us, and/or for some inexplicable reason seemed to deplore us: were it not for the challenge presented by your mind-boggling behavior and insane antics, we would not have had a single thing to write about. Eternal thanks for all the great fodder.

—M and J

Marcelle would like to thank everyone who has ever taught her anything worth knowing: To Maureen, who taught me how to be a big sister (and when to stop being so much of one). To Paul, who taught me that tenacity always pays off. To Ryan for teaching me to be a mother. To Quinn for teaching me to be a better mother. To Liam for teaching me that I didn't have to be a perfect mother. To my brothers, James, Clayton, Roger, and Christopher, who taught me many things I probably should never have learned (but am glad I did). To Francine Kenney for teaching me that if you really want to be good at anything, the quest for learning should never end. To Gertrude and Dolores for teaching me that friendship is a lifelong affair. To Lee Ann and Wendy, who taught me that a lunch (or a good bra) can save your life. To Sister Karen Donohue for teaching me the common prepositions. To Dr. Warren Roberts for teaching me about the illuminated manuscripts. To Michael Batterberry for teaching me how to write without putting people into a deep sleep. To Trish Hackman, who taught me how to get in sync with my damn PDA. To Julie Mautner for teaching me how to Chat & Hum. To Beverly Stephen, Kelley Regan, Wendy Marcus, Monica Velgos, Debra Tristler, Cara Schlanger, and Christine Tsingos, who taught me that you never forget the best people you ever worked with. To Dr. Janice Marks and Dr. Anne Knott, who taught me that I infinitely prefer female doctors. To Michaela Reilly Wilson, who taught me that what you wear and the way you wear it counts. To Francis Jeffords, who taught me how to pull a weed and plant a seed. To Tom Matthews, who taught me most of what I know about wine. To Kevin Patrick, who taught me never to take a day for granted. Additionally: thanks to all the guys who asked me to proms (yeah, you too, Frank) and thanks to James Lamprecht, C.J. Zaharas, Jonathan Silvers, Robert Cenedella, Alan Richman, the Peck-Frame family, Karen Kirk, Rudi Sodamin, Becky Nezin, Bill and Linda Hanf, Greg Sandusky, Amber Clark, and my godchildren—Theresa Mary Emmanuel, Erin Ann, and Danny—for making me smile just to think about you. Thanks again to Simon & Schuster, this time for giving this book the publishing date of January 11, the birthday of James Brendan Golding, one of the finest and most courageous men who ever walked this earth. And, finally, to The Divine Boss of the Universe, thanks for use of the groovy planet.

—M.L.D.

To Patricia Caplen Greenky, thanks for being mom, sister, babysitter, eagle-eyed proofreader, and my ultimate girlfriend. To Lynn and Sharmon Greenky for being the ultimate big sisters. To Brett and Seth, thanks for doing what big brothers do best, torturing me into the toughness I needed to survive at work. To Paula Herz for your sweet optimism. To Leslie and Peter Tilles, thank you for a lifetime of devotion. To Tracy and Marc Zand and Ivy and Jonathan Palmer for being my oldest friends who don't tell all my deepest and darkest secrets. To Stuart Brownstein, the best friend, and business guru a girl could ever ask for. To Colin Cowie, my personal Professor Higgins, thanks for your fabulous guidance and friendship. To Diane Gordon, thanks for always being by my side and on my phone. To Craig Lamb, thanks for always being by Diane's side. To Lisa Rogen, Jason Alexander Nixon, and Paige Herman, thanks for your infectious enthusiasm for all my ideas. To Abby, my adopted little sister, thanks for being such a positive force of perspective in my life. To Tess Ghilaga, who always shows me the bright side of things, no matter how gloomy the outlook. To Samantha Reiss, thanks for being my very own personal publicist. To Mary Beth Wright, thanks for showing me the ropes and how to avoid getting hung up in them at work. To Ken Rosenblatt and Amy Prentiss, my closest cousins, thanks for your constant interest in my life. To Lissa Schaus, thanks for a lifetime (literally) of listening to my sagas. To Nick Matarazzo, my friend and mentor, thanks for all your insights. To Whitney Casey, thanks for putting me on CNN, let's do it again sometime soon. To Cella Irvine and Hart Hooton, thanks for the endless support. To Emma, thanks for all the love. To Jesse Kornbluth, thanks for keeping my inbox filled. To Susan Servetnick, thanks for the memories. To Laura Fernandez, thanks for bringing order to my life and spareribs to my table. To Sarah Cotsen, thanks for being the all-time volunteer. To Brigitta Horvat, thanks for being my international spokesperson. Thanks to Alyson and Al Galishoff, Gary Herman, Tia Wou, Jill Toom, Theresa Barone, Jill Abramson, Jaime Stevens, Jessica Freiser, Blu and Steven Kokin, Liz and Jordan Cahn, Lauree Dash, the Schlessingers, and the Sandows for cheering and nudging me forward. And finally, thanks to the brilliant and dedicated Dr. Joyce Wyden for always helping me to see new angles.

—J.G.H.

Contents

Intro Deductions

Hey.

Welcome to our book.

Let's start out with a question: Does the world really need yet another career book for women?

Answer: Yep. It needs this one.

There are about a gazillion "success" guides out there telling women how to manage their careers. Several of them are loaded with great hard-core advice for playing with the big boys and hauling your butt up the corporate ladder. So why are we all here today?

Well, it's like this: when we first started out, at the time in life when we *most* needed useful career advice, you couldn't have paid us enough to wade through one of those tomes. Standing in the bookstore, leafing through those dense books, it was clear that the lofty advice didn't directly address us, the Lost and Clueless. Jocelyn was a party girl dying for a big break that would land her in the entertainment field. Unfortunately, she was trapped in assistant-hell in a huge gray monolith personality-free advertising agency where everyone wore dark suits. She was suffocating and wanted to breathe in the fresh air of a fabulous paycheck, an exciting career, and a zestier office attire policy. Marcelle, who at the time couldn't decide if she wanted to be a starving actress or a starving writer, found herself in a dinky advertising agency where she spent her days staring at a phone that never rang. All she knew was she was starving anyway and couldn't even act like she enjoyed a job that was clearly nothing to write home about.

In those first few years we were in the working world, there was *nothing* on the bookshelves that spoke to us in words that we could relate to. We didn't have enough experience in the professional world even to understand what many of the über-accomplished authors were saying. And we couldn't stomach sober instruction from some overachieving Stanford MBA who had walked out of school into a six-figure salary and now wanted to tell us how she "made it," while in the meantime we were defaulting on our student loans because we were making so little money we had to choose between paying bills and eating.

No. What we really could have used back then was straight-from-the-hip advice from a woman who had risen through the corporate ranks, had made some hideous mistakes, and was ballsy enough to be truthful—and politically incorrect if need be—about what the real problems are when you are a woman blindly squirming around in the bottom half of the heap.

Basically what we wanted was a paperback to love and dog-ear to death filled with practical and true words to the wise from a funny, smart-mouthed Big Sister type who could get us to stop whining and start laughing, and who would tell us in no uncertain terms what to do at work and how to do it.

Problem was, there was no such book. Years later, after we had taken a few spins around the corporate block ourselves, we were stunned to discover that there *still* wasn't anything in the bookstores addressing the real issues women face every day that wasn't too stuffy, too self-important, too new age-y, or insufferably sanctimonious. A great, practical, down-to-earth and fun-to-read office guide for women simply didn't exist.

Until now, that is.

The book you now hold in your hands is the basic training manual we would have killed for at any point in our first years in the job market.

We just never dreamed we would be the ones to write it.

How Low Can You Go?

You see, when we started out in the work world we were just two girls—not of the Hilton sister variety, but of your average, everyday, nobody, know-nobody variety. The salaries and the respect level of those first positions couldn't possibly have been any lower. And we didn't know how—or if—we would ever get out from under.

At first we clung to the popular misconception that by working hard we would automatically be rewarded and get promoted. We relied on our impression that good opportunities invariably came to the best, most qualified, and smartest people. We discovered à la rude awakening that it almost never works that way.

After a couple of years of not knowing what we didn't know, each of us having endured multiple dead-end jobs and countless humiliations (many of which were, uh, self-inflicted), we began to study other professional women and men who were higher up in the pecking order than we were. Trying not to reveal our deep ignorance, we began to ask questions like "I want to move from here to a position in the commercial production department, what should I do?" and "I really want to do more writing, where should I start?" Many of the answers we heard revealed that the GPS is different for girls than it is for guys, and we began to understand how to navigate the corporate maze and began to move in the right direction.

Truly, what saved us, though, was our lightning-bolt revelation that things would never "just work themselves out" at work—unless we *made* them work out.

Out of Nowhere

Fast-forward eight years from the dark days in our respective office pits of despair to the point at which our lives intersect in 1996.

Jocelyn is executive director of new media programming for Hachette Filipacchi, a high-profile, glamorous Big Important Media Company that publishes *Premiere, Elle, Metropolitan Home,* to name a few. Jocelyn has the impressive high-tech job of producing websites for twenty-five Hachette magazine titles. She has oodles of responsibility and a lovely staff of forty-five to boss around. Jocelyn takes long business lunches with editors at Manhattan's best restaurants, has a great window office with an actual door, and jets off routinely on celebrity-elbow-rubbing biz trips. Oh, and Jocelyn has plenty of $$$ to support her groovy clothing addiction. Sweet, but not without sweat. Marcelle is editor in chief of *Eating Well* magazine, which at this time is owned by the same Big Important Media Company, and she gets to watch Jocelyn picking pretend lint off John-John's Armani in the elevator on her way upstairs in between advertiser lunches.

Naturally, Jocelyn didn't arrive in such a swell job direct from entry-level land. No, she came by way of her first break—which she orchestrated herself—landing a gig as an event planner for Philip Morris. From there, Jocelyn was recruited to be the senior promotions manager of a new division being formed at the N. W. Ayer advertising agency, which managed sports and entertainment sponsorships for AT&T. Later, she joined Wenner Media (publisher of hip titles *Rolling Stone, US* magazine, and *Men's Journal*) as a manager of event marketing and was rapidly promoted to director of a new broadcasting division, where she created TV shows such as *Rolling Stone Style Show* and *US Hot Zone Show.* Each job was clearly a step up, each one more challenging and fun than the last, landing Jocelyn *exactly* where she wanted to be: in broadcast and new media production.

As editor in chief of *Eating Well* magazine, Marcelle writes a column for each issue, complete with a glam photo of herself that her mom and dad like to point out to strangers in waiting rooms at doctors' offices. She lives in Vermont, and she runs the magazine and manages all the nice editors and designers while nipping in and out of the test kitchen for a bite of something sublime. Once a month or so, Marcelle abandons her idyllic rural life and her office overlooking the sunflower field to hit Manhattan for city-style hustle-bustle meetings with other editors, execs, and advertisers. She travels around the country to meet and greet and eat. She realizes she's arrived at the top of the food chain one night in a San Francisco restaurant while in a tête-à-tête with Julia Child over some orange roughy.

Marcelle had jumped to the Big Hachette Media Show from a cozy midsized company, M. Shanken Communications, where she held the position of managing editor of *Food Arts* magazine for seven years. It was the best cubicle job in the world. Sure, she worked insane hours, but she learned more than anyone really ever needs to know about fine food and cooking by hanging out with the likes of chefs Paul Prudhomme, Charlie Trotter, and Emeril Lagasse—long before he ever said "BAM!" But more importantly, it was here that Marcelle became *exactly* what she had always wanted to be: a writer.

So how did we, essentially two suburban know-nothing girls, rise from twenty-something know-nothings to top-level players for a Big Important Media Company by the time we hit our thirties? Truth is, sometimes we still can't believe it ourselves. But here's what we do know:

1. It was painful.
2. It didn't *have* to be as painful as it was.
3. We worked harder than sweatshop girls.
4. We didn't *have* to work as hard as we did.
5. We took risks.
6. We could have taken *more* risks.
7. If *we* managed to maneuver our way into dream jobs, *anyone* can.

Almost Famous

Over the course of our own professional paths, we became self-appointed career advisors to a handful of our girlfriends who were struggling at and confounded by work. Having found our particular brand of down-to-earth straight talk "refreshing" and "lifesaving," they told their friends to call us, and in turn, those women told their younger sisters, who told their girlfriends, and so on. These days, we affectionately refer to all these professional women, which number in the hundreds annually, as The Girls Who Call Us.

It's business as usual for one or the other of us to get a call from some woman we've never heard of in some career somewhere in the world who has been given our number by a friend of a friend who told her that we would give her cut-through-the-nonsense analysis on whatever her work dilemma du jour happened to be and solid advice on how to get a grip on it. Over the years, the whole thing has grown organically into this wild, spindly-branched phone tree that reaches across the country and as far afield as Sydney, London, and Munich.

The curious thing, though, is no matter where The Girl Who Calls is from, or how old she is, or what she does for a living, the questions always end with the same four words: "What Should I Do?" Check this:

"I take *everything* personally. I spend so much time second-guessing myself, and I can't help but think that my coworkers are *trying* to make me sweat. What should I do?"

"I think my boss hates my guts, and I have no idea *what* I've done wrong. What should I do?"

"I'm scared to voice my opinion or stick up for myself at work, because every time I do, I get shot down the *second* I open my mouth. What should I do?"

"I just got out of school and discovered I'm qualified for *nothing.* I just can't seem to get a really good job. What should I do?"

♟ "I don't think anyone at work knows how smart I am—they treat me like an idiot. What should I do?"

♟ "I love my job, but I'm afraid I'm going to get fired. What should I do?"

♟ "I hate my job and want to quit, but everyone tells me how lucky I am to have *any* job. What should I do?"

♟ "I'm reeeeally uncomfortable talking about money. I don't even know where to begin to have this kind of discussion. What should I do?"

♟ "I work like a *dog,* so how come I don't seem to be getting anywhere? What should I do?"

We've heard and answered a million of these "What Should I Do?" questions. And, from what The Girls Who Call Us tell us about the results they've gotten at work from taking our advice, we've become pretty damn good at it.

We think it's rough out there in the working world and have come to the conclusion that every working woman needs a Big Sister. We have become the Big Sister mentors to The Girls Who Call Us—we tell them straight up what they need to hear, help them structure viable plans, regale them with our own tales from the office dark side, and, when necessary, tell them to knock it off. And now we're inviting you to the inside, to become One of The Girls.

Oh, and btw: some of The Girls Who Call Us are men. While our male friends do give us some insights as to how guys operate, and have demystified the psychology behind some of the more alien male office behaviors, basically they still call us with many of the same "What Should I Do?" questions as The Girls. But since our boys *hate* it when we lump them in with The Girls, we gave them their very own cool-sounding epithet: Guy Spies. Makes 'em feel better about asking us for directions.

Why Are We Here?

We wrote *The Big Sister's Guide to the World of Work* because after a few years of listening to The Girls Who Call Us detail all their work traumas, we realized that the questions, problems, and recommendations were giving us a nauseating case of déjà-vu-induced vertigo. We can't get them *all* on the phone, and we became utterly exasperated at the thought that there are *millions* of fabulous, smart, capable, talented women twisting themselves into emotional macramé year in and year out, asking the same questions but not finding satisfying or otherwise useful answers to them.

And, frankly, once we really started thinking about it, we buckled down to put the whole working scene for women in perspective because we were really pissed off that lots of the career advice floating around out there actually makes girls feel bitter and filled with self-doubt because they were not raised to play by the boys' rules.

What's in It for Y-O-U

Now, if you are just starting out in the World of Work, you might not think any career advice pertains to you just yet. Wrong. What happens in the first ten years of your career will likely determine the overall quality of the next twenty-nine.

And, clearly, if you are standing there in the business section of the bookstore reading this, it ain't because you want to learn how to knit.

You are looking for help and some answers to those nagging questions all tangled up in your brain basket. You need look no further.

If you are a young executive who sailed through the entry-level and lower-management parts of your career but then ran into nasty snags and mysterious happenings such as office "politricks" as you moved up in rank, this book is for you. Likewise, if you are still in school and wondering about the future, or if you have been out of the cozy, idealistic, and equitable womb of higher education for a few years and can't figure out which end is up in the World of Work, this book has your name on it.

What follow on these pages are our work tools and rules and tips on how to deal with fools. You'll learn exactly what you need to know so you can stop being stressed, make more money, get your job under control, and cruise smoothly to the career and lifestyle you want.

Curl up with this book awhile, and . . .

- **You will completely abandon any idea you might hold that you simply have to Pay Your Dues** and wait for something or someone *else* to make it all better.

- **You will learn how to identify and avoid the common and not-so-common types of office quicksand** that suck women in and sink them up to their necks before they even realize they stepped in something nasty.

- **You will base your career decisions not on what every negative person in your life thinks** but rather on what you *know* in your heart you want and have the potential to do.

- **You will know exactly how to find the time to get what you want** instead of spinning your wheels with busywork and worrying about pleasing everybody damn else.

- **You will know what to do to put yourself in the right place at the right time** and what you should wear and talk about when you get there.

- **You'll learn how to make the corporate system work for you instead of against you,** no matter what industry or job you find yourself in.

- **You'll laugh out loud** because we happen to think work is an intrinsically funny topic, and the ability to laugh at it is an invaluable skill in any profession.

And that's just for starters. By the time you finish the book, you will be armed to face the forces of evil and opportunity in corporate America. You will:

- Know everything you need to know to get the job you want
- Have the relationship you want with your boss
- Have the confidence to set your own course
- Be living the life you want the way you want to live it

If you adopt only two of our ideas and they make your life a better place to live and work, then we've done our job, and you, sweet sister, will be in a better position to succeed at yours.

—M & J

miss
Orientation

If you only knew what nobody bothered to tell you . . .

Useful Terms: What We Mean When We Say . . .
Girlogic What makes sense to us: play nice
Guylogic What makes sense to them: win at all costs
PMS Political Misery Syndrome, a work-induced condition
Nah-Nah-Nah-Nah-Goo-Goo I've got a great gig and you don't

Once upon a time, there was a bright, wide-eyed girl from Long Island named M, who was working as a potted plant outside some big mucky-muck advertising executive's office making approximately two cents per hour. Why would a college graduate (magna cum laude, thank you very much) be a secretary for a man who did so little he clearly didn't need one? The answer was obvious: it was all because she couldn't type.

All the "good" jobs for women—those fantastic opportunities listed in the *New York Times*—required 50 wpm on the typing test.

Around the same time, M's high school friend and two-time prom date Frank, who was walking around with a similarly useless liberal arts degree (OK, so it was from Harvard), didn't have to take a single typing test and, through a contact from his old neighborhood, got a job with an actual livable $$$alary trading foreign debt at a big old bank. Frankie couldn't type either and had never so much as balanced a checkbook.

Hmmmmmmm . . .

Meanwhile, there was a bright, blue-eyed girl from Buffalo named

J who came to the Big City and also got a job at an advertising agency making two and one-half cents an hour. J, who *could* find a Q on a keyboard, was an assistant to a woman who mentored her in the ways of Madison Avenue—instructing J that her main objective was to keep the pencils sharpened at all times.

J moved to New York City to seek her fortune with her college boyfriend, Keith, and he, like M's friend Frank, got a job in foreign trading at a big old bank, making big-old-bank buck$$$.

Double hmmmmmmm.

Why would J, a college graduate, be working as an assistant for an obsessive-compulsive with a pencil fetish? Because unless you were Someone's Daughter, it seemed that the only jobs available right out of school were as Someone's Assistant.

Surrendering to the Pink

In those first few years of working in those brain-optional "pink-collar-ghetto" jobs, each of us remembers thinking: "Oh my God, I can't believe *this* is my life. I am *nothing.*"

Not only did we have *nothing* jobs (while it seemed that everyone *else* had interesting, exciting careers) making *nothing* $$$, but our coworkers seemed stupid and petty, and the only time they paid attention to the fact that we were even alive was when we did something wrong or when our skirts were too short. To add insult to insanity, we were treated as if feeding paper into the fax machine was probably more responsibility than we could handle.

Things were Very Wrong.

What we really wanted was one of those "good" entry-level jobs, where you might actually *learn* something and get a smidgen of R-E-S-P-E-C-T. But *those* jobs, the ones with the word *assistant* at the beginning of the title rather than at the end, seemed to go either to those who knew someone's father's brother's son's boss or to the genetically challenged of our species, who happen to be missing fallopian tubes.

We were mortified. We thought we were losers. We couldn't fathom why in the heck we'd gone deep into tuition debt and sat through four-plus years of communications classes simply so we could type tabs for hanging folders and feel dumber than doorbells. Ding-dong.

Kate Hudson Never Had *These* Problems

What was the difference, we wondered, between us and Dawn the account exec, who was only a year or two older than us but making the big $$$, wearing the designer clothes, and living a sassy single life in the doorman building, unlike the dumps we lived in with our neurotic, diet-obsessed roommates? And why oh why was it that Dawn didn't seem to let *anything* ever get to her personally?

Did Dawn know something we didn't? "Nah, couldn't be," we thought. It was less painful for us to assume that Dawn had a daddy who made her life easy, which, granted, was unfair of us, but occasionally absolutely accurate.

And as long as we were bitching, we also wondered why our male friends weren't feeling as tortured as we were.

In the heat of those moments, we just couldn't figure it out. We thought that our lives would remain in the below-average category for all eternity because we didn't happen to have Ivy League upbringings, well-connected relatives, or the ability to use a urinal.

Bitter? Party of two?

Hard Knock. Who's There? You. You Who? Precisely.

We couldn't *possibly* have known then what we know now. Why not? 'Cause nobody bothered to tell us. There wasn't anyone.

We had no savvy, smart-mouthed older sister to set us straight.

Neither one of us had parents who worked for a real company (one orthodontist, three teachers). We had no mentors to tell us what we might be Doing Right and what we were definitely Doing Wrong.

But we know now. Boy, do we know. How did we learn? Ah, dear little sister, the ever-so-hard way—*NOT* a strategy we recommend. They say you have to be burned to learn, and let's just say we were torched like campfire marshmallows.

Now we know how it goes: it all starts with a handshake, a smile, and a "Welcome aboard." The next thing you know, you are sobbing in the ladies' room because you can't figure out why Sally in marketing *Hates Your Guts* and why Jeff in sales is *Always Trying To Make You Look Bad*. "What did I do?" you sob. "Why are they all sooo mean?"

Any of this sound familiar?

At some point in the beginning of your working life, it probably dawned on you that things were *WAY* harder than you thought they would be. But, you know, you're not alone. We too used to think it was just us, but over the years we've discovered that *countless* women (and, OK, a handful of guys)—even females pretty far up the food chain—suffer in many of the same ways.

What most of us didn't realize is that the instant we started working for any corporation, we were transported to an alternative reality on an alien planet known as Officepoliticus, where all the rules about fairness, achievement, success, and rewards are dramatically different from everything we were ever taught.

Yesterday All Your Troubles *Were* So Far Away . . .

Over all those years you spent at school, you learned that if you did the work, you would get all the credit that was due you. The harder you worked, the more credit you got—maybe even bonus points.

Basically, if you did pretty much what you were supposed to do—no matter what you looked like, no matter how you dressed, no matter how fabulous or stinky your attitude, no matter what your gender or orientation, no matter if you asked a zillion questions or not one—you were promoted to the next grade and were eventually rewarded with a lovely diploma that even had your name spelled correctly. Mom and Pop threw a party and people mailed you money.

So far, so good. Then you got your first *real* job.

It Starts with Those Painful Periods . . .

When you first arrive at a new job it can be truly perplexing because it all looks and feels so familiar—so innocent and tidy, with grown-ups going about their Business. When you get there, things seem normal enough. You *think* you understand what's going on.

Then you start to notice the weird stuff. The things that defy logic. Girlogic, that is. Ironically, the qualities that make us girls such great human beings can totally trip us up at work. We work hard. We try to play fair. Most of us try to make sure everyone feels good and equal. We try to make everyone happy because life is better when *everyone* is happy.

Problem is, for the most part, kill-the-guy-with-the-ball Guylogic still drives the prevailing system, and Guylogic is all about winning. And, frankly, most guys don't care as much as we do if they make a mess while trying to score points.

If your own sense of fairness is disrupted frequently enough, you'll end up stupefied like we did, with an acute case of work-induced Political Misery Syndrome (PMS)—an epidemic disorder of the mind most frequently found in the female population of Officepoliticus.

What Cramps Your Style

Women (and, OK, some men) develop Political Misery Syndrome because they are not aware that every single thing they do or don't do at work is being observed and interpreted.

Everything.

Just as it is with politicians on the campaign trail, everything you say (or don't say) in the office, how you say it, to whom you say it, whom you eat lunch with, who your friends are, how you deal with officemates, when you show up and when you leave, etc., can determine how you are treated, how quickly you are promoted, and how much license someone will take in hassling you.

Unfortunately, in the office, the most innocent of actions can be perceived as sinister or manipulative; the most manipulative maneuvers can be perceived as sincere and appropriate gestures. Most of The Girls Who Call Us completely resist any behavior that could possibly be construed as "political." Girlogic: "I'm just not a political person; I'm not manipulative. Why can't I just be myself?"

Answer: Because it's *all* political anyway.

You don't have to like it, but you do have to live with it. What counts in the office has virtually nothing to do with the truth; what matters is the *perception* of the truth. Your personal reality is about as relevant as your shoe size. Until you recognize this fact, you are at risk for a case of Political Misery Syndrome that all the Midol in the world can't fix.

To see if you currently suffer from work-induced PMS, see if you have any (or all, God forbid) of the top ten symptoms:

1. **Confusion.** You lack perspective; all events are relatively equal in terms of their importance in your mind. Every single project or misunderstanding is a big fat hairy crisis, and you are too befuddled to see any humor in anything.
2. **Oversensitivity.** You allow office conflicts and slights to hurt you, stress you out, and adversely influence your behavior.
3. **Obsessiveness & compulsiveness.** You feel undervalued, so you work harder and harder, which makes you feel even more taken advantage of, undercompensated, and overworked.
4. **Paranoia.** You feel like you are being excluded. More days than not, you are afraid that you will get fired.

5. **Boringness.** Your primary topic of conversation, no matter what time of day or who your audience is, is your job.

6. **Bitterness.** You spend tons of time enumerating the countless reasons all the stuff you really want from your career is completely unattainable, and then get resentful when you see others achieve the exact wish you had in mind.

7. **Major rage.** You stew in a cauldron of negativity, looking for people to blame, sue, and be mad at. Your primary office skill becomes creating dramas and dragging others into them.

8. **Denial.** You ignore the fact that you think your job sucks, you make no plans, live exclusively for the moment, spend all your money on shoes and Champagne instead of paying your phone bill, and hope that somehow it will all magically straighten itself out down the road.

9. **Relationship trashing.** You drive away your boyfriend and other significant people with nonstop bitching about your sorry situation. J did this, more than once.

10. **Stupidity.** You crash your car—just about total it—on the way to work, and still go and put in a full day anyway. M actually did this, but once was enough.

The Story of Oh . . .

There is only one remedy for Political Misery Syndrome—and no, it's not shopping. The one, repeat, *one* cure for chronic acute PMS (don't blink; you'll miss it) is:

Options.

Options are oxygen.

Without options, your company becomes your life-support system. You live in a state of paralyzed fear that your boss will pull the plug and that you don't have enough skills to get another job that's as good, or *any* job. So you work harder, become paranoid, enjoy less.

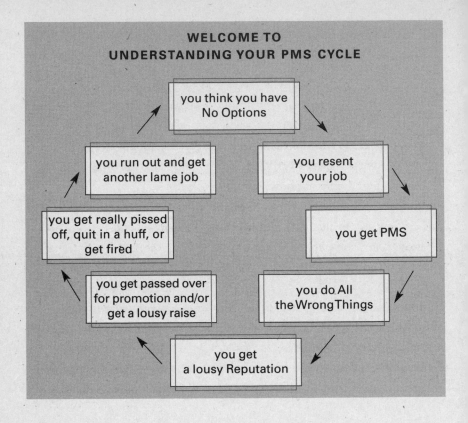

**WELCOME TO
UNDERSTANDING YOUR PMS CYCLE**

you think you have
No Options

you resent
your job

you get PMS

you do All
the Wrong Things

you get
a lousy Reputation

you get passed over
for promotion and/or
get a lousy raise

you get really pissed
off, quit in a huff, or
get fired

you run out and get
another lame job

Taking Stock of Your Options

Most of the women we know think that Options are a luxury they just can't afford. We call this the Girl Option Paradox (GOP): women *love* when Options are *offered* to us, hence our great devotion to shoe shopping, yet because most of us are hard-wired to value commitment, many of us feel obligated to stay in the bad relationship that is our job. Girlogic: spending time *creating* Options seems like "cheating."

It's different for most men. Some ancient directive from the Divine Boss drives guys to sow seeds hither and yon, constantly laying the groundwork for a more attractive position. Our Guy Spies tell us that pondering possible Exit Strategies begins before they take on *any* commitment. Guylogic: not having Options is not an option.

For women, though, monogamy is our default mode. If you have PMS or are potentially at risk for it, which, btw, we think almost all women are, the first thing we need to do is get in there and change the power management settings on your control panel.

Here's our tech support:

Step 1: Write down your new mantra. "I *must* have Options; they are an absolute necessity for the life and health of my career and for my sanity." Repeat daily.

Step 2: You have to learn *how* to get them. The rest of this book will tell you *everything* you need to know. You will soon discover that Options *are* one of the most luxurious things in the world to have.

Step 3: You have to make the *time* to create Options. You'll have to learn to be more selfish (yes, the *S* word!). If you are like most women, multitasking your head off, the things you need to do for *yourself* are usually at the bottom of the priority pile—if they make the list at all. We'll fix that right up for you in Chapter 11, "*Y-O-U: The Ultimate Planning Machine.*"

Honey, you have to *believe* that you, and you alone, can manufacture good Options for yourself, and not let *anyone* convince you that you can't. People in your life—well-meaning and otherwise—might try to brainwash you into believing that you have no Options. Why? Because if you had *choices,* you might *change,* and people really don't like it when others change anything more significant than their underwear. Really. It drives them completely mental.

THE JUST-LIKE-THAT FACTOR

Even if you think that you don't *need* Options because you love, love, *love* your job, your boss, your commute, your colleagues, and the

(continued)

soap in the ladies' room, you still must be out there building up Options. Why? Because even if you don't want to be a career girl or climb any ladder whatsoever, you still need to protect yourself from The Just-Like-That Factor.

The Just-Like-That Factor is responsible for the saddest cliché in working life today. Our girlfriend is going along, minding her own business, working at her job, giving up large hunks of her personal life and most of her emotional RAM in order to guarantee her job security, which, after years of devoted service, she believes she has achieved.

Then *BAM!* One day, for whatever reason, or no reason, she and her usual morning bagel are completely blindsided by the pink-slippered fairy and it's O-V-A-H. The job is gone, and our friend is left alone with not much more than the overtures of outrage from her unaffected office buddies and her big old Kate Spade full of resentments wadded up like so many used Kleenex.

- **Just like that,** the life you knew for the previous [insert number here] years is O-V-A-H.

- **Just like that,** you have to clear out your desk (or have it cleared out for you) and leave the building immediately. Your key, phone number, cell phone, and the email address everyone in the universe has used to contact you for years: gone.

- **Just like that,** the computer that has all of your personal stuff on it—not to mention a record of all the Internet sites you've ever visited—see ya.

- **Just like that,** you have no place to report to in the morning, and the people you used to chat with at work—and all your other friends, for that matter—don't have time to gab or commiserate with you: they're all too busy working. Buh-bye.

- **Just like that,** no matter what your financial obligations, the paychecks stop coming, and the future you were banking on—poof!

(continued)

- **Just like that,** you find yourself in the psychological tailspin of your life, and suddenly what's happening on *All My Children* seems like critical information. All the issues that were life-and-death vital at work yesterday—vaporized.

- **Just like that,** it's O-V-A-H and you're O-U-T.

The Just-Like-That Factor is not just reserved for sinners, slackers, and sad sacks. Just because you've been on the job for fourteen years, show up early, work late, never take sick days, skip lunch, get the job done, and accrue obscene amounts of vacation time because you are too devoted to take it, you will not be exempt from The Just-Like-That Factor.

Getting laid off might have *nothing* to do with you, your devotion, or even the important work you do. You really just never know what those bean counters are doing all day, let alone what they are thinking, and honey, *anyone* can get canned faster than they can say: "What resumé?"

Don't believe it could possibly happen to you? Can you say "Enron"?

Think about it.

You've Got a Friend . . . or Do You?

When you are trying to psych yourself up to explore your Options, be especially wary of your boss. There's a breed of bosses out there who *love* to make employees believe that they have no choices, because choice implies decision making, and decision making means power, and many bosses *hate* perceiving power anywhere but in the mirror.

When M worked at that advertising agency in New York, she didn't think she had any Options because her boss, Charlie, *told* her she didn't. M viewed Charlie more like a buddy than a boss (hint: *never* do this). He confided in her his shrink's ludicrous advice and regaled her with his dramatic adventures with devious dry cleaners. Charlie gave M a sense of security that he had her best interest at heart and convinced M that she was virtually unemployable anywhere else because, as he told her so often, she "had no real marketable skills."

It wasn't such a stretch for M to believe that, especially after the completely hideous time she'd had getting the lame job with Charlie to begin with. Not to mention that M was subject to the universal fear that "there are no jobs out there."

What M took way too long to figure out was that Charlie *liked* having her sitting outside his office. He liked the way she handled the important tasks of watering his plants, ordering his carefully prescribed lunches, and answering his phone—the two times a day that it rang. He loved his office ornament and didn't want her to go *anywhere*. M didn't think there was anywhere *to* go. So she stayed far longer than was good for her.

You must keep your head up. If your boss tells you in any way, shape, or form that you have no skills and no potential and that you should consider yourself lucky to have any job, get out! A truly great boss will encourage you, help you devise a plan, and ensure that you develop the skills you need to get to the next level. If you wind up with one like Charlie, you'll go nowhere fast; you won't even get promoted within the company.

With Friends Like *That* . . .

Other times, we think we have no Options because often the people we trust the most, the ones who are supposed to love and support us, are actually our Evil Network of Negativity. Instead of giving us a leg up and encouraging us to take risks, they push us down—in that ever-so-well-meaning way.

J was working at an ad agency in Boston as an assistant to Demi, an account exec, who, while only two years older, was snotty beyond her years. Demi would give J only menial tasks, would not lift a finger to train her in ways that could help J get promoted, and, worse still, spoke to J as condescendingly as Paris Hilton would to her chihuahua, Tinkerbell.

Understandably, J wanted to quit. But she didn't. J had moved to Boston to be with the boyfriend (read: potential husband) and knew no one else. J's boyfriend and other friends made the situation and her misery even worse by *constantly* reminding her that she *Had No Money.*

J's Evil Network of Negativity said incredibly supportive things like: "Well, how would you live if you quit?" Or: "Where are you going to get the money to figure out your life?" People in her life played on her fears rather than giving her the confidence that she *could* succeed at something else somewhere else. They thought they were doing her a favor by being *realistic* for her. But it was no favor. She forced herself to stay in a job that was damaging her.

You've got to learn who is in your own Evil Network of Negativity. No matter how much you may love those you've identified as particularly unsupportive, you've got to cut them off from your decision-making process. So, for example, if you tell your parents you want to be a preacher and they tell you you don't have a prayer, *stop* speaking to them about your career. If you don't have support and encouragement from *someplace,* those Options will be harder to come by than Manolo Blahnik stiletto boots at Payless.

How Can Anything That Feels So Righteous Be So Wrong?

Political Misery Syndrome is not a condition you should ignore for long. It can do a number not only on your career but on your life as well.

During her Beantown stint, J's ego was out of control. Rather than spending her time at work looking for a way to leverage her lousy job into something at least less lousy, and instead of being mindful of the image she was projecting, she did, as many of us with work-induced Political Misery Syndrome do, All the Wrong Things.

J couldn't see that she was threatening to Demi. J was skinny and wore her sexy New York clothes to work. In her relatively conservative Boston office, *that* got her plenty of attention—and it drove Demi (aka the person with the power), insane. J kept her desk a complete mess and acted as if she didn't care about anything, which only served to make Demi look more mature, more in control, and far better by comparison.

Meantime, while J was busy acting out all over the place—chain-smoking at her desk, coming in late, telling her personal saga to anyone who would listen—and being totally miserable 24/7, her relationship with Boston Boy crumbled like your first attempt at making piecrust. Coincidence? Hardly. Serious relationships can't survive, let alone thrive, in an environment of eternal misery and complaint.

Likewise, M's perceived lack of Options in those early years also gave her a raging case of PMS. M believed that she was *way* too good and *way* too smart for some of the early positions she held, and broadcast her opinion at every opportunity to people in and outside her office. The result: the perception M sent out was not that M was smart, sophisticated, and dee-lightful, but rather that she was a chronic complainer and stuck-up. No one wanted to listen to it.

In defense of our rather brainless behavior in those first few jobs, however, no one had ever mentioned the importance of Options to us. Instead, almost everyone we complained to said: "You have to Pay Your Dues—Nah-Nah-Nah-Nah-Goo-Goo."

So we paid and we paid and we paid. What did we get for it? A worse case of PMS, not to mention broken relationships, sleep deficiency, and a wardrobe of outdated duds.

As far as we're concerned, the nasty little phrase "Paying Your Dues" is a convenient way to dismiss griping entry-level people who are sick of being treated like a remnant of industrial carpeting. It's *so* not helpful.

What *would* be truly helpful to women just starting out in the working world who feel miserable and/or useless because they can't seem to get a job that they feel good about, and to women with a few years in the job market whose jobs have them more twisted up inside than pantyhose in the spin cycle and who can't figure out why they are not getting anywhere no matter how hard they are working, would be to tell them that they *do* have power and they *do* have choices.

In fact, most women need to be told (and retold) that they have everything they need to succeed in their careers.

And that, dear, is what we are all about.

Chapter 2

Harder . . .
a little to the Left . . .
now Up . . . Ahhhh

Why claw your way to the top when all it takes is a little well-placed scratch?

Useful Terms: What We Mean When We Say . . .
Uppity Uppers Anyone with more power and influence than Y-O-U
Invisible What you are at work unless you put in appearances
Backscratch A favor large or small
Scratch Pad Where you keep score

Our friend Robin was trapped in Dues-Paying Hell like a passenger who's just dying to get anywhere but can't 'cause she's terminally fogged in at O'Hare.

Robin had landed a sweet job in product marketing at a software development company at a time when it was practically minting money. She watched as coworkers were being given these phenomenal opportunities in call-your-own-shots positions because the company could not keep pace with its own exponential growth. Robin, however, remained in the eye of the big let's-promote-everyone-and-their-dog blizzard. But she wasn't exactly standing still.

Screwed, Again . . .

Robin was moving, all right—she just wasn't getting anywhere. Over a five-year period, she had had seven different jobs at the same company and worked for five different bosses. You would think all this exposure to new people within the organization would make Robin blissfully happy because exposure breeds Options. But our poor friend Robin was completely freaked out and miserable. Why? Because each of her moves was lateral: she got no additional responsibilities, no cool title change, no extra money, and no more respect than she had before. Nada. What she did get was Political Misery Syndrome.

After each job move within the company, Robin figured that if she just worked *harder,* surely someone would notice and the next move would be to a much better gig with much better bennies. Robin kept her head down and worked incredibly hard, only to be moved to an identical interior windowless office next door—over and over again. She became totally self-absorbed and self-pitying about the unfairness of it all. Unfortunately, this didn't do anything to help her sorry situation. In fact, it became something of a self-fulfilling prophecy: no one sees leadership ability in a person who never lifts her head.

Something About Mary . . .

Contrast Robin with our friend Mary, who started out as a PR peon at a local television station. Within a few short years, she was promoted to director of marketing. Mary was not killing herself, she was happy with her job, and she was completely PMS-free.

So what's the difference between Robin and Mary? Was Mary doing a better job at following her daily horoscope to the letter? Was Robin doomed by bad karma? Nope. In this particular case, it had to do with personality. Robin is a fabulous girl, but at the time, you had to go waaaay out of your way to find out. Robin was *always* such a downer that getting to know her was actually *work:*

You: Hey Robin! What's up?
Robin *(looking at her shoes):* Um, nothing. Same ol', same ol'.
You: Right. Um, so how's your summer shaping up?

Robin *(looking at her cuticles):* It sucks.

You: What's wrong?

Robin *(looking at the ceiling):* My boss is driving me crazy. I have a pile of work that I never seem to get through. You know . . .

You *(now looking at your shoes):* OK, well, then . . . Listen, things will look up soon. See you later at Trisha's party?

Robin *(looking at her watch):* Can't. Got too much to do.

You *(walking out, thinking, "What a drag"):* Oh, right. Um . . . sorry. Bye then.

Political Misery Syndrome had turned Robin into a hard-core, dark-cloud Eeyore. Mary, on the other hand, cruised onto the promotion express lane by being her sweet little self. She smiles a lot. She's pleasant to be around. It's incredibly effortless to feel like you know her. With Mary, you don't have to sit around and worry what she thinks of you (of *course* she likes you!):

You: Hey Mary! What's up?

Mary *(looking right atcha with a big smile):* Hey, sistah! Things are great! Thanks! I haven't seen you all week. How'd things go for you?

You: Pretty good, thanks. I finally landed the South Mountain Surveying business.

Mary *(animated, still smiling):* No way! Oh my God! That's *sooo* amazing. Good for you! You deserve it, hon.

You *(now also smiling):* Thanks! So, I'll see you later at Trisha's party?

Mary *(smiling as she walks out):* Absolutely. See you then.

You *(saying to yourself):* She's *so* great.

The big difference is that Mary has a great attitude. Attitude isn't everything, but it's a big slice of the pie, pumpkin.

The truth is, most of the working gals out there are not born with a naturally attractive attitude and the political instincts Mary got when they were handing out useful personality traits. But just because we're not all perky little cheerleaders doesn't mean that we can't get to the top of the pyramid.

Don't Despair, Be Aware

Robin is the extreme. She didn't know that an important step in creating Options was to have the awareness to make some simple attitude adjustments like smiling at people, saying hello, not making a beeline for her desk every morning, and, particularly, blowing out the candles at her personal pity party. Company does *NOT* love Misery.

While these to-dos might look so simplistic that they seem incredibly stupid, all these things can make or break you at work. Why? Because unless you *make* yourself Visible, you are invisible!

Let's repeat that one: no matter how hard you work, you are *invisible* to the people with the power to help you unless you make yourself Visible in a positive and memorable way.

A stellar attitude can make up for a lack of skills, but no matter how talented, productive, or dedicated you are, if you have a negative or otherwise toxic attitude, people will avoid and/or ignore you. Robin continued to be off the radar screen because no one in particular—not those five bosses, not even Robin herself—was making damn sure that she made a regular blip. Robin was one note, and a sour one at that. She didn't know to connect with coworkers and build mutually beneficial relationships. She never made time for social interactions and never made herself available to lend a helping hand. She was too busy working to be bothered with anyone else, so nobody bothered to be bothered with her.

Sure, you could, as some do, make yourself Visible by, say, wearing spike heels, screaming-red lipstick, and crotch-grazing skirts every day, but that approach in most environments, unless you happen to work in a strip joint, is Reputation suicide (see Chapter 6, "Be a Girl with a Reputation").

Mary, being the perky, upbeat, and intellectually curious person that she is, naturally connected with the right people during coffee-fetching chats and postmeeting hangouts. She expressed her enthusiasm for the company and became Visible in a very positive way. When the time came to fill the marketing director spot, the Uppity Uppers immediately thought Mary the obvious choice.

You want to be the *first* person who comes to mind when someone important needs something or someone. And it ain't gonna happen if you work, work, work with your head down every second of your work day and never show your face or reach out and touch someone.

You Scratch My Back . . .

Getting noticed for a swell disposition is basic training. After that, you need to move on to the more advanced obstacle course of becoming politically savvy. Guys make themselves not only Visible but also memorable in their office worlds by employing a form of accepted corporate intimacy that comes naturally to them, known as The Backscratch.

A Backscratch is a favor large or small, and these favors are incredibly important in the lives of men (as in "I gotta go see a guy about a favah") and therefore in corporate America.

You know how most guys can't remember much of anything—not what you wore, not who you saw, not that you asked them to pick up toilet paper—but they can easily remember the score of a 1992 Raiders-Giants game? It's because guys keep score. And favors are a quantifiable, scorable item. Guys know that to make themselves Visible, they've got to get out there and scratch the backs of the most influential people in the office—and make sure that all those scratchees know the score. This is the basis of all politics, office and otherwise.

A favor can be something you actually do for someone to help him get his job done, or it can be something like putting him in contact with someone else who can help him. A favor for someone at work can be something of a personal nature or even something as minor as just giving him your time and attention as you listen to whatever is on his mind.

Like all things political, The Backscratch is about perception—and this is where many people, both male and female, crash and burn. If you give the impression that you are loyal only to yourself, your career will choke, sputter, and stall faster than your Volvo after you filled your tank with watered-down gasoline. Certainly, being competent at your job will move you up in the first few years of your career, but beyond that you will have to establish your Reputation—which is what will take you up or out or bury you alive at your desk till you wake up when someone is shaking your shoulder and telling you that you can withdraw from your 401(k) with no penalties now.

To a large degree, your Reputation will be built on the goodwill you've built up with people whom you've worked with over the years. Assuming you are at least reasonably good at whatever it is you do, the equation works like this: the more favors you do, the more people who favor you, the more favorable your Reputation.

Scratch from the Top Down

Every person you encounter in the office presents you with an opportunity to give relief from some itch—a need real or imagined. That means that there is *always* something you can do to cultivate mutual feelings of loyalty.

Remember that fable about the eternally grateful lion that had the thorn in his paw pulled out by a little insignificant I-should-eat-you-for-lunch mousie? Same deal. The trick here, though, is to concentrate more on scratching the lions and less on the mousies.

This might seem an obvious point, and so it is, but it's a surprisingly overlooked one. Take our friend Paula, a secretary at a nonprofit. Paula's boss is constantly pissed off at her because if he asks her to do something, rather than dropping everything else she's working on and doing him the favor of accomplishing what he wants when he wants it, she puts his stuff on her big to-do pile. No good. Paula essentially makes him wait in line while she completes a dozen other time-sucking tasks for a random assortment of underlings or whatever else *she* thinks is the priority at that moment.

Paula doesn't have the bad attitude her boss thinks she has; she just works on the first-come-first-served model—which makes perfect sense in Girlogic and at the deli counter. But seeing as how she's actually *trashing* her position with her boss, who, ignorant of Paula's fair-is-fair, Girlogic rationale, has come to the conclusion that she's just slow and passive-aggressive, Paula's not doing *herself* any favors.

Come raise time, the boss will have a major case of amnesia about the fact that Paula did an unbelievable amount of work for countless people to keep his office running smoothly. He'll only remember that it takes her forever to get stuff done for *him*—so she'll only get a 1 percent raise, while everyone else gets the standard (whopping) 3 percent. Poor Paula. Literally.

Extra! Extra! Fuhgeddallaboudit

One of the problems lots of The Girls Who Call Us have is that once they get into doing a Backscratch, they want to throw in a scalp massage too. Your Girlogic will tell you that throwing in the bonus of the scalp massage means you did extra—that's good, right? That's showing initiative, right? No one *asked* you to do it, so you would think you should be given some kind of award for *such* dedication. Right?

Sorry, honey, you lose: you raised the bar on yourself by creating a performance expectation and doubled your workload doing something that won't be noticed or get you anywhere because no one else thought it was important enough to ask you to do it in the first place.

Most women are not instinctively discriminating about whom they do favors for. We're just helpful, nice people who generally want to help anyone who asks us—and even some who don't.

Guys, on the other hand, scratch almost exclusively when it's in their best interest to do so, and they stop at the point when they've found the itch. In short, guys are strategic scratchers—they get noticed not for the fancy extras, but for the speed with which they accomplished the *requested* task. And let us tell you, men won't scratch just any old back either.

Take one of our Guy Spies, Jake, for instance. Jake is VP of engineering for a dot-com. You would love this guy. He'll do you the favor of showing a little personal interest, make jokes with you, nod interestedly when you speak, and promise he's on your side. You'll be convinced he's totally your ally, until you realize that he won't actually *do* anything for anyone unless it is clear to him that the request is specifically on his boss's agenda. Jake—who walks out the door every single day at 6 p.m. sharp, waving ta-ta to the late-stayers—is the one who consistently rakes in the boss's public praise, the big bonuses, and the juicy promotions. Sickening, ain't it? Well, not if you're Jake.

Too Flaky

We would never want to suggest that you girls should stop being girls and ignore your natural instincts to do favors and help folks out in order to get ahead at work. There are a couple of books out there that recommend this strategy and, frankly, they make us feel like hurling.

What we are saying is that we think it's wise to be more conscious of *all* the favors you do in the workplace, not only to become aware of all you do in a single day and pat yourself on the back for being such a swell gal, but also because consciousness will lead to a personal strategy and greater efficiency. Focus all that energy, honey.

You need to know where you are spending your time, so you can direct your energies into more than just spinning your wheels. Give yourself a quick test:

1. **Turn a notebook into a Scratch Pad.** For one week, write down every single time you do someone a little favor and how long it took. That

means every time you make the coffee run, help someone get a dinner reservation, answer a question that has nothing to do with your own job, or have a conversation that is totally irrelevant as your workday tick-tocks away, you jot it on your Scratch Pad.

2. **After a week, circle *all* the favors that you think could somehow elevate you in the esteem of your boss.** Chances are that those circles are pretty few and far between.

3. **Put a check mark next to all the items that were done for people who are in a position to potentially help you in return.** That is to say, people who could either advance your career someday or make your current job significantly easier. How did you do on that score?

Personally, we've found that organizing our minds and actions on paper is the best way to be conscious. Your Scratch Pad will get you in the habit of running a quick little cost-benefit analysis on every activity you undertake in the office to see where your energies are being spent. This review will give you the courage to utter that all-important, infrequently used little word: *No.* By all means keep score for several weeks, but hey, sister, don't leave it out on your desk.

Put yourself in the habit of primarily doing favors that build good-will with the Uppity Uppers and influential peons: the boss's secretary, for example, is in an amazing position to give you great information about what's going on in the company and to talk you up and make you Visible because she has the boss's ear, keeps his schedule, and deals with everyone else your boss has business with. Keep score in your notebook until you're finding that *most* of the activities you undertake during your workday beyond your actual job description potentially benefit your career and/or day-to-day experiences rather than simply sap your energy.

One final thought: don't just wait for people to come to you with requests for your help. Intentionally *seek out* ways to assist others that will improve your standing with people who can hook you up with bigger and better Options. Got it?

GIRL'S GUIDE TO GOOD WILL
HUNTING & BACKSCRATCHING

Like virtually any other relationship-oriented activity in the workplace, The Backscratch is a game with rules that no one will actually tell you but which you are expected to know nonetheless. S'ok. *We'll* tell you.

The most important rule is that you *never* say the following three words: "You owe me." If you say *those* words, *YOU LOSE.*

The Backscratchee *knows* he owes you one. To actually come out and say he does is to remind him that at some point he needed your help—when in retrospect he will usually think that he could have done it without your assistance. Besides, saying "You owe me" is bad form.

- **Eyeball the situation.** Step back and assess whether the coworker might interpret your offer as presumptuous or patronizing: "Let Mama help you, pookie-poots, 'cause you couldn't *possibly* solve this big nasty problem by your own silly little self." If you so much as *think* it could go that way, skip it entirely.

- **Favors are offers, *not* advice.** Do not say anything that starts with the words *"I just think you should . . ."* or *"You must . . ."* Those phrases mean you aren't a helpful, loyal, sympathetic party, but an obnoxious buttinski or potential backstabber trying to make your coworker look bad. *Always* say: "Is there anything I can do to help?" That way, the coworker actually *asks* you for help and is less likely to feel threatened by your ability to provide it.

- **Don't let anyone pressure you into doing something you don't want, or feel equipped, to do.** If you *do* agree to do something you would rather not do, remember, it was your choice. Breathe not one word of complaint.

- **No martyrdom.** If you do someone a favor, don't keep reminding the coworker about it while you are doing it: "You are gonna owe me big time for this one!" No bitching, no guilting.

(continued)

- **Statute of limitations.** You can't give a Backscratch, never collect on it, never keep in touch, and then waltz through the door 42 years later asking for the favor of his next dance. You must renew contact at least once a year—at the very least, send an annual holiday card.

- **Never demand payment.** Ask the coworker for the favor you want, and make no mention of the previous assistance you gave her. If she can't deliver the requested favor, be gracious and let it go; she'll still owe you one. If she outright refuses, then you know the score with her—she's a User Jerk. In that case, be tactfully unavailable to her for future help, unless, of course, she's your boss. (See Chapter 12, "Hail to the Chef.")

When someone helps you out above and beyond the call of duty, make sure you appropriately acknowledge the favor. One of The Girls Who Call Us, Lola, was trying to help out young Stacy, who said she was trying to start up a business. Lola gave Stacy tons of time, advice, and equipment, among other favors. Stacy said "thanks" when she picked up the computers, but she never stopped to follow up with even so much as a "thanks again" email. The next time Stacy contacted Lola, it was to ask for yet another favor. This time Stacy was ever so unavailable to help. Honey, don't ask for another favor from the same person if you never appropriately acknowledged the first. Hint: think handwritten note or small giftie.

J once helped Lisa out with her business plan, and as a thank-you, Lisa sent a gift certificate for a massage. J did not *expect* anything in return for her assistance, but she was so surprised and touched by the gesture that she has *never* forgotten Lisa's thoughtfulness. That was years ago, but to this day, J feels very loyal to Lisa and will *always* give Lisa a hand with anything she needs. That's how it works.

Sharpen the Claws

Mostly, think about a favor as something that you do for others, rather than something done for you. If you want to be able to give a good

Backscratch, you'll need to grow those nails a bit and give them some shape. We're talking skills here, mama.

Ask yourself this: "What do I have to offer that other people might need or value?"

For example, J can talk to anybody. There has never been a time in J's career that she hasn't tried to engage people, hear their stories, and look for ways to help them out. Over time, not only has J developed a queen-size contact base, but she has made it a policy to connect people with one another for their mutual benefit. J is constantly thinking not so much about what she can do for someone but about whom else she can connect him to in a way that helps both individuals simultaneously. J lives to join people with people, and people with ideas.

You need a lawyer? Business plan? Sellable concepts? Web designer? Hairdresser? Nanny? Need to get in touch with the president? J's your girl. But her favorite Backscratch is connecting contacts who need work with other contacts who need to make a hire. J has been so effective at this particular double Backscratch that when people—even friends of friends of friends—are looking for a job or know of a job, J is the first person they call, which, btw, gives J first dibs on any job *she's* interested in.

M uses her way with words. When people need something written or edited, they call M, who has by now "looked at" or rewritten countless cover letters and resumés for people at all levels—many of whom end up in very interesting positions. Resumé writing is an awesome tool for racking up points with a diverse group of players.

Likewise, M has gotten a lot of mileage with her marketing writing experience. She's helped many start-up companies develop brand names, slogans, marketing proposals, positioning statements, websites, press releases, and the like—all as favors. When the businesses take off, the entrepreneurs *always* return to M to handle their advertising and marketing. Hint: start-up companies usually need tons of goodwill work to get off the ground, and if they fly, you've got a first-class window seat.

Doing unto Uppity Others

If you are just starting out, maybe you think that you don't have many skills that are of value to anybody. Wrong. You definitely do. It took us years to build up those skills that serve us—and others—so well. You have to be patient with yourself, but in the meantime, here are a few classic favors that anyone at any level can do:

- **Cheerleading.** You know that company newsletter you never read? That's where you can find out what people outside your department are doing. If your boss or an important coworker has written a book, is speaking in a seminar—work-related or not—or is doing anything else that you can participate in or be witness to, go go go, girl. Show your support; you can be sure the other company execs will be there too. If you can't attend the event, shoot off a congratulatory note. *Everyone* likes to be noticed.

- **Newbie-sitting.** Go out of your way to meet new hires and be very helpful to them; they will remember you for a long time. It will take you ten minutes to walk down to someone's office, shake her hand, and tell her to call your extension if she needs any help with anything. New hires will be touched by the welcome-aboard note you send the week they start; J still has a box filled with them. You never know where a newbie will eventually land or whom she will end up influencing.

- **Pinch hitting.** If you know a coworker (or your boss) is on an impossible deadline, volunteer to help! You might not get the credit for helping him because it was his job in the first place, and he probably won't want to make it look like he couldn't handle it by publicly acknowledging your participation, but he *will* remember the assist. Be prepared to kill yourself for no immediate payoff, but years down the line, that gesture of support could come back around again in a big way. M had a few such opportunities to help coworkers out over the years, and those people became her best sources of information and her staunchest supporters in the office. Even now, M would feel completely comfortable calling one of those former coworkers if she ever needed help with *anything*—business or personal.

Matchmaking. Anything you can do to help someone else find a job will be remembered—even if she doesn't get it. If you know Patti is dying to break into PR, and you know Paul the Publicist, make the introduction! This is an easy Backscratch. Even if you don't know anybody, anywhere, keep an eye on the job boards, and if you see a position that might be interesting to someone you know, mention it—discreetly, doll, discreetly.

Sacrifice flying. Step up to the plate and volunteer for the thing *nobody* wants to do. This is a high-profile Backscratch. When something comes up and there are *no* volunteers, jump on it! Lots of people will be relieved and grateful if you take it on. Then send perfunctory updates on the hideous task to all involved to remind them of your heroism. This is a favorite move of J's. She has looked like a stud and earned appreciation from execs by handling the kind of dirty work that was clearly not in her job description, like the time she cleaned up the mess in the front hallway that her boss was bitching about. *Warning:* don't go looking for chores that nobody in her right mind would take on and just do them—no one will notice! Wait until the Uppity Uppers *request* a volunteer.

Offer tendering. Whenever possible, offer a solution to execs and other influential people who mention a problem in passing. Think on your feet and gently offer to help. Be prepared to follow through and make good on your offer, but nine times out of ten, you get the credit for volunteering to help out but don't have to do the deed. *Warning:* don't make an insincere offer that you are not in a position to, or willing to, deliver on.

Face saving. If you see someone making an error, step in—cautiously. These are the most valuable and the most dangerous Backscratches.

Warning: make sure you don't make anyone feel stupid or negligent when you point out his oversights, do it in private, and don't tell anyone else about the problems. Be careful with this one.

 Info passing. Read those industry trade magazines and other publications so you can clip and send articles to people you think will be interested in seeing them. It's a great way to make contact or keep a relationship humming along.

On your Scratch Pad, think of other ways that you can help people who are in a position to potentially help you. Awareness breeds opportunity.

Our Exclusive 60/40 Solution

We *know* what you're thinking: "God, who has time for any of that nonsense? How am I supposed to actually Do My Job when you guys are telling me that I've got to get out there and find the right backs to scratch and then scratch 'em?'"

Backscratching and other Visibility strategies we'll be recommending throughout the book will take a hunk of time, no doubt about it, so you'll need a reorg of your typical day. But fear not. We've got the perfect solution for you.

We want you to think of yourself as a magazine. You are a fabulous, interesting, must-read glossy. A magazine must have a healthy percentage of advertising to thrive. In fact, if it doesn't have ad pages, it will wither away and die. Same goes for your career.

Your forty hours a week in the office should break down precisely like an average American magazine's ratio of advertising to editorial content:

 60% content. In your case, this is the actual job-description work you do for your company.

40% advertising. In your case, this is time spent becoming Visible by Backscratching, networking, and building your Reputation by promoting yourself within and outside your company.

The 60/40 Solution is about taking all that unfocused time at work—there's probably more than you think there is—and focusing it. It's about being conscious during the day and creating opportunities to be Visible and connect with people inside your office and out of it. Forty percent of an eight-hour day is three hours and twelve minutes. You already have one hour free—it's called lunch. Take it. Use it. Make it work for you. Rather than working at your desk during lunch, work the phones. Call people you've met in your industry and feed them interesting tidbits you picked up in the trades or online. On a nice day, ask a coworker if she wants to take a walk and eat lunch in the park. Come up with excuses to make a lunch date with someone in the public relations department. Troll the job boards and see if you can find something interesting that someone in your office would want to know about: "Hey, Jake, did you hear that our competition is looking for a new VP of engineering?"

That leaves another two hours and twelve minutes to spend on making yourself Visible. To alleviate your guilt at this point, because maybe you are thinking, "It's just not right—my employers pay me for forty hours of *'work'* work," we'll tell you that the exact things we suggest you do to fill that time will not only make you Visible and thus give you more Options but also will make you *more* valuable to your employer. The more you know about your industry, the more people you know and who know you, the more skills you acquire, the more value you offer your company.

What some might view as standing around not getting anything done and socializing, Option-minded workers see as deliberately moving their careers, and their companies, forward by taking time from their "work" to "network." There's a fine line between not working and networking.

Sometimes Done Is Better Than Perfect

Still wondering how in the world you can squeeze even one more wafer-thin to-do in your life when you're putting in ten-hour days just to do what you do already?

Honey, something has just got to give.

Let some of that work slide, but not stuff your boss specifically asks you to do. Don't be such a perfectionist about *everything*. You will always have too much work on your plate, so don't worry about things piling up—they will anyway. Time is a funny thing. Those of us in high heels tend to use up all the allotted time available to do a given task because we are obsessed about Getting It Right—down to details no one else under the sun would ever notice or value.

When it comes to getting a particular objective met, focus on it, do your best, don't obsess, and move on. See Chapter 11, "Y-O-U: The Ultimate Planning Machine," for tips on how to streamline your workload.

If you follow the 60/40 Solution, you will definitely be Visible—to the right people. Be conscious. Be deliberate. Plan to work as hard on your 40 percent as you do on your 60 percent.

The funny thing is (or maybe it's sad), your boss and coworkers won't notice that you've changed your operating model for a long time. It's like wearing supersexy underwear to work—you may look same old same old, but you know you're doing something that makes you feel more confident, sexier, and more powerful.

The 60/40 Solution can put a challenge and a thrill into your current position that might not be there otherwise, not to mention open up possibilities for future opportunities that wouldn't have existed at all if you had not taken the time to put yourself out there.

Which is exactly what networking is all about.

DO *YOURSELF* A FAVOR

If you want to be Visible, a good place to start is by reminding people you exist. Notes are great ways to sustain relationships and keep you in the front of people's minds. The trick is to represent yourself well.

Go out and invest in some quality personal stationery. Get something really nice—50 pound stock—with your name embossed on the cards and your home address engraved on the matching envelopes. Now go out and buy a roll of a hundred stamps and one nonleaky, nonsmudgy black pen. Keep it all in a cool-looking box right on top of your desk.

In a world of sloppy email communication, good stationery is a smart investment. It reflects your status as a classy, forward-thinking, prepared, and professional person. The fact that you have your home address on the envelope (not the letter itself) makes it truly personal and demonstrates your desire to connect as a person to the recipient. Handwritten notes are so rare in business exchanges that sending one off is a distinctive and elegant touch that will make you more memorable.

Use your fancy new stationery for everything. Collect business cards at every opportunity, and write to the person who gave you one immediately: tell her how nice it was to meet her, and perhaps put out an invitation for a lunch date. Always toss *your* business card into the envelope, so the person has it for her files, is reminded of your professional status, and can respond via phone or email if she so chooses.

Find other excuses to write people quick little personal notes. Some of our favorites include:

Thank-you notes for anything and everything
- Thanks for the job interview . . .
- Thanks for the meeting . . .
- Thanks for support in the meeting . . .
- Thanks for lunch . . .
- Thanks for sending that info on your company . . .

(continued)

- Thanks for that great article you wrote about my company . . .
- Thanks for your input . . . [*be careful not to come off as sarcastic or defensive if the input was negative*]

Was-thinking-of-you notes

- Saw an article that made me think of you . . .
- It has been a long time since I've seen you—we met at the trade show last fall, and I was wondering what is new with you. I'm working on . . .

Special-event notes

- Happy birthday . . .
- Happy anniversary . . . [*at the company or wedding anniversary*]
- Condolences for your loss . . . [*do these because it is absolutely the right thing to do, and we know firsthand that it is a meaningful gesture even from someone who we barely know*]
- Happy holidays . . .

Seeing-you notes

- Looking forward to seeing you again at the meeting next week . . .
- It was nice to see you at the meeting yesterday . . .

Invitation notes

- I'll be in Cleveland next month—would you like to get together? . . .
- Are you going to the National Association for Television Producers annual conference? Perhaps we can meet up . . .
- Was wondering when you'll be in town next . . .
- Would love to buy you a drink . . . [*you can certainly extend an invitation via phone, but we recommend that you*

(continued)

take the opportunity to first write a note several weeks in advance, get your business card in the person's hand, and then follow up with a phone call (if you have not already received a response) when the date draws closer.]

Don't be paralyzed by the prospect of writing. You don't need to be Shakespeare. Use simple sentences. Keep the notes direct and to the point. It's a good idea to scratch it out quickly on scrap paper first to avoid a trash can full of your beautiful new stationery. Whatever you do, don't make it harder than it has to be—don't spend an hour constructing a five-line note. Remember that you are a charming and delightful person, and people love to get handwritten notes from charming and delightful people. Once you get in the groove of writing notes, it will become as automatic as punching in your PIN at the ATM.

Chapter 3

you are
Always Looking
for a Job

Opportunity doesn't knock, it Hums

Useful Terms: What We Mean When We Say . . .
Chat A nice meaningless conversation that creates a sweet Hum between
two people
Hum That happy little sound you hear that lets you know things are working

Many women think of networking like exercising: something that's good for them, that they know they *should* be doing, but that they just can't find the time or the motivation to do. Plenty of The Girls Who Call Us *hate* the very concept of networking. Girlogic: networking is slimy, manipulative, superficial, and mostly for people who have no life.

Yet every single career-building book in the universe will tell you that networking is the single most important thing you can do to keep your Options open. We agree. Personally, though, we think the problem here is the word *networking*. When people use it as a verb, as in "I was out networking last night," we want to *gag*.

Machines network. Human beings talk.

Networking is actually just Chatting—having a simple, meaningless conversation that creates a Hum between two people. Relationships—and we're talking real relationships here, not just a bunch of names in your Rolodex that you've "collected"—begin with "hello" and are built on a series of Chats.

Once you've established a nice Hum with someone, she becomes your Chum, and you become hers—notice that nice reciprocity part? Getting the Hum going assumes that during your Chat you formed a *mutual* interest in each other. And we're not necessarily talking only about bigwigs who can hand you your dream job.

Really, isn't *everyone* you know good to know for some reason? Even if it's just that they make you laugh?

Getting One Pump in the Door

You've already got a bucket of Chums—it's called your address book. All of those people—family, friends from high school, people in your office, friends of your siblings—found their way into your little black book for *some* reason. You might not think of these Chums as valuable assets in your Option arsenal, but they are: they all have their own connections to other potential Chums that could quite possibly change your life.

We can't tell you how many of The Girls Who Call Us got jobs through a friend of a friend of a friend. Check out how three of The Girls Who Call Us got their most recent jobs:

- **Alison** got a job as a headhunter (when she had zero experience) through a former colleague's husband's sister's contact.

- **Allison's** dad knew somebody whose secretary knew somebody who knew somebody to get her a job in public relations.

- **Alyson** and her sister met a guy at a dog run. He dated Alyson's sister, and Alyson got a job as an Internet retail site producer at his company.

The moral of the story here is not to go out and get a dog, although people do tend to get Chatting with complete strangers on the street who have either dogs or babies. The point is to start broadcasting in a chatty, nondesperate, and positive way, to anyone you meet, about what you do and where you think you would like to go next.

We mean to anyone, anywhere. When J was a senior in college, while she was waiting on line to get into the ladies' room at a bar, she struck up a conversation with the woman in front of her. After a quick little blah-blah-blah on where they both lived, J casually mentioned that she was a communications major and was looking for an internship at an ad agency. Well, turns out the lady on the loo line just happened to be a senior manager at an advertising agency, and before the two of them could even see the stalls, she gave J her card. As soon as J got back to school, she dropped Ms. Senior Manager a note reminding her of their conversation. Ms. Senior Manager arranged for J to get a fab internship for the summer. Hummmmm.

Beyond Ho-Hum

When something is humming away, it's working in the background. Don't you just love it when you hear the washing machine running? It means you are getting something done, and, really, your effort was pretty minimal—you shoved the clothes in, dropped in some soap, pushed the button. Whoosh.

When things are humming, productive work is getting done. So you Chat to get that nice Hum going between you and a wide and diverse crowd of people. Think of it all as music in the background of your work life. Whoosh.

Our careers, as opposed to the string of early hateful J-O-Bs, did not *start* until we learned to Chat & Hum. We originally thought that we needed to follow all the conventional job-hunt routes—classified sections, job agencies, temp agencies. Obviously some people find success down those avenues, but the best jobs we ever cruised into, and the best jobs that most of the people we know landed, were the direct result of Chatting & Humming. It's a fact: most people get the good jobs the same way they get good dates—because someone "fixed them up."

People's willingness to help each other can be amazing. The fact is that most people like to make good things happen because you are *giving* them power to do so—the godlike influence to change your life. Plus, when someone helps you get a job, you owe her, *and* the person she helped out by referring wonderful you owes her. It's a Backscratch!

Sealed with a Kiss of Lipstick

When J wanted O–U–T of the hateful Boston ad agency job and away from her dreadful boss Demi, she told her friend Linda that she wanted to meet Linda's Chum Brigitta because Linda had said Brigitta worked in event marketing—which is exactly what J thought she wanted to do with her life next.

Linda brought J to a party that she knew Brigitta would attend. J got a little Chat going with Brigitta, who mentioned that she liked J's lipstick. J, who at the time was just this side of signing up for food stamps, ran out the *next day,* bought a tube of the same lipstick she had worn to the party, and sent it off with a note to Brigitta. Alas, J heard nothing more from Brigitta as the months rolled away, and J's Political Misery Syndrome raged on while she was under Demi's thumb. J assumed there was no Hum happening with Brigitta.

Six months later, though, while aboard an Amtrak to New York, J spied Brigitta. J plopped herself right down and began Chatting with Brigitta, who immediately mentioned the lipstick. Huuuummm.

During the conversation, Brigitta revealed that she was planning on leaving her event marketing position at Philip Morris to return home to Europe:

Brigitta: So, ya, I'm going to leave my job and go home to Munich.

J *(jumping out of seat):* Are you *kidding* me?

Brigitta: No. I'm ready. Why?

J *(trying to steady herself):* Brigitta, I am *dying* to get into event marketing. Can you please tell me what I can do to get my foot in the door at Philip Morris?

Brigitta: Do you have any event marketing experience?

J *(passionately):* Absolutely none. But I will *kill* myself, I mean KA-ILLL myself, to learn it. Can you help me?

Brigitta *(sold entirely on the strength of J's unbridled enthusiasm):* I don't see why not.

True story. Brigitta helped J land the job that she herself was vacating, and even trained J before she jetted off to Germany. A little Chat, a little Hum, and a little lipstick did more for Jocelyn's future than her four years of college could.

You can't expect to connect with everyone. And there is such a thing as trying too hard. But if you have a *sincere* instinct to follow up with someone you just met, or even send a small gift as J did, follow it. It might take you nowhere, or it might take you exactly where you want to go.

A little gesture that you make—be it a letter or a lipstick—to a relative stranger that shows you really *were* listening to her when you were Chatting and thought about her *after* the discussion enough to take some kind of action is a fabulous Backscratch. It confirms in the other person's mind that yes, there was a some-hum-thing there. She'll be touched and impressed—and she *will* remember you if you run into her on the train six months later.

No Mistletoe but Got a Job to Go

That's how it works. Opportunity is random, yet not random. M gained entrance to the coveted world of magazine publishing simply because she went to a Christmas party. M was unemployed and feeling very loserish and didn't really want to go that evening, as she didn't really know the hostess, Elena, who was the new girlfriend of M's friend Greg. M felt she had *nothing* to say for or about herself, but she slipped into a smile and went to the party anyway. And it changed her life forever.

> **Elena:** So, M. Did Greg tell you I just got an amazing job at a food magazine called *Food Arts*?
>
> **M:** Yeah, he mentioned it. Sounds like a great job. Good for you.
>
> **Elena:** So, where are *you* working these days?
>
> **M** *(wanting to fib and say she was applying for grad school, but deciding to come clean):* I quit my lame job last week. Right now I'm open to anything. I want to try lots of different things to find the right fit. Uh . . . um . . .
>
> **Elena:** I think they are looking for someone to do some grunt work at the magazine. Do you want to meet the editor?
>
> **M:** Absolutely. Thanks. *Great* party!

M had never worked at a magazine, couldn't cook anything besides English muffins, and *still* couldn't type, but she said "Absolutely" anyway. M started as a temp, was made a full-time editorial assistant within one month, and ten months later became the managing editor, all thanks to a little Chat & Hum with a friend of a friend at a tree-trimming party.

These two jobs that each of us secured through incidental Chatting & Humming were the launchpads for all of the success that followed. If *we* did it, anyone can.

Chatting & Humming Rules

Networking really *is* like exercise. It's good for you on multiple levels and has untold benefits that you might never actually see. Just as there are lots of fun ways to get physical activity besides thumping the Stairmaster feeling like you are getting nowhere, there are plenty of entertaining ways to Chat & Hum. Here are a few of our favorites:

If you are a gym rat, go to the best gym you can afford. Ask around your office and sign up for the gym that the execs go to. Nothing like Chatting & Humming in the showers. *Don't* try to chat with people when they are working out, though. Pretend you are serious about exercise. Suck up a spinning class.

Take every possible opportunity for training. Go to seminars, trade shows, and as many professional development classes as your company will foot the bill for. If they won't pay for any, tell your folks you want a gift certificate to the local college or other continuing-education venue for your birthday. Get in those classes and sharpen those claws.

If your industry involves travel opportunities, take them. Don't be the one stuck home watching the phone board not light up, unless you are doing it as a deliberate, heroic favor that someone influential will truly appreciate and remember. Once we strong-armed our friend Ayn, a shy divorcee, to go on a press trip that she didn't want to go on. But off she went. Ayn ended up Chatting & Humming like a pro and came home not only with a bunch of great new Chums but also with a most excellent guy who later became her hubby!

If you are traveling for work—say, to a trade show—ask around to find out who else in the industry, or in your office, is going. Call each person on the list, introduce yourself if you don't already know him or her, and make a date for a meal, a quick coffee, or a floor walk during the show. Invite people to see you at your booth, babe.

When traveling, skip room service. Don't eat cheap; use the expense account to Chat & Hum with Most Uppity Uppers who are willing to be seen in public with you.

Go to every single stupid company function. The picnic, the Christmas party, the award ceremony. Smile. Bring your most handsome and/or accomplished escort with you to get those colleagues buzzing, a close cousin to Humming. Do *not* get sloppy drunk no matter how much you feel you need to relax, and don't Chat about work except to drop the most subtle clues about how *interesting* the projects you are working on are.

 Be a do-gooder. Find a charity to actively support. It can be in your church or temple, the local schools, Habitat for Humanity, United Way, whatever. It gives you something to say about yourself, you'll feel like a good and noble human being, and chances are good you'll meet some high-powered executives there. Part of the secret of truly successful people is that they make time to volunteer. The COO of Royal Caribbean International and Carnival Cruises, presumably a busy guy, once took the time to train for ten months, covering seven hundred miles, to be in shape for the New York City Marathon. He ran it in five hours and twenty-two minutes and in doing so raised $300,000 for the Cystic Fibrosis Foundation. Find a cause and make the time to support it—you'll never be sorry.

 Go to your alumni reunions: high school, college, camp, it matters not. Just go. You have a natural connection with these groups.

 Go to places where other professionals who are not necessarily in your industry congregate. Art shows, adventure tours, adult education classes, the bookstore, lecture series, book readings, and the like. Read the weekend section of your local paper to find out what's happening where, and go, Flo, go.

 Join industry groups and other professional organizations and participate in them as much as possible. *Do not* put off doing this for even one more week. If you don't know which to join, that's a *perfect* question to ask an exec to begin a mentor relationship. And no, sending in $25 for the PBS fund-raiser and getting a tote bag is not what we're talking about here. Try something more like the Association for Women in Communication (womcom.org). Go on your industry website and see what associations look good to you. You can sign up online for most organizations, and the membership dues are tax-deductible. The relationships you build in a professional organization will outlast just about any job. When you join, recognize the commitment you are making—everyone else will. We learned the hard way that giving organizations you join a priority in your monthly schedule is Ka-Roo-Shill.

Build your base of Chums through a variety of social events that expose you to new people and new interests. Join a book group (or start one) or form a dinner group, and each month have one person in the group bring a new person as a guest. Tap into the local college. Talk to everyone.

Are you getting the idea here? Get out of your office, get out of your house, get out of your rut, and get looking for a job—everywhere and anywhere. And no matter where you find yourself, be it the Laundromat or a lecture, make it a point to connect in some way with the people you find there. You just don't know if that person sitting next to you at jury duty could be the connecting thread to your future unless you strike up a little Chat. (OK, here's our dirty little secret. We call it Always Looking for a Job, but normal people call it Having an Interesting Life. *Sssshhh.*)

HAVE THEM FROM HELLO

Helllooo???!!! Have you ever thought about *how* you say the all-important word that starts every single Chat?

Don't just mumble hi. Put some energy behind it, like you would if you were meeting a hot date! Look people dead in the eye. Smile to feel more energized and confident. Let all those folks know that you have something invaluable to offer: a pulse.

(continued)

Once you get past hello, to the How-Are-You? portion of the ritual, the answer should be delivered with equal energy and enthusiasm. We call this the Have-a-Pulse Hello Rule. M's usual response to "How Are You?" is either "Perfect" or "No complaints!" J typically says "Fantastic!" or "Fabulous!"

Giving an energetic hello might seem insignificant. It's not. Saying something enough times will make it come true. Hogwash, you say? No, darling, brainwash. If you constantly remind people that you are fantastic, that will be the word they consciously or unconsciously associate with you. You are what you say you are. The more you say it, the more you become it.

Beyond that, here are other reasons to think about spiffing up your greetings:

- **It is critical to adjusting your attitude.** If you do it consistently, you will develop the *habit* of responding positively and enthusiastically—it's really hard to say "Fabulous!" without putting some energy behind it. *Nobody* wants to hang out and Chat with a sourpuss. Improve the mood, Jude.

- **You don't know who is standing behind you in Starbucks.** Perhaps it's a potential husband. Perhaps it's a job opportunity. If you do this long enough in your office and out in the world at places you visit regularly, people will remember you years after you've left, long after they've forgotten those who could never bother to flash a smile and make an imprint.

- **It saves time.** When you give someone an upbeat hello, it's really hard for him to then turn around and start bitching about how miserable his life is, in which case it would be nearly impossible to extract yourself from the exchange without looking like an insensitive clod. In the process of lifting yourself up, you lift your listener up as well.

- **Following the Have-a-Pulse Hello Rule creates intrigue and interest.** When you are cheerful, people will say (or at least think), "What are you so happy about?"—giving you an invitation to be positive about the big deal you just closed, the successful completion of an important project, or whatever. If you keep it brief, it's bragging without seeming to brag. *Voilà*—instant, productive self-promotion without coming off like a blowhard.

Inner Monologue for Outer Dialogue

Lots of The Girls Who Call Us tell us that they hate going to "networking" events or joining organizations and attending the functions because of those awkward moments when they don't know anyone, have no one to introduce them around, and have *nothing* to say.

We agree. It can be difficult for anybody, particularly for the shy and otherwise tongue-tied. Even company functions, where you more or less know everyone, can be painful. But to get the Hum going, you must be able to Chat—which is why we are going to take a few moments here to teach you to be a Chatty Cathy.

Being a Chatty Cathy means that you can engage a perfect stranger in conversation. It's not so tough when you get the hang of it. The key is to project a positive aura as often as possible—no matter how many legitimate reasons you have to be miserable. A good attitude is imperative to producing the best Hums; have you ever actually heard anyone Hum when they are depressed? Here are some things to ponder to put you in the mood and get you in the swing of the thing.

- **You are *not* alone.** Everyone experiences anxiety or dread when faced with meeting new people. It's called being human. We all fear rejection to a certain extent. Make it your mission to put *others* at ease; it will help you forget your own jitters. Generally, the more experience we get under our garter belt with any activity, the lower our anxiety level. The more you Chat, the easier it becomes.

- **Think of something that makes you smile.** Seriously. Before you speak to anyone, think of a dirty joke or anything else that will give you a little face-lift.

- **You've got nothing to lose.** Ask yourself this: "What's the worst thing that can happen if I go up to that senior VP and ask him about his holiday plans?" This is not an ass-kiss thing. This is simply being a human being engaging another human being who shares the common bond of working for the same company. Go for it.

Bond in the bathroom. When you're confronted with a roomful of people and you can't seem to make yourself go stand near enough to a group of them to get pulled into the discussion, go to the ladies' room and start chatting with someone in there about the decor. Walk out with her, and then confess: "You know? I really don't know anyone here except you. I'm Jocelyn."

Position yourself well. If there is a bar, belly up. Traditionally, you can always talk to the guy in the next seat. If there's a line, get on it and say something positive or funny to the person in front of or behind you.

Be the first person at the event. The next two people who come in will wander over to you faster than coffee can stain a silk blouse.

If you see someone you want to meet, plan what you will say, then go up and introduce yourself. "Hi. I'm Marcelle, I read that article you wrote in the *Wine Spectator* on Château Margaux. It was intoxicating. . . ."

After you start a conversation, don't worry if they don't start Humming with you. Don't take it personally: assume they are just thinking of something else. Just because you toss the ball doesn't mean the other guy feels like playing catch. Move on.

Read the next section for some opening lines to try on for size, and before you go out to an event, prepare, prepare, prepare by thinking of other topics to discuss (see "Puh-leeze, Not the Same-Old Same-Old Story" on page 55). We've also found it exceedingly helpful to have a few really *good* jokes in your pocket, particularly if you'll be Chatting with men.

Have confidence that once you get past those first few awkward moments of Chatting, you'll begin to relax and it will all start to flow.

Girl Gambits

Get out there and practice Chatting with strangers in different venues using some of the ice-chippers below. When you get really good at it—and you will—a fun place to practice is on the plane with the captive audience provided by the person strapped down next to you.

We like to play a little game. We see if we can engage our seatmates and keep them interested long enough to get them to tell us *their* life story. A surprising number of them do. Hint: ask your frequent flyer if he's headed home or out—we've always gotten tons of mileage with geography questions. But *puh-leeze,* honey, if you *can't* get your seatmate to play along with your little Chatting game, let the poor guy read his paper.

- **Find something to compliment sincerely.** This is easier to do with women than men: "Fabulous earrings, where did you get them?" She'll say, "From a little boutique in Santa Fe," and you can then carry on to discuss Santa Fe. . . .

- **Make a *true* positive comment about the event or venue.** It's got to be a good observation, because if you say the place is nice and it's obvious to anyone with eyes that it's peeling-wallpaper tacky or beige-brown drab, you've thrown your taste into question.

- **Express a point of positive anticipation.** "I'm really looking forward to the seminar session today; it looked fascinating in the program!"

- **Talk about food.** Everybody eats. Everyone likes to eat well and talk about it. Tell her that you are looking to make dinner reservations and ask her if she knows what's good in the area. Ask her which dish she selected at the luncheon. Discuss what you liked about the food at the events. Again, be mindful of taste: if those runny egg burritos were inedible, don't rave about how delicious they were.

And, of course, you can always talk about the weather. Hint: to get conversational momentum, rather than just saying "Nice day," compare the weather to some other location so you can continue talking about the place. So say: "I love it when it's sultry like this. Reminds me of New Orleans in July—steamy. Have you ever been to New Orleans? . . ."

You Must, You Must, You Must Increase Their Trust

Once you break the ice, your goal is to build trust, which is where the Hum starts to happen. The easiest way to do that is to ask questions about *them*. Don't interrogate anyone by rifling off 42 canned questions in a row (which will only get you branded as nosy and pushy), but listen to each response and then formulate your next question based on what he just said.

The more you engage someone on the topic of himself, the more he'll feel you actually understand him, even if you are not saying much. Generally speaking, most people don't really listen—they are too busy waiting for their turn to hear the sound of their own voice—and most people don't feel heard.

The more you can make someone feel like his words and thoughts and stories are interesting and important to you, the stronger the relationship you will build. To do this, you must learn to truly listen.

This takes a certain amount of sensitivity and practice, especially if you are nervous and/or used to being the one doing all the yakity-yakking. J was in a friend's office. Said friend, a classic Babbling Barbie, was blathering about how her sister was taking a supersaver to meet a friend in California. Barbie's boss stared at her glassy-eyed. It was clear to J that the boss couldn't care less and was wondering how to escape the torture of Barbie's drip-drip-dripping. But Babbling Barbie didn't pick up on his cues and kept right on gurgling. J saved the boss—and

Barbie—by interrupting with a question about what the boss was working on.

If you are Chatting about something, watch your audience. Look for signs of disinterest—looking over your shoulder, checking the watch, yawning, eye rolling, arm folding, and edging out of the room, for starters—and if you see your audience squirming, cease and desist with your dreary dripping. Turn the topic back to *them* and watch them perk up—it's like adding water to a wilting plant.

You don't need to work so hard to impress people. The more they feel *you* are impressed by *them*, the more impressive they will find Y-O-U. (For more talking tips, see Chapter 9, "Speaking of Talking.")

THE NAME GAME

The biggest problem we had when we were first learning how to get that Hum going (neither of us particularly good at carrying a tune) was terribly absurd. We could Chatty Cathy like there was no tomorrow. Then, when we met our new Chum again, we could remember what she'd worn or what she'd eaten the last time we met, but we had *tons* of trouble remembering the most important thing about her— her damn name.

Sometimes we'd even forget it thirty seconds after we were introduced.

God, what an awful feeling. Some people have no problem with the name thing, but others really struggle with it. We know, because we can't tell you how often we've been called Michelle and Joyce.

To block out the name block, try these tricks:

- **Slow down and pay attention.** To remember a name, you first have to catch it. Make sure you heard it. If possible, verify what you heard against what you can see on a name badge. If not, spell the name in your head and visualize the letters. Say to yourself: "I *will* remember Jocelyn's name."

(continued)

- **Repeat her name.** "Hi, Jocelyn, it's so nice to meet you. So, Jocelyn, which company are you with?"

- **Discuss her name.** "Jocelyn, what an interesting name," or for a more traditional name: "I've always loved the name Mary. My favorite aunt was Mary. . . ." Then stop and ask a question about her name: "Were you named after someone in your family?"

- **Associate her name.** Quickly think of other people by the same name. If you don't know any other Jocelyns, say so, and it will help the name stick: "I have never met anyone with the name Jocelyn before! It's a great name."

- **Connect the face with the name.** When you meet someone, as soon as you've heard her name and repeated it, stop for a sec, and in your head create a descriptive rhyme about the person: "Jocelyn is smile-lyn; Paul's the guy who's not too tall." It's silly, but it works.

Search and Deploy

Aside from putting yourself in lots of locations where you may run into fascinating and possibly influential folks, you also want *intentionally* to seek out *specific* individuals who are in a position to lead you where you think you might want to go. Once in a blue moon, what we want in life does get dropped on our doorstep—but mostly we need to go out there and find it.

Many of The Girls Who Call Us reject the idea of trying to meet someone so they can "use" or exploit her. Certainly, there are people out there who do this. You know, frankly, it really doesn't work like that. If someone is going to help you, it's because they *want* to.

Rather than dwell on what a certain person might be able to do for you, spend time thinking about all the reasons people in your life already are lucky to know you. Think about what dimension you can add to someone else's life. Are you a great friend? A compassionate person? A hoot to have around? Rather than concentrate on what you can *get,* think about what you can potentially *give* this person—professionally and personally.

It's perfectly appropriate to make yourself known in the world to anyone and everyone. People, particularly those with some kind of power, are *always* looking to connect with people who have something to offer—that's *how* they got powerful in the first place. Our question to you is, don't you think you have something to offer?

Of course you do, silly wabbit.

Put Your Face in the Right Place

If you have a specific career goal in mind, or even a general idea about an industry or a type of office culture—like casual, all-girl, creative, strictly nine-to-five, mostly moms, stay-all-night singles—go out there and expose yourself to people who you are relatively sure might be able to help you get what you want, or at least can tell you where you can find someone else who can.

To figure out who you might want to meet, keep your eyes peeled and your ears open. Read your local business section; hit those industry groups and functions; run searches on the Web for the particular industry, find the local ones, and read the websites' "About Us" pages; ask your Chums if they know anyone in [insert industry sector here]; read the trade journals; find out when the trade shows are and see if you can get a ticket. For example, suddenly we are keenly interested in meeting some bookstore owners, and you can bet your buppy that we'll be at Book Expo—a trade show neither of us has ever attended—before this book hits the stores to chat up the bookish moms and pops.

That whole six-degrees-of-separation thing is really true. You are closer than you think to knowing the people who can get you where you want to be. Seek long enough and ye shall find, sister.

Single out a person (or group of people) who you would like to get to know, make it your business to put yourself in places where you could possibly get an introduction, and begin Chatting to get a Hum going. This is *how* you put yourself in the right place at the right time. And it ain't no crime.

Now, if you finally meet someone you've been trying to connect with and the whole thing is a complete bust, don't sweat it. Sometimes the Hum doesn't happen with the first Chat (bad timing). Sometimes you *never* get the Hum (bad chemistry). Realize that there are others out there with whom you are more in tune, and move on.

All's Well That's Eating Well

M's biggest career move happened because she went out of her way to Chat with a particular person. M stayed at *Food Arts* as managing editor for seven years and loved it, but about five years into it she heard that a new food magazine called *Eating Well* was being published out of Vermont—a place where she had fantasized about living since she had her braces off.

For a year or two, M watched this publication. Meantime, M continued to receive invitations to the bazillion industry functions for the food press. Each time, while RSVPing, she would ask the public relations person who alse would be attending. Finally, it happened. A PR person told Marcelle that Sam, the editor in chief of *Eating Well,* would be going to a wine tasting. M arranged with the PR person to be seated next to Sam at the event. They Chatted. They talked food. They talked wine. They talked publishing. They talked New York and Vermont. They talked Shakespeare. They found the common ground between them and got the Hum going. They exchanged cards. M followed up with a note inviting him to eat someplace fabulous next time he was in town.

After that, Sam would occasionally call and ask M for a small favor—the name of a good food writer, a copy of *Food Arts.* M would drop *everything* else she was doing to accommodate the requests. M didn't think there was anything to be gained by helping Sam because she assumed that the editor-turnover rate at *Eating Well* was nonexistent. M wanted to keep up the Hum because she liked and respected Sam *and* he was in a leadership position in her industry.

Then one day Sam called to ask M for another favor—he wanted to know who she thought would be a good candidate to fill his shoes in Vermont.

> **Sam:** Hey, Marcelle, I got promoted to publisher.
>
> **M:** That's fabulous, Sam! So who will run the magazine?
>
> **Sam:** Well, actually, that's what I'm calling about.
>
> **M** *(breathless, waiting for him to pop the question):* Really . . . you mean . . .
>
> **Sam:** Yeah, I was wondering who you think is down there who's qualified and would be willing to relocate to Vermont to take the editor position.
>
> **M** *(hiding her disappointment):* Sam, I've got *just* the person.
>
> **Sam:** Really? Cool. Tell.
>
> **M:** I know this great editor who has been working in an executive editorial position on a food magazine for seven years who might be interested.
>
> **Sam:** Wow. Sounds perfect. Who is it?
>
> **M:** Sam. It's *me*.
>
> **Sam:** Right. Yeah. Duh. Of course! We *should* talk. . . .

M knew at least half a dozen people who were more qualified for the job than she was at the time. But she didn't give Sam a single other name. Sam eventually did hire her, and she moved up to the Green Mountains.

Straight up, we'll tell you that targeted Chats will not always be *that* successful, but if you don't *try* to meet people who might be helpful to you, it's unlikely that you will just stumble across them at Applebee's.

Also, you have to let go of the expectation that someone will help you. Note that M's quick *Eating Well* story occurred over the course of several *years*. To sustain a good Hum, you have to find the value of the relationship, not just your original goal in meeting the person, and keep the Hum going. Again: be a human being. Let the relationship be the point, and let go of all possible outcomes.

PUH-LEEZE, NOT THE SAME-OLD, SAME-OLD STORY

How many times a week will someone say to you, "What's new?" And how many times a week will you reply with some unremarkable remark like, "Oh, nothing much" or "Same old, same old"? You should *always* be able to answer this question—not endlessly, mind you, with all me-me-me-speak, but by quickly getting to a positive point that makes you look good.

At the beginning of each month, take a few minutes to jot down What's New with you in each of the following categories. They should all be positive—no new aches, pains, or crises. If you can't fill a category, clear the decks, honey, and make something happen for yourself.

- **The good book.** You should always be reading a book. Even if it takes you months to finish, be reading a book. Be prepared to *briefly* discuss your opinion on the writer and the topic.

- **Learning.** You always want to project that you are *constantly* learning. Talk about that art course you are taking, tap-dancing lessons, something you learned on the Internet or on the news. Tell people about your *plans* for learning. People are incredibly impressed by those who make learning new things a priority.

- **Work.** Talk about the most interesting thing you are working on, and say why it's interesting. This might be a stretch for some, but think about it, find it, offer it up. Never, ever miss an opportunity to tell someone something great about the work you do. You'll be a welcome breath of fresh air.

- **Cultural.** Discuss the trip to the museum, the movie you just saw, or a trip you're planning, but not what you saw on a major network during prime time.

(continued)

- **Personal news.** Positive only! Not the dog-tail amputation—although that *is* fascinating—and not the nursing home story, puh-leeze. This can be a move you are planning on making, a birth in the family, a cool vacation, whatever. This shows that you do have a personal life that is important to you and potentially interesting to others. Don't get too personal, though—so *do* mention that your sister has six kids, but *don't* mention that each has a different daddy.

Remember to keep your stories pithy. Stop talking once you've made your pithy point. We like to punctuate our stories with the ever-useful "Thanks sooo much for asking." Follow up your minispeech with a question about the other person. (For more on the importance of having your very own opinion, see "The Duh Dwarf" in Chapter 7, "Be Snow White & Deal with Your Dwarves.")

Everyone's favorite topic is always himself. Engage, engage, engage.

Chapter 4

hiring
Hell

How to survive an interview with a vampire

Useful Terms: What We Mean When We Say . . .

D-O-N-E You have a better chance of getting in a lip lock with Ben Affleck than you do of getting this job

NEXT! Don't quit your day job

Gut The largest consideration as to whether you are shown your new workspace or the door during an interview

Resumé Either a birth announcement or an obituary: a piece of paper that isn't important enough to get you a job but is important enough to keep you out of one

Getting a foot in the door is *huge,* but it's only 50 percent of the equation. The other 50 is how you do in the interview. Trouble is, we used to think getting in the door was a full 80 percent. Maybe that little math issue is why so many of us who get into an interview on a referral from a Chum completely blow it.

Many interviewers like to pretend that an interview is a discussion. It's not. It's an audition. In a discussion with someone, you might be inclined to do something ridiculous, like relax and be yourself.

The goal for a job audition is to *look* like someone who is being relaxed and herself, but who is actually being highly strategic about the personal information she reveals. You *only* want to divulge information to the interviewer that will tell her:

⚇ You are the right person for the part.

⚇ You will make her life easier.

⚇ In no way will you ever become a liability to her or to her company.

For the entire interview, you are onstage playing the role of your perfect self—who happens to be perfect for the position.

Twenty Ways Your Mouth Will Blow It for You

Even if you've never auditioned for so much as a high school play, think about auditions you've seen in movies. What's the primary activity? Reading the lines from the script, of course.

When you open up your mouth in an interview, there are a number of faux pas that will have the interviewer calling: "Next!" These are the worst mistakes we've either made or seen other people make on job auditions:

1. **Speaking too softly.** It is perceived as passive, helpless, and/or not dynamic. You're making the interviewer work too hard to hear you. It's exhausting. What? NEXT!
2. **Speaking too loudly.** It comes off as abrasive, brash, and unpleasant. Hush yer mouth. NEXT!
3. **Mispronouncing words or not using them correctly.** Imbe-silly-alic. NEXT!
4. **Digressing.** Answer only the questions asked. Don't ramble on about yourself without making a point related to the question. Your job in an interview is to *prove* you can listen and respond appropriately. And if you don't, you will be perceived as a bore. NEXT!
5. **Speaking without any energy or enthusiasm.** If you sound like a dial tone, or speak in that lazy way we all do when, say, we've been in a

dead sleep and answer the phone at 2 a.m., the interviewer will feel a strong urge to check your pulse. Uh, Hul-low? NEXT!

6. **Apologizing**. Unless you seriously do something wrong like spill coffee on the interviewer, which you won't because you won't accept coffee if offered, *don't* say you're sorry. Whatever you're apologizing for, the interviewer might not have noticed anyway, and you've also just communicated that you made some kind of mistake, which you probably didn't. Sorry. NEXT!

7. **Giggling, nervous or otherwise**. Giggling is just annoying; don't do it. Ask yourself this: would *you* hire a man who giggled? No way. So what makes you think that you would hire a woman who does? Tee-hee! NEXT!

8. **Name Dropping**. Dropping names is *obvious* and often U-G-L-Y. It's a big fat turn-off. Don't drop a name unless specifically asked about someone. The interviewer may *know* the person, so *don't* fabricate and don't exaggerate; this is not your resumé. J once knew a guy whose name was dropped, and so she called him to see what he thought of the candidate she had just interviewed. He said: "Never heard of her." NEXT!

9. **Baby talk**. This is the *worst*. You wouldn't think anyone would *ever* do this, but they do. Try this: ask a female colleague about her pet. About half the time, she'll automatically go into cutesy-wootsy mode and gush about her little snookum-doo. Say, *"Yes, I have a cat,"* and leave it at that. Woof. NEXT!

10. **Acting coy or flirting**. You might get a date, but you won't get the job. And on the very off chance that you *do* get the job, it will likely come with an expectation that you will be responsible for duties not listed on the original job description. Nice cleavage. NEXT!

11. **Talking about problems or sex—or sex problems**. Don't talk about being a woman or how *hard* it is to be a lesbian—someone actually did this in an interview with M once—or how *hard* it is to be a single girl or how *hard* it is to be a married girl with children. In fact, don't bring up children at all, as they are the direct consequence of sex.

Interviewers are not permitted to ask about your offspring, and as hideous as this truth is, many people don't want to hire someone they know will use personal days because of a sick child. No kidding. NEXT!

12. **Cracking a distasteful joke.** Did you hear the one about the two female writers—one of them a Jew, the other a Catholic? NEXT!

13. **Arguing with the interviewer.** Some do, you know. Lots of women become argumentative in order to show backbone. M once pulled a "Do you really think so?" in an effort to show spunk. She was sunk. NEXT!

14. **Cursing.** If you curse pretty much daily, you might let one fly in an interview. Watch it, damn it. NEXT!

15. **Giving one-word answers.** Don't just give yes or no answers. They'll peg you as being defensive and/or passive-aggressive in a New Yawk minute. Oh, and while we're on the topic, the word is *yes,* not *yeah.* NEXT!

16. **Bringing up salary, benefits, vacation time, etc. on the first interview.** If asked what you are looking for, try to deflect—tell them you want to focus on the Big Picture of where you fit into the company. They love that. (For pointers on how to negotiate the salary, see "A Deal is a Deal—Let's Make a Good One" on page 73.) Whatever you do, don't carry on about how undercompensated you are at your current job because the interviewer will assume (a) you are too expensive and (b) nothing will make you happy. NEXT!

17. **Complaining.** Don't complain about a single thing—not the weather, not your tight shoes, not the smell in the subway, and for God's sake not how long they kept you waiting. In an interview, never bad-mouth anyone, *ever.* Especially do not bitch about current or former bosses or colleagues or companies. If you do, you will be telling the interviewer that you are about as loyal as Linda Tripp. NEXT!

18. **Excuse making.** Don't make excuses for anything. Not time gaps in your resumé, not promotions you didn't get, not the degree you don't have. If *explanation* is called for, say something positive: say you were volunteering, consulting . . . say you were writing your first

novel. Whaddevah you do, don't say you just couldn't get a break! NEXT!

19. **Being arrogant.** There are no small parts, only small actors. If you indicate that you are too good for anything, it will be too bad for you. NEXT!

20. **Presuming.** Don't tell the interviewer he reminds you of your ex-boyfriend, your father, or anyone else, for that matter. It won't help you, and it's annoying. Mommy? NEXT!

Fatal Distractions

Aside from all that talking, there's the matter of the rest of you. The interviewer will definitely have some strong reactions to things she *doesn't* want to have to see, smell, or deal with in the office every day.

First of all, no matter what shape your body is in, if you drag it in late to the interview, you are D-O-N-E. There is only one excuse good enough to show up late for an interview, and that's the fact that you were mugged on the way in. Which, btw, did happen to one of The Girls Who Call Us. *And* she had to borrow 20 bucks from the interviewer for cab fare home. *And* she got the job—pretty hard not to be impressed by someone who shows up for a job interview right after she's been assaulted. Talk about a dramatic entrance.

Once you show up promptly for your interview, *nothing* about your body—at least nothing that can reasonably be helped—should be disturbing to the interviewer. She will not hear one brilliant word you say if she is distracted beyond repair.

1. **Slouching.** We're sorry, did we wake you? Slouching says no energy, no grooming, no self-awareness, no confidence. Even if you are a slumper by nature, pretend for half an hour that you are interested, have a pulse, and have respect for the interviewer.

2. **Asphyxiating.** The interviewer will not be able to concentrate if you are freshly drenched in CK One or any other pungent perfume.

Besides, he might be allergic, or maybe that's the same fragrance his hated ex used to wear. Our scent suggestion: nothing smells more like success than soap.

3. **Being a smelly cat.** You *can't* smell like anything bad, including but not limited to: McDonald's, the cab, cigarettes, coffee, BO, the bar from last night, stinky socks, or any other smelly smells. Brush your teeth right before the interview. Altoids, darlings, Altoids. (Note to selves: see if we can get Altoids to create an interview mint.)

4. **Bad-mouthing.** Speaking of teeth: yellow ones are a yucky distraction. You want to smile, smile, smile (but no giggling). If your teeth look anything like the inside of the coffee cup you left on your desk yesterday, go get 'em shined at the dentist. Bleach 'em baby. Bleach 'em.

5. **Gum chewing.** You definitely don't want the interviewer to come anywhere near thinking the word *cow*.

6. **Clock-watching.** Don't check your watch. *You* have all the time in the world; the interviewer does not. *Never* say you have to get back to work—the interviewer will think you are presumptuous and/or don't care enough. If you are not sure how long the interview will take, take a personal day. Whatever you do, don't yawn, no matter what time it is.

7. **Clammying.** Sweaty anything is O-U-T. Just because you are nervous, doesn't mean you're allowed to let them see you or, God forbid, feel you sweat. Give those hands a good wipe before you shake. If you are prone to upper-lip sweat, bring a hanky. Wear a jacket too, babe.

8. **Nightmare nailing.** No chips, no outgrowth, no polish on the cuticles. Go neutral on the colors—no flaming red, no decals, no Howard Hughes–length nails. And definitely don't show up at an interview with your nails bitten down to nubs. Oh no, she might be a hair chewer too!

9. **Chewing on hair.** And, while we're at it, unclean hair. Again, we're back to the merits of soap.

10. **Weeping.** Big girls don't cry. No matter how nasty an interviewer may

be or how hard she might try to unnerve you or make you look stupid—which some *will* do—do not spring a leak until you are way off the premises. It does happen. One of The Girls Who Call Us told us about a male interviewer who told her that her haircut was "unbelievably unattractive" and that it was distracting him. She cried on the spot. Um, she didn't get that job, but then again, who would want to work with *that* guy, anyhow?

For a whole bunch more on what your body language says about you, see Chapter 10, "Some Body."

No Thanks, I'll Just Puke

Here's one of the dumbest ways we put ourselves at a disadvantage while interviewing: not eating!

Interviews make us nervous, right? We don't want to eat because we are paranoid we'll get some unfortunate seed irreparably stuck in our teeth. We're afraid we'll throw up. We spent too long drying our hair and left no time to eat. Bad moves, sisters!

You've got to feed that body appropriately before you go on a job interview. Otherwise you will be flaky and shaky. You'll get that glucose low and your concentration level will fall through the floor. Eat a good healthy breakfast, just like yer mama told you. Hint: not eating will also make that breath of yours stinky; see Fatal Distraction #3 above.

Two more nutritious thoughts for you:

- **If you are going up against a guy for the same job, we think there's a high probability that he ate something.** They are *always* eating something. And they don't spend as much time on their hair. He's got more fuel than you do, honey.

- **You have no idea how long you will be there.** What if they *love* you? You could be there for hours and hours, and if you arrive having eaten nothing more than a breath mint, your stomach will lurch into an incredibly resonant chorus of the *1812 Overture.*

The worst case of this happened to M when she was interviewing for the job at *Eating Well,* a magazine about the impact of food on health. Hello, Ms. Irony? While trying to secure the position at the helm of this publication, M almost passed out from hunger during an interview that she expected would last two hours, tops, but ended up taking all day.

We say, forget about the diet on interview days: go for the egg-and-cheese sandwich on a poppy-seed-free bun for maximum protein power.

Consult the Wardrobe Mistress

An interview is not just another meeting. Not that you should go to any business meeting looking like an unmade bed, but you'll never get scrutinized as closely as when you are auditioning for a job.

For example, J always prefers to hire people in the warmer months because one of the first things she looks for in women candidates is toe overhang. If that foot is hanging over the front or back of a sandal: D-O-N-E. J's rationalization: "If this broad doesn't even know her own shoe size . . ." In winter, J pays particular attention to the interviewee's overcoat. Is it worn? Ripped? Torn? If so, out in the cold, baby.

Our Guy Spies tell us that women will be judged far more severely on their appearance than men will be on a job interview. We agree. A guy doesn't have to have great shoes—just shined ones. A guy can wear a suit that's several years old as long as it's in good shape and fits well. A guy going on an interview doesn't have to accessorize; as long as the tie is remotely the right width and tied in a smart knot, he's good to go.

Your clothes, however, *will* count. You need to make a strategic choice when picking out what to wear to an interview. Your costume, including your makeup, should say:

- I'm confident.

- I'm creative.

- I can fit in.

- I have self-respect.

- I am respectful.

- I am a together individual.

No matter what industry, it's probably best to stay on the conservative side for the first interview. It's expected anyway. But try to have one element of your outfit that stands out—a cool scarf, an antique necklace, fab shoes. Wear glasses—if you don't really wear them, get smart frames with glass in them and pop them on your head as a hair ornament. Guys with great ties get remembered.

When selecting interview clothes, do our Big Sister Screen Test T. Stand in front of a full-length mirror, look at yourself, and ask yourself aloud: "Would I hire me?" The answer *has* to be yes or you don't have a prayer.

Give Good Gut

Actresses know that in order to snag the part, they must deliver a performance that causes an emotional response in their audience. And while no human resources professional will *ever* admit this, most hires are made on an emotional basis—it's called a Gut. In fact, our Guy Spies who have done lots of hiring told us that Gut is the single most influential factor in whether they hire someone or not—be it a man or a woman.

Here are a few of the ways you can give interviewers good Gut:

Feel powerful. Do whatever you have to do before you go to make yourself feel your own power. J once learned an invaluable lesson in an acting class in college. The professor said that the student actors should always rehearse and perform in the exact shoes they feel the character would be wearing. He believed it would make them feel the authenticity of the part. To this day, J will always drop the bucks for the perfect shoes for every occasion, and she swears by it. If wearing sexy underwear or having a $100 bill in your purse gives you a feeling of power and confidence, make sure you do it for every job interview. When she would go on interviews, M always had a professional manicure less than twenty-four hours old for just this reason.

Eye contact. Look the interviewer in the eyes as often as you can. When we are nervous, we tend to not look people in the eye. If you don't, though, the interviewer is likely to think you are lying. If you stink at looking people in the eye, look right between (on the bridge of the nose); the interviewer can't tell the difference. Practice this—you *can* do it. Looking people in the eye comes from habit, not heredity.

Handshake. Not too firm (owieee), please not too soft (eeewwwee), no limp wrist, no clammy mitts (wipe 'em!). Thumb joint to thumb joint. Practice this too. Ask your close guy friends to evaluate your handshake on a scale of one to ten. Keep working on it till they all say ten. Also, don't wait for someone to stick out his hand. You go first. And don't stick that hand out there without the smile. If you are on the receiving end of the dead fish, try not to wince, and don't wipe your hand on your thigh if you've been clammied.

Connect. Say something nice—"Nice shoes," "Beautiful office," "Cool tie,"—which in essence tells the interviewer, "You make good choices, of which I will be one." But don't try *too* hard.

Read the signals. If they've capped their pen, you are talking too much. When they stop taking notes, stop talking. If they close their pads, look at their watch, or drum anything, including fingers on foreheads, shift gears, stop pontificating, and ask a supersmart question: "This seems like a fabulous place to work. How long have you worked here at Sider Road Media?" Make sure you say the name of the company correctly!

Be comfortable in silence. Sometimes interviewers are just thinking, or they might be trying to test how quickly you become uncomfortable. Don't feel the need to fill the void with babble.

Make her job easier. Chances are good the interviewer is not prepared. Make it easier for her by bringing several crisp copies of your resumé— make sure it is the *exact* same version you sent to the company originally. Also arm yourself with some intelligent questions: "How does this job position fit in with Broken Record, Inc.'s main mission?"

Honey, make sure you know what the mission is. To prepare the best questions, go to the company's website and read the "About Us" section. Also surf through the industry association's website. Some of The Girls Who Call Us admit that they never check out the company website until *after* their first interview, when they are *sure* they are really interested in the job. Most of the time it's too late at that point, and the second interview never comes. Do your homework *before* you go.

RESUMÉ PILATES

Your resumé is not just a listing of your professional experience; it is your brain on paper. A great resumé, and we don't mean just the contents of it, can open a door even if you don't have the exact skills the company is looking for. A sloppy resumé will slam that same door shut even if your experience is exactly aligned with the available position.

Resumés and cover letters are the first line of attack for a company to thin out the crowd. You have a mistake, use poor grammar, don't sell yourself enough, or sell yourself too much—say hello to the reject pile.

(continued)

An interviewer can't afford to overlook stupid mistakes on a resumé or cover letter. If the hire turns out to have been a bad one, out comes the personnel file, out comes the offending resumé, out goes the person who disregarded the obvious problems this hire presented on paper. Long story short: the hiring person can get royally screwed.

Conversely, if a candidate looked good on paper but turns out to be Nightmare Nancy, the person who recommended the hire can point to the strong resumé and great presentation and say, "Who could tell from this that this woman was an ax murderer?"

These days, people are whipping off multiple resumés on home computers, each one specifically tailored to the job they seek. Unfortunately, this leads to sloppy resumés on lousy paper with bad presentation and stupid slip-ups.

Whether you have one version of your resumé or one thousand, each and every one needs to be proofread by a really good copy editor or, better still, a professional resumé-writing service.

Get that resumé into shape, girl!

- **A resumé shouldn't be a last-minute proposition.** When you slam one together over the weekend, you are bound to make mistakes. And when there is a mistake in your resumé, D-O-N-E. More than once, J sent out a resumé that said *right* instead of *write*. She didn't even realize it until—much to J's humiliation—some prospective employer pointed it out. Oops.

- **There are lots of resumé writers and websites; punch in "resumé writer" on your favorite search engine to find one.** Like finding a shrink, though, you might have to work to get a good one, and like a bad shrink, a misguided resumé writer can do more harm than good.

- **Once a year, get your professional writer to give every version of your resumé a tune-up.** We suggest you mark this to-do your calendar on April 16—right after you've sent in your income tax return and have fresh perspective on just how much you are not making. PS: resumé writers are a tax deduction!

(continued)

- **Don't fold your resumé.** That's like putting on a hot little black cocktail number and throwing a sweatshirt over it. Go out, get a cool little folder with two pockets, put your resumé in one side, put your cover letter in the other, and attach a business card with a nifty spiral paper clip from Italy. Find them at flaxart.com. Pop the folder into a large envelope and use a printed label for the address (Avery big labels #5164). None of this will cost you very much, but it will make a big difference. Companies are used to receiving and producing slick marketing materials; if you package your resumé professionally, it will show you as a highly savvy, together prospect who knows how and when to go the extra mile.

Tell Me About a Time When . . . You Wanted to Crawl Under a Rock and Die

Like theories of education, bad ideas come into vogue in interviewing. The latest is the behavioral interview. Sadistic HR people find them effective for making people squirm—um, we mean for finding the best hires.

If you don't know that you will be walking into a behavioral interview, especially if you've never faced one before, you're basically screwed.

Behavioral interview questions always start with these six evil little words: "Tell me about a time when . . ." For example: "Tell me about a time when you took a public stance on an issue and then had to change your position." Blugh–huh!

OK, you draw a complete blank, and you've now got four seconds to formulate your answer before the heat starts creeping up your face and your hands are sweatier than your date's were at your junior prom.

Try another one (these are *actual* sample questions): "Tell me about a time when you were unwilling or unable to make the necessary sacrifice to achieve a goal." Go ahead—try to talk your way out of that one, sweetheart. We're talking interview hell here.

You've *got* to be prepared for the behavioral interview. We're pretty sharp and think fast on our tootsies, but we wouldn't want to face one of these things without a crib sheet. These questions are *designed* to break you and to see how quickly you degenerate into negative thinking. They are *designed* to test your discretion. They are *designed* to foil your plans of sailing painlessly in to a new position.

Go to mvnu.edu/prosptrad/candc/behavior.html (Mount Vernon Nazarene University) for a list of particularly nasty sample questions. The University of Nebraska—Lincoln also has good stuff on their site (unl.edu/careers/prepare/behavioral.htm). Get your hands on behavioral interview questions, sort out your stories, write them down, and be prepared to give answers that *always* spin positively.

Thanks for the Torture

Unless you got a bad feeling and know that there is no way on earth you would take the job, your job interview is not complete until you run home, grab your classy engraved stationery, and handwrite the interviewer a sweet note of thanks. Mail it that *same* day, Ms. Emily Post.

Be sure to send a thank-you note to each person you interviewed with. One of The Girls Who Call Us, Sasha, a sales manager, told us that she once was looking to hire someone as her personal assistant and interviewed a woman who sent a thank-you note to Sasha's boss, whom the candidate had also met, but *not* to Sasha herself, who had the final call on making the hire. Needless to say, that candidate was D-O-N-E.

Some people who *are* savvy enough to write the thank-you note make the mistake of thinking it is like a secondary cover letter, and they pitch themselves again. It is not. Now that the interviewer has met you, the thank-you note should be a cordial reminder of what a swell human being you are—and what a swell human being you think he is:

> Dear Mr. Dracula:
>
> I just wanted to drop you a quick note to tell you what a pleasure it was to meet you today and to thank you for giving me so much of your time. I have to say that now that I've been to AnneRice, Inc., I'm extremely excited about the prospect of joining your team in the role of Unit Import Manager. I know that hiring is a difficult process. If there is anything I can do, or if you need additional information to help you make your decision, please feel free to call me at any time. Consider me at your service.
>
> Again, thank you so much for your time, and I look forward to hearing from you soon.
>
> Best,
> Lucy Bloodworth

J usually never even reads the thank-you notes. J says, "One LOVE stamp or Christmas stamp in July, and that candidate is O-U-T." When she does actually get past the envelopes, she scans the letters for spelling errors and checks out the quality of the applicants' handwriting. *Everything* counts, so puh-leeze don't use a mess of one-cent stamps.

Leave the Phone Alone

Once you've sent the note, consider the event over. Lots of The Girls Who Call Us sit by the phone. Don't do it. Expect that you will *never* hear from those people again, no matter how great you thought your interview was. Move on.

Those folks are *busy,* and also they might just not have a sympathetic bone in their bodies. Just because you don't get called in a reasonable amount of time doesn't mean you don't have the job, but it doesn't mean you are still in the running either.

At the end of the interview, ask with whom you should follow up. If they say they will call you, don't call them until 48 hours after they said they would call you. You may call *once*. Keep it simple. Just tell them you were wondering where they were in their hiring process. Don't remind them that they said they would call last Tuesday. We're pretty sure that some of The Girls Who Call Us were actually strong candidates for jobbies and took themselves out of the running because they stalked the interviewers on the phone and with email. To resist the temptation to keep checking in on the status of your application, think: caller ID. Don't touch that dial!

Gulp: The Agony of Defeat: Swallow It

Be a good loser. If you don't get the job, don't be a jerk. When they tell you—if they tell you—you didn't get it, be gracious and grateful, no matter what. Tell them that you know it was a very hard decision to make and that you are so appreciative of being seriously considered for such a great job. If you can't tell them in person or on the phone, write it in a follow-up letter. Again, keep it simple: "Thank you for considering me. It was a pleasure to meet you."

Listen up. You *must* do this. Approximately 50 percent of all new hires don't work out. You never know how close you came. Besides, the person who got the job might have another offer somewhere else.

M was not the first choice for editor in chief at *Eating Well*. The publisher first hired a woman who looked better on paper. M accepted the defeat cheerfully; after all, she still had a great job. M took great pains to let the interviewer know that there were no hard feelings: she called him and told him she thought he'd made a good choice and she understood why he made it. Then she dropped him another note thanking him for his time and told him that if he needed any assistance in the future, he should feel free to call.

Six months later, he did. The editor who was originally hired had to leave the position for personal reasons. As first runner-up, M was the only candidate. Had she been even *slightly* pissy about not getting the job in the original search, there's no way the phone would have rung with a second chance.

A DEAL IS A DEAL—LET'S MAKE A GOOD ONE

When you start out on any long trip, do you fill the tank only halfway? Three-quarters? No. You top that sucker off with as much as the tank will hold. Why? Because you want to get as far on that trip as you can on one tank; you're not really sure when you'll come across that next filling station, are you?

When you start a job, you *have* to think in terms of filling that salary tank to capacity. We can't tell you how many of The Girls Who Call Us started new jobs thinking, "Well, the salary isn't that great, but when they see what a hard worker I am, they will adjust my salary upward to make it right and fair." Nope, nope, *nope*.

J started a job and shortly thereafter found out that she was making far less than another equivalent senior executive who was hired around the same time. J marched right into her boss's office to request a salary bump to even it all out. No fuzzy dice. J's boss pointed out that J's salary was a reflection of the deal she herself had negotiated when she signed on. He told her that he wouldn't even *discuss* a raise until it was time for J's yearly review. "Take it or leave it," he said.

In most cases that initial salary *is* negotiable even though the hiring party will try to make it seem like she's locked into a fixed price. But don't worry about seeming greedy by asking for more: negotiation is expected.

No matter what business you are in, no employer will give you more than the market rate. If you ask for $80K as a starting salary when your skills are typically more in the $30K range, it truly does reflect unkindly on your sobriety and sanity. However, negotiating

(continued)

reasonably shows that you are a good negotiator, and the interviewer will increase her perception of your value because you know your own worth. So, to prepare to competently negotiate a salary:

- **Find the going salary in your region for the job title.** Go on monster.com and select "Earn what I deserve" from the "Today's the day I . . ." on the home page. You will find the salary wizard, so you can run the numbers. If you know people in the industry, you can also ask them about salaries. Don't, however, ask people for their personal income number; that's tacky and taboo. Rather, ask people, particularly people you know who are frequently involved in the hiring process, about the current market *trends.*

- **Pick a number that will make you *happy.*** Seriously, so few people think about this part. It's not just about taking what you are given. You are signing your *life* away here—what's it worth to you? Then add 10 percent to your Happy Number. Your final number should fall somewhere within the salary range uncovered by your research. If not, it's the Breathalyzer for you, sister.

- **Figure into your analysis any other costs associated with this job.** Is it a longer commute? Add $$$. Will you require a fancier wardrobe that needs dry cleaning? Add $$$. Figure in *any* changes you can anticipate, such as added meal costs—add breakfast $$$ if your old company provided bagels, and if there is no office coffeepot, add $$$. Daily javas add up, Caffeine Queen.

- **Determine your bottom and middle numbers.** Lock your bottom, middle, and Happy Numbers in your head before you go in there to negotiate.

- **Recalculate your current salary.** If the interviewer asks you the old "What's your salary now?" question, *know* that she is looking to keep the offer as low as possible. What she will do is figure out a percentage bump, based on your current salary, that she thinks will satisfy you. If you can't sidestep the salary question, round up: add in what you would guess would be your raise in the current year, plus any bonus, and use *that* number to reflect your current salary. It's not lying. It's projecting. It is kosher to *reasonably* estimate up based on your anticipated income. One of The Girls Who Call Us recently got a job offer after revealing her actual salary to a prospective employer. Before she accepted the offer, she got an unanticipated 10 percent salary hike at her current job—and now the salary at the new job was lower than the old one. But don't go nutty inflating your current salary. If you overinflate, it will be as obvious as double-D breast implants. Hint: never reveal your actual current salary to a headhunter, no matter what they say; they *will* report it to their client! If asked, say politely: "I'm looking for something in the $50K range."

- **If they ask you for a number, try not to give it**. We've both hired people who spat out a number that was well below—as much as $20K—what we were authorized to offer. We thought, "Great: they're happy, we're happy. Problem solved." If asked what salary you are looking for, say, "Well, I've done some homework on this, and the range seems to be between $2 [your bottom number] and $5 [your Happy Number + 10 percent]. What's the range you have budgeted for this position?"

- **When they make an offer, don't accept immediately.** Thank them for the offer; don't show disappointment or glee. Tell them that you will go home, crunch some numbers, and get back to them. Usually they will give you a deadline. Chances are the number will be lower than what you want. Be prepared to go back and tell them your Happy Number. Use common sense—if your Happy Number is 40 percent higher than their offer, you are not in the same ballpark, and you might have to counter with your middle number plus 10 percent wiggle room. They will tell you they need "to crunch the numbers" and will come back again to you with something probably 5 or 10 percent lower than the number you gave them.

- **Be prepared to walk away if they don't come close to your deal-breaker number.** If you are not happy with your salary, you will be anxious and unhappy—never a great place to start a new life life. But before you walk away from a job you think you are dying

(continued)

to have because they are offering you less than you currently make, ask about the other benefits that might make up for a lower salary: bonuses, health insurance, flex spending (AFLAC!), 401(k) plans, profit sharing, car allowances, moving expenses, stock options, and salary reviews at intervals of less than a year. At that point, feel free to ask for the moon—you've got nothing to lose.

Money isn't everything. Don't leave a job you are really happy with for $5K or $10K more unless you are sure that the new position is one you really want. It might sound like a lot of money, and so it is, but if you divide it by twelve, the financial impact isn't worth leaving a job you adore. Conversely, to *not* take a job that you think is perfect for you because it pays less than the job you have currently and feel lukewarm about is equally self-defeating. You can't put a price on day-to-day happiness.

Chapter 5

a whole
New World

How to avoid office alien-nation

Useful Terms: What We Mean When We Say . . .
Culture What you'll find if you put the office petri dish under a microscope
Alien That would be you
Ego Ecosystem The fragile world in which you live Monday to Friday, nine to five

When you first started your job, the nice people in human resources, or some reasonable facsimile thereof, gave you a whole stack of glamorous paperwork associated with your fantastic new life: health insurance forms for when you get sick, worker's comp forms for when you get maimed, 401(k) forms for when you get decrepit, and the designation-of-death-beneficiaries form for when it all finally kills you.

In that hefty orientation packet there was an innocuous-looking, nondescript piece of paper that you had to sign swearing that you are not an alien. And sign you must, or you would never see the light of pay. But you lied. You *are* an alien.

You are a complete *alien* in a whole new world until you fully understand the culture of your office and figure out how to assimilate to your new environment. If you are truly to succeed at work, your mission, Ms. Alien, is to figure out how to stand out *while* you are fitting in.

Our mission is to tell you how to do just that.

Mastering the Microcosmic

In the petri dish of office life, it's all about culture. Of course, with the dawning of the New Economy, people, most notably MBAs and insecure, twenty-eight-year-old CEOs, use "office culture" as a code phrase meaning anything from "We're child-friendly" to "We're basically children—wanna see our ping-pong table and Coke machine?"

Yup, "corporate culture" is a big, fat, vague buzzterm that everyone and their HR department throw around *all* the time, but The Girls Who Call Us usually ignore its vital relevance to themselves. Attention, dear reader: all that corporate culture crap that might seem like nothing more than marketing hype to you should be the *primary* factor that determines how you *behave* in the office.

Corporate culture is *not* just what a company *says* about its environment. It's the Ego Ecosystem of your day-to-day reality. The truth is, when it comes to Officepoliticus, you *gotta* sweat some of the small stuff—we're talking microscopic. In those first few jobs, we each spent an embarrassing amount of time as *National Enquirer*–worthy two-headed aliens that no one would take quite seriously due to a series of incidental cultural insensitivities on our part.

For example, when J started a new job in a super-duper corporate setting, she showed up that first week toting a five-foot floor lamp through the lobby because she hates that nasty overhead lighting. Coworkers stared in Alfred Hitchcock horror as she passed: clearly, the lighting was good enough for *them,* but this broad, this *new* girl? "Nooooo, she's too *gooood* for fluorescent."

An innocent mistake, but one that didn't make J look too bright. Anytime you introduce an obvious change, no matter how minor, to a highly codified culture in which you are a newcomer, it will be seen as alien behavior. And ya might just find yourself being left in the dark about a lot of what's going on around you as a result.

It's so simple to inadvertently criticize what you find in a culture you are new to. One of The Girls Who Call Us, Barbara, a sales account executive for a handbag manufacturer, started a new job and immediately began making myriad suggestions to her fellow salespeople and other coworkers about how to improve the office environment and the business itself.

From her first day on the job, she wanted to change the way *everything* was done. Barbara began rapid-firing memos to execs about how the processes should be altered and improved, what software they should all buy to be more efficient, and on and on. She kept it up for a month, until she became conscious of the resentment that was building around her.

What she saw as being passionate, helpful, and enthusiastic, her colleagues saw as attacks on how they had managed the business before she arrived. Essentially, she was slamming them. Barbara never managed to heal those relationships, and she left the job within four months; none of her suggestions had been taken.

When you enter a new culture, if you see areas for improvement, you must be careful to introduce your ideas gradually, and when you do so, be sure that you are sensitive to the fact that what you have found at the new job is the result of someone's decisions and someone's work.

We never stopped to consider that. In fact, we were completely mystified when what we considered minor episodes seemed to be such big fat hairy deals to others. We just couldn't understand why things were the way they were instead of the way we were *sure* they *should* be. We didn't know the rules, and we were *pissed* that no one would just *tell* us. As we matured, though, it dawned on us that everybody at work was just too damn busy to explain what we should have been able to see for ourselves if we just would have opened our eyes: if you refuse to fit in, you should get out.

In this chapter, we'll help you put your office under the microscope so you can study its unique culture. Understanding the Ego Ecosystem will help you avoid stumbling into culture craters that you thought were little divots. Not only that, but you will also discover how to put yourself in the right place at the right time, scratching the right backs so you can shine like Sirius, the brightest star in our galaxy.

Let's Do the Time Warp . . .

Time bends, sister. Each office culture has its own time zone and its own concept of "regular hours." Honey, there ain't no such thing as Standard Office Time.

Understanding the Time Culture in your organization is of the essence. One of The Girls Who Call Us, Sigourney, for example, was viewed as a foreign body when she said: "Isn't it a bummer to have an eight a.m. meeting?" She knew she'd blown it when her coworker, smiling at a nearby Uppity, replied: "Oh, I am *always* here by seven, and I *never* leave before ten. In fact, the *rest* of us are in the same boat." Sigourney didn't yet understand her company's time culture: although she frequently stayed late in the p.m., she never asked, and didn't realize that she was strolling in hours later in the a.m.

A given office might have any number of time zones, and you need to adjust yourself to each one you deal with. For example, the subculture reflected in your division or department might have a very different dynamic from the overall culture of your parent company.

When J was working in a start-up new-media division, the pace was insane, and everything and everyone was fast, fast, fast. But the parent company was established, plodding, highly bureaucratic, and procedure-happy. J quickly learned that when she worked with people outside her particular department, she was in a time warp and had to slow it down: she spoke slower, had to deliver detailed printed proposals instead of zipping out off-the-cuff emails, and had to have incredible patience—and not take it personally—while hearing *nothing* for days and days from the Most Uppity Uppers for answers that could easily have been issued in ten minutes.

Here are a few of the office culture timetables to check from time to time:

Pace yourself . . . accordingly. What's the general pace of things? Is everyone rushing around looking ever so busy? Then you probably should not be practicing your Zen meditative walk through the hallways. Are people mellow in their speech patterns? Then don't let your tongue zoom at NASCAR MPHs.

The times they are a-changin'. Do you have all the time in the world to generate that proposal—but it had better be purr-fect? Or is sloppy better than seconds wasted? You can tell which option your culture finds more acceptable by which tends to receive more praise from Uppities. Btw, Uppities tend to measure efficiency against how long *they* think it should take to accomplish a task, not how long it actually took *you* to do it. *Always* ask your Uppity *when* she wants delivery. You just might need to turn that project around like Speedy Gonzalez. See, señorita?

Watch the daily tides & swim accordingly. Observe when people wash in and when they wash back out. In some cultures there are high expectations of overtime without pay, and the on-the-dot nine-to-fiver is perceived as an annoyingly anal alien. You don't need to directly mimic the timing patterns of your culture, but the closer you match your coworkers' schedules, the less alien you will seem.

Ponder the monthly phases of the paper moon. Know what the company policies are and how the process works. If expense reports *must* be filed monthly, don't turn in six months' worth at once, whining you didn't have the time to do them. M did this all the time, and in doing so she both brought into question her administrative abilities *and* irritated the nice accountants. Worse, though, was what happened to one of The Girls Who Call Us, Jean, a printing-equipment salesperson. Jean got stiffed to the tune of almost ten grand when she didn't follow the policy and file her expenses routinely. Because Jean was so hell-bent on selling and completely ignored the climate in her company, she wasn't tuned in to the signs that it was going under, and she let her expenses pile up for almost a year. She was unexpectedly laid off, the company went bankrupt, and she never saw a dime of the money she'd spent out of her own pocket. In a highly bureaucratic culture, internal paperwork is an essential part of your job responsibilities, and in all other cultures it's still important and you *must* stay on top of it, no matter what else you have going on.

Adjust seasonally. When's crunch time? Which department gets slammed, when, and how often—annually, monthly, weekly? Don't be running to accounting asking for a copy of your W2 from three years ago during the stay-all-night height of budget season. If you *know* when the worst times are for each person and division, you can put yourself in a great position to do favors by being Miss Sensitivity and offering to help out. Do a quick coffee run for the accounting team before you punch out for the night. Or do as J used to do when she knew particular departments were pulling late-nighters and drop off a sympathy six-pack or a bottle of tequila and a few shot glasses.

Check up on the annuals. Read the company handbook and ask coworkers how often people tend to get promoted. Is it every third Friday, or only in sync with the viewing of Halley's comet? If you *know* that people are promoted regularly, feel free to go in after six months on the job when you've exceeded expectations and ask for a bump. If promotions are next to never and you ask for one prematurely, you are *doomed:* stingy cultures call this "entitlement."

Watch the other guy's watch. Everyone has good and bad times of day—not to mention the month. Make it your business to learn coworkers' cycles and chart them on a mood forecaster spreadsheet, which will help you predict the most auspicious times for meetings, requests, and delivering bad news. "Lucas: won't answer questions till after 5 p.m." "Elias: crabby before lunch; cheerful after." "Tia: don't speak to her until she's drained her second cup of coffee." "Gary: has 3 p.m. deadline every day."

Ⓐ **Show them a good time sensitivity.** In every culture: Don't keep people waiting. Don't say you'll call back in two minutes if you *know* it will be twenty. If you need help, ask: "Is this a good time?" If you call a meeting, keep it as brief as possible by being prepared.

Look for the Uniformity Label

Oh, this one drives us *nuts* with The Girls Who Call Us. So many of them tell us, "Look, I have *my* style, and I'm *not* going to change it. I'm *great* at what I do! What does the way I *dress* have *anything* to do with my abilities? How *dare* they try to tell *me* how to dress!"

We *agree!* But tough doodly-doo for all of us. The way you dress in the office has a *ton* to do with your abilities—it can get them completely ignored!

Even if there is absolutely no written official dress code for your office, there *is* a dress code. The whole thing about office attire is a very sensitive issue because it pits individual style against the collective culture—dicey stuff. Dressing too distinctively can seem like an act of disloyalty against the culture.

When J was working in the Boston advertising agency, even though that company prided itself on its culture of creativity, virtually everyone wore superpreppy clothing. J, not one to be straitjacketed, clung to her New York City Sexy Mama look. On days when she wore something even remotely conservative (as in not skintight), a nice older gentleman, who was clearly trying to help her out without getting himself sued, observed that she "looked nice" and gently suggested that when she wore foundation makeup she "looked better."

When J finally got the hang of the conservative thing, she then landed a job at *Rolling Stone.* J spent months frumping around that terminally hip office culture in Ann Taylor red or blue suits, opaque stockings, and practical pumps, all of which she later realized pegged her for a big fat D-U-D. Finally a colleague tipped her off that the

French twist *had* to go. J regrouped and regroovified her wardrobe to fall into step with her hipper-than-thou coworkers.

Think of it this way—when it's snowing out there, you don't take it as an affront to your personal sense of style or your intellectual capabilities that you need to pop on a pair of boots instead of slingbacks. Check out the clothing climate of your office:

- **Think of uniforms.** They show *belonging* to a group. Same thing in the office. If you outdress coworkers by a league, they will perceive you as "too good for the rest of us." If you underdress by a mile, guess what? "Clueless D-U-D." Look around and check out the message that others are sending with their clothes—groovy/hip, status-conscious, classic, authoritative, trendy, powerful—and align your working wardrobe accordingly.

- **Dress Uppity.** Check out what the respected execs are wearing and follow suit. Never conform in a way that makes you look bad, though. If all the women have bowl haircuts and you think that cut will make you look like one of the Three Stooges, skip it. Pay close attention to when Uppity Uppers tell you they like an outfit, and wear it regularly, but no overkill. Pull together other outfits that give a similar look and feel.

- **Icon eye candy.** Within the context of your office culture's uniform, create a Visual Signature—an item of clothing or style that people identify with you. M has white hair and always wears an antique cameo ring; J never fails to turn out in fabulous shoes. Ladies, the world is our oyster when it comes to creating memorable Visual Signatures: all most guys have to work with are their ties and wherever their hairline happens to fall.

Is It a Workstation or a PlayStation?

Everyone knows about the corner office—the bigger the office, the more powerful the person. The better the view, generally the more influential the inhabitant. No news there. It's just a big ol' corner office cliché.

But we want you to look beyond square footage. You can learn a ton about your company's culture just by checking out coworkers' desks.

When M started with *Food Arts,* it was a small, chaotic start-up environment. Pretty much anything went—everyone's desk looked like the aftermath of a hurricane. M's desk was always piled precariously high with all manner of manuscripts, folders, and month-old newspapers. Then, when the magazine was purchased by M. Shanken Communications, a more established publishing firm, and moved to far posher quarters, M brought her start-up mentality with her. Her desk was *always* a disaster area—that's how we show people we're busy, right?

Once M bothered to look around, though, she realized that all the coworkers in the cubicles around her pretty much kept their stuff in nice neat productive-looking piles, and you could land a plane on the clear surfaces of the executives' desks. M realized she looked not only out of place but also out of control by comparison. She cleaned up her act.

Take the desk litmus. Are the desks orderly? It might indicate a highly structured by-the-book environment. Are there lots of kitschy paraphernalia strewn around—rubber nuns and Barbie dolls in various states of undress? You are probably in a creative culture. Keep the state of your desk in a manner that meshes with that established pattern. If there is a wide culture gulf between subculture styles in different divisions, then subtly follow the lead of the company execs.

Cultish or clannish? Do people display lots of family photos, or none at all? This can tell you how much or how little to talk about your personal life. Hint: no photos can mean that employees don't want to let the Most Uppity Uppers know that they might have other obligations and priorities beyond their loyalty to the company. In this company cult culture a fifteen-hour day is likely to be an expectation rather than an exception.

Ⓧ **Status cues.** If all the Uppities have Palm Pilot docks on their desks, don't be dragging your gigantic day planner to meetings with all those Post-it notes bursting out of it like New Year's confetti. Pick up the cues, follow the clues.

Ⓧ **Tell no tales.** Don't let your stress show on your desk. Put the bottle of Rolaids in the drawer, okaaaaayyyy?

Ⓧ **Desk destination.** Be strategic about what you are communicating with your workspace. Rotate in *objects* that fit the culture and generate interest and discussion on their own. For example, in the creative culture, keep your paper clips in some handmade pottery. In the techno culture, display the latest prototype gadget. One of The Girls Who Call Us, Natasha, a graphic designer, displays classic toys like Slinkys. Natasha's coworkers come over to visit just to fiddle with the latest toy and play a while. Hummmm. Conversely, stacks of black binders are good for the boring android corporate camper look.

Space: The Vinyl Frontier?

Take a look at the decor. What are its pretensions? Is there expensive framed Belle Epoque artwork on the walls? Then you are probably in a place where a "cultured" image counts, and you can be sure the Uppity Uppers never miss the Sunday *New York Times Magazine* and always know what's on the best-seller list.

Are there illustrated posters on how to be a good corporate camper plastered through the hallways, like there are at AOL headquarters? Then you'll be wanting to use the words *upgrade* and *proactive* a lot. Is there an implied emphasis on innovation? Renew that subscription to *Wired*. Is it grunge youthful? Then perhaps you *can* keep your nose ring in and use your purple marker after all.

Check out the parking lot: what kind of cars do the execs drive? If it's a bunch of Lexuses, Porsches, or Aston Martins, you know that luxury status items count in this office culture big time. If there are SUVs, you are dealing with a whole other status mentality—the active lifestyle wannabe culture—so you probably want to let it be known that you own a snowboard. And if the parking lot is full of rusty trucks and nasty old Volvos, then you know that these people probably care more about good value and faithfulness—or, quite possibly, just driving everything into the ground.

See where we're headed here? Map out what you think is the underlying cultural system and message as expressed by the physical office spaces and align your head space with it. Whatever the culture seems to esteem (is it outsider art? vintage tools? brainy Mensa-esque quarterlies?), educate yourself. It's not tough, since there's a website for everything (europuppy.com—need we say more?). To succeed, you need to understand the culture and clearly fit into it, but not conform to the point that you lose your individuality and become invisible.

When M. Shanken, which publishes *Wine Spectator,* purchased *Food Arts,* M didn't know a claret from a clarinet, her entire exposure to wine up to that point having been provided by swill with screw tops and fruit-sopped sangria. Even though M didn't work on *Wine Spectator* herself, wine was clearly the epicenter of the company's culture—the huge glass wine cellar in the lobby was a pretty good tip-off. M made it her business to first teach herself a little bit through reading and classes and then asked some *Wine Spectator* editors to mentor her further.

She would speak to these colleagues/wine experts about how much she was enjoying the classes she was taking, ask them for advice, and give them updates on her progress. Eventually, sensing her sincere interest, they began to invite her along to in-house wine tastings and wine events around the city. She was candid about what she didn't know, was respectful about asking to be included, listened carefully to the lessons, learned quickly, and showed her appreciation to them for having shared their time and knowledge. She became highly Visible within the larger company and formed great and lasting friendships with those mentors.

In fact, if you are in a culture where everyone knows about something you don't, it's a great excuse to begin Chatting with coworkers so you can build a relationship that Hums for years. Get yourself interested in the topic with a little research, tell someone in your company about your desire to know more, and ask them to help you learn. People are always flattered when you ask for help and make it clear that you trust them to teach you well.

So focus some of your energy on building skills and promoting the subjects that the atmosphere seems to suggest it values. For example, if the place seems on the cheapy, chintzy side, become an efficiency expert: look for ways to save a dime and toss them up to the executives. If the walls are filled with press clippings, start learning the ropes of promotion and showing your support for the PR effort. If your company slogan is "Think Different," then no matter what your job description, it's your job to come up with innovative ideas that will help the company grow. This is what we call being the Synergizer Bunny—you keep going and going to develop and display yourself as a person who not only fits into the culture but enhances it.

You get the idea here. Hop to it!

Tapping In to the Chatter

Observe *how* and *where* people communicate with each other in your office. Where do people gather to Chat? Is it the coffee room? Is it the mailroom? Is it Colonel Mustard in the conference room with a rope?

Check out where and when people do the most Chatting and be there, baby. Frequently morning is the best time to Chat & Hum around the office before the heavy lifting commences. We've told many of The Girls Who Call Us to show up half an hour early just to get in on that prime Chat bonding time.

 Alien intruder. Be careful not to barge in on coworkers' chats unless there is an obvious opening for you to do so. If people are obviously engrossed in a tête-à-tête, say hello, but be sure not to insert yourself into the conversation.

Subjects matter. Catch the general drift of office chitterchatter. Is it all work? Mostly work? If so, do not start in about your new boyfriend, your old mother, your "about last night" stories. If coworkers routinely discuss personal matters, you *must* join in and bond with them. Pet talk is always a safe topic, but please, not in that all oozy snookum-poo-speak that makes people want to cough up a hairball.

Cover your privates. The most common mistake people make when Chatting is that they say things that make them look bad or reveal too much. Stay mindful when you are blah-blahing and never say *anything* that will make you look U-G-L-Y, shows poor judgment, or will otherwise give someone a bad impression. For example, even though it's chic to be on antidepressants, the knowledge that you take them will most likely change someone's image of you. Don't get anxious about it; just keep the old trap shut about the bats in your belfry.

HOTBEDS OF HEARSAY

Gossip is probably the way most news spreads through your office, and you really do want to be on that grapevine. Most people tend to think of gossip as coming in only one flavor: malicious. It's just not true. Really, anything that doesn't come directly from the source or isn't officially pronounced is considered gossip. Gossip can be anything from where Dominique got that fabulous deal on her cool shearling coat to buzz about the company relocating to Montana.

Gossip can help you prepare for what would have been an ugly surprise, like the time J tipped M off that *Eating Well* was going to be folded by the parent company. And if you find out through the grapevine that the COO was squeezed out for attacking the CEO, you'll be less likely to tell the CEO when you run into her in the elevator what a great loss it was that he left the company.

(continued)

In other words, gossip will keep you in the know and on your toes. Here's how to manage unofficial office communications:

- **Be a bystander.** If what you hear as the rumor mill spins is primarily personal dirt, it's best to be very busy at those moments when the worst blood is being spilled. If you do happen to hear some exceedingly damaging stuff, don't repeat it. Repeat: don't repeat!

- **Give to take.** In a gossip culture, you must supply tidbits as well as digest them or most people will eventually stop feeding you anything. Keep an ear to the ground for innocuous morsels that are work-related, and pass them around strategically to a *small* group of reliable sources who are in a position to return the favor. Don't blab everything you hear to everybody, otherwise the word about you will be that you are an indiscreet gossipmonger.

- **Avoid temptation.** If someone confides in you with a particularly important piece of information, like the fact that they must fire someone you know, don't use it as currency in the gossip market. Keep it *to yourself.* Discretion builds friends for life. Nothing busts trust like a betrayal in favor of a cheap gossip thrill spill. J once told a colleague that she might fire a subordinate. The colleague immediately told the subordinate the bad news. Tides changed and J didn't need to let that subordinate go after all, but she never told the blabbing colleague so much as the time, let alone anything important, ever again.

- **Grains of salt.** Never confuse gossip with gospel. Listen and consider carefully before you repeat or take any action. Even if the gossip is benign information, it could still be incorrect, and repeating it could make you look foolish. Assume what you hear is true and brace yourself accordingly, but sit on it. Some gossip might make you nervous, such as impending layoffs, and you will be tempted to discuss it to calm yourself. Resist the urge and work on your resumé instead, girlfriend.

- **Playing post office.** Remember that *anything* you say to *anybody* about *anything* will be repeated and attributed to Y-O-U. As you are Chatting, keep in mind that what you say might be taken out of context later, and you will probably be misquoted.

Internal? External? Eternal?

Pay careful attention to how the company communicates to its employees. Are there lots of companywide memos? If so, who sends them? If anybody and everybody memos the entire staff all the time, feel free to email the universe with requests for participation in the paper recycling initiative. *But,* if companywide memos only come down from on high, do *not* send memos of any nature to the entire organization.

Check out the tone of internal communications—is it friendly and chatty? Pithy? Punny? Putrid? Observe and learn, lady.

Function follows form. Try to tailor your communication style to that of the company's culture. If email is the primary form, don't be walking the halls looking to poke your head in someone's door with every incidental observation. If yelling from office to office is the mode, don't be Miss Formal Fancy Pants and have every communication start with "As per our discussion of 4 August . . ."

Plagiarize to synergize. Copy the tone, style, and format of the corporate communications, so don't use that ivy background and 26-point fuchsia Comic Sans font on your emails if the company emails are froof-free. For language points, see the "Cool 'Tude Dude" section on page 92.

Kindly in kind. Specifically focus in on how *individuals* communicate, and reply in kind to *each*. Some people resent too much email; others don't want to hear from you unless you put it in writing. Is the boss a one-word email kind of guy? Then no *Les Misérables* epic-length replies. But be careful not to come off as abrupt, as some bossy bosses can dish it out but not take it. Always sign off with a "thanks." Does the Uppity Upper hate being caught on the fly? Then don't say, "I'd like a quick word with you." Instead say, "I'd like to schedule a quick meeting." Same meaning, different planet.

Meetings of the Mindless

Are you in a by-committee culture? Are people huddled together frequently with the conference room door shut? Are meetings highly formatted and planned or spontaneously constructed and BYOB casual? Who attends? Who doesn't? Do people ask lots of questions or sit quietly like kids in detention? Are the meetings stress fests or snooze fests? Do Uppities tend to kill the messenger? Watch it all and learn your company's meeting culture.

If Simon says bring pastry, bring pastry. If people never interrupt each other, don't interrupt. If it is always formal, don't call a meeting and then show up without a written agenda. If decisions are always made in premeetings, hold one before yours.

Take the time to prepare. A good place to start is knowing what the topic is.

Know how to run a meeting. It's a skill, not an art. Don't let people go off onto unrelated tangents; keep it on track and you'll look like a star. If you don't *really* know the ins and outs of running an effective meeting, ask someone outside your company for advice and coaching; always pay close attention to those in *your* office culture who you think do it well.

COOL 'TUDE DUDE

When J first started at *Rolling Stone,* she had never worked for a magazine before. Her boss started blah-blahing about "rate base," and J had noooo clue what he was talking about. J was smart enough not to say, "Excuse me, but what the hell is a rate base?" She knew that to reveal her ignorance would have branded her as a know-nothing outsider alien. Instead, J bluffed her way through it by re-

(continued)

peating back more or less what he had said to her: "Right. Rate base is key."

To fit in, you must keep up with the jargonese of your industry. Read at least one or more trade magazines every month, and check out your company and industry websites. Learn the language and speak it, sister.

- **Adopt the lingo, Lois.** If everyone is walking around saying, *"What are the deliverables and next steps?"* then don't *you* be saying, "When will you get me that thingy and what d'ya wanna do now?"

- **Don't overuse any one term**. You'll become the jargonhead joke of your office if you do. Make sure you *know* when a *buzz-phrase* is dated and don't use it. We were sooo sad when "I'm swamped" was replaced with "I don't have the bandwidth." Thank God we had the RAM to handle it.

- **Introduce a new buzzword.** Go to the job sites, click on your field, and read the job descriptions—it's a great way to pick up the latest buzzwords in your industry. Check out wordspy.com for the new word evolutions and convolutions in our language and talk about them.

- **Don't pick up bad habits from your officemates.** Cliché overkill is the worst: "I hear ya." Poor grammar ain't nothing too good neither. Here's the rule: if your boss doesn't say it, don't you say it.

Observe the Movements of the Stars

Follow the leaders, follow the leaders, follow the leaders. We can't say that enough. No matter where you are in the company, do your very best to keep an eye on the executives. Hint: it's a good idea to know who they are and what they do. To find out, go to your company website and read the bios, or ask around.

Observe how the leaders lead. Get to know their styles, listen carefully to the behavior they publicly praise, and repeat it. M once worked with a CEO who practically canonized another VP for presenting a report in PowerPoint. You can't *believe* how fast M taught herself to use PowerPoint.

We know what you're thinking, and we're telling you right now: this is *not* sucking up. It's responding appropriately to the culture cues. M didn't go in the next day and say: "Boss, you were riiiight. Ooooh, PowerPoint is soooo special. You are soooo wise . . . that must be why *youuuu* are the boss." M just put her next report in PowerPoint because her boss had expressed that preference. Ignoring the boss's stated or inferred preferences is not ass-kissing avoidance—it's active passive-aggression. (For more boss biz, see Chapter 12, "Hail to the Chef.")

If you don't have direct access to Uppity Uppers, do your best to make yourself known to them anyway. J used to literally follow company execs to the deli so she could "bump into them." It might sound a bit absurd, but she did some major bonding there in front of the cold tortellini salad. One VP from the deli became the friend, mentor, and office champion who helped J become Visible to other Uppities within and beyond the walls of that particular company. Btw, they are *still* friends.

Take a few risks (the old bump while getting a grinder at the deli) to meet your company Uppities. Chat & Hum in the elevator, at office functions, wherever, and find the common ground. Execs and managers in other divisions who take a shine to you will tell you far more about what's *actually* going on in the company than your direct boss probably ever will! J had the inside scoop on *everything* because of Mr. Tortellini from the salad counter.

Then there are the invisible leaders. These are the people who are not necessarily in the big offices; they might not have the fancy titles. It might be the most low-key person in the company, but she or he is the most trusted and most *influential* person in the company. We call these coworkers the Rainmakers.

The Rainmakers are the people who know how things work.

They know how to make things happen in a company. They are the eyes and ears of the Most Uppity Uppers, and God help you if you inadvertently piss off the Rainmaker—we're talking major downpour on your career parade.

One of The Girls Who Call Us, Anita, was a newly installed director at an Internet service provider. The CEO initially bragged to all about what a superstar performer Anita was. And she was. This gal was a dynamo of productivity and efficiency. Anita, however, needed the cooperation of the quality assurance department to keep her own division running smoothly.

Anita, who was stubborn and fearless, would inform the head of quality assurance in ever-so-snotty emails and a few snide face-offs how he was "screwing everything up." The quality assurance guy was intensely mellow in the face of Anita's browbeating. Anita was gone within six months. The quality assurance guy happened to be an old college buddy of the CEO's, and while it's almost impossible to know for sure, our guess is he was the Rainmaker.

The Rainmaker could be a senior exec, the Most Uppity Upper's assistant, or just some nondescript employee whose job function no one is exactly sure about. You just don't know. Finding the Rainmaker is like trying to catch snowflakes on your tongue—seems like it should be easy, but you're never entirely sure when you've been successful, which is why you should plan on being professional and courteous with *everyone*—rain or shine.

Changes in the Wind

Corporate culture is like the weather—it *can* and *will* change. Sometimes a production glitch or missed deadline will cause a sudden storm, but things soon return to normal. Other times the environment undergoes a dramatic change caused by some cataclysmic happening—a new tornado of a CEO comes aboard and rips through the joint, and life never returns to its original state. Change can also happen over time, through erosion, and you suddenly notice no one seems to be doing things "they way we've always done them."

Change is the one thing you should count on, Grasshopper. You need to put up those alien antennae and observe how the execs respond to change—however and whenever it happens. If there's a big shift in culture, you *must* be prepared to move with it. You might not like the change as it happens—but if you show that you are resistant toward it, you are in for a big culture shock yourself.

We've seen this again and again when a new manager comes in and wants to change the way everything is done, even if it means undoing all the stuff that was accomplished in the last six months. The staffer kicks up a nasty dust storm, relying completely on her tenure to see her through. But when the dust settles, the new manager is still there, and the girl is nowhere in sight.

You must be on the lookout for and adapt yourself to every change. Even when you get promoted, you will, once again, be an alien until you figure out the culture at your new higher elevation. The air is thinner at the top, which can cause dizziness, delusions, and disillusion—not to mention that increased risk for heart attack. Don't overexert yourself unduly trying to prove that you belong there at the top. Stay cool, baby, stay cool.

be a Girl with a Reputation

Make a good name for yourself and don't leave home without it

Useful Terms: What We Mean When We Say . . .

Mashed Tofu Bland, lumpy; may be full of good protein and low in fat, but fundamentally unexciting

Reputation The thing that will take you UP or O-U-T; not necessarily based on reality

Credit You win

Debit You lose

In our mothers' generation, all a woman had to worry about was whether she was perceived as a "nice girl" or a "bad girl." Back in the day, a Reputation meant something exceedingly nasty and was to be vigorously avoided. Today, though, if you don't have a Reputation, you're going nowhere fast and nothing is easy.

These days, if you live and breathe, you have a Reputation for something. Now, the way we see it, you have a choice. Either you gear your actions and behavior to control what people think and say about you, or you take your chances and let people brand you as they will, accurately or not. Alternatively, as many do, you can let people you encounter out there in the world think a whole bunch of random nothings that adds up to a hodgepodge we like to call a Mashed-Tofu Reputation—lumpy and unmemorable.

Honey, your Reputation is your most important career asset, bar none. A good Reputation will get you UP, a bad reputation will get you O-U-T, and you may never get back IN—anywhere.

There Are Some Things That Money Can't Buy

Here's what we want you to do: think about your Reputation as your credit rating.

When you are young and broke, you're not likely to spend much time pondering your credit report; you're not running out to buy any big-ticket items, you're just trying to make ends meet. You can get credit—even before you establish any history—simply because Visa, MasterCard, and all the rest want your business and are willing to give you the benefit of the doubt.

It's the same deal when you get those first few jobs. Whether or not someone referred you, you are an Unknown Entity and are being given a shot to prove you were worth the risk she took in hiring you.

You must remember, however, that while it's insanely easy to get into huge trouble with credit cards in only a few months, it can take years to get out of debt, can compromise your ability to purchase the things you *truly* want when you want them later, and can hang over your head for years after you've long forgotten what you purchased to get yourself so deep in the hole to begin with, as in "Whatever *did* happen to those three-hundred-dollar lavender cowboy boots, anyway?"

Your Reputation works *exactly* the same way. The more you conscientiously do things to establish good credit in those first few jobs, the stronger your professional Reputation credit rating and the more confident you will be that you have a decent idea about what people out there are saying about you. The more debt you rack up—intentionally or unintentionally—the longer it will take to undo it, and you will be perceived as a Bad Risk if a prospective employer decides to ask around.

Finally, if you never bother to establish a Reputation in the first place, and the day comes that you want that big chance, few will want to take *that* risk: "Her resumé says she's been in the industry for ten years. But if she's really as great as her credentials, how come *I've* never heard of her?" NEXT!

The Girls Who Call Us frequently insist that they can't control their personal or professional Reputation: "People will just say anything." And sure, it's true; there will always be people who try to trash our good names professionally out of jealousy, political manipulation, or generalized bitterness, or they will downplay the fact that we are good at our jobs by attaching negative adjectives to our personality when describing us. To this fact of life we say: So what?

Everyone has detractors. We're pretty sure even Mother Teresa had her critics. And God knows we've sure had ours. There are plenty of people out there who, we are relatively certain, have gobs of unpleasant things to say about us—some of it reasonably accurate, because, being human, we've made our fair share of blunders, and some of it patently false, because anyone who receives a degree of success or attention invariably suffers garden-variety ill will—just ask Martha Stewart. But for every detractor out there, we figure we've got about fifty other professional people in many industries saying, "Oh, I love those two—they are the best."

Just like your credit report, your Reputation is a numbers game. You cannot please all of the people all of the time, but if you can favorably impress the majority of those you meet, your credit will be good in all the places you most want to be.

What's in a Name?

Every credit card in the world has two things that identify it with Y-O-U: your name and a number. Nobody, however, will remember your numbers (your sales figures, the hours you worked, how many new accounts you brought in, etc.), and if you *can't* get them to remember your name, it hardly matters what else someone might remember about you: "Oh my God, I met this amazing account exec from Tulsa. She would be just purr-fect for the new sales position. Let's see, she takes belly-dancing lessons and only eats raw food . . . Damn! What was her *name*? . . . Oh well."

It might seem like a stupid little detail, but every marketing person in the universe knows that you put your brand name out there not only in the bold type but also in the fine print. You *must* put your name on everything you do at work. Oprah didn't get to be Oprah by calling her show Clyde.

The more people hear and see your name, the quicker you can build a kick-ass Reputation. When she was a managing editor, M became known to a Most Uppity Upper because she signed off *legibly* on an invoice and submitted a pack of them to accounting with a cover sheet summary that also had her name on the top. The Most Uppity came into M's boss's office one day waving an invoice and said, "Who the hell is Marcelle Langan DiFalco?" M, who happened to be sitting there, said, "Uh, that would be me." The guy asked his question about why a particular expense had been approved, M explained, he was satisfied, they Chatted & even Hummed a bit, and thereafter the guy, who happened to be the *owner* of the company, knew who M was—face, name, *and* job description.

Put your name on every paper you touch, as many times as is reasonably possible; in the $15-billion-per-year promotional products industry, it's called imprinting, and it's effective as hell for building name recognition, which is why you'll see T-shirts, baseball caps, and every other imaginable item emblazoned with corporate logos. Your name *is* your logo, baby—use it so others choose it.

Cover me. Put a nice crisp cover sheet on top of reports with a big headline for the title or topic followed by your name demurely on the bottom: "Submitted by Mary Oliver." This habit also can help prevent credit theft of your brilliant ideas and work. Use fax cover sheets and cover letters for *everything* you send anywhere. Put your name, not just your company or department, on each.

Name me. On Word documents, go to View, click on Header and Footer, and put your name and the date on the file—it will show up neatly on every page. And while you are in there, sugar, do everyone a favor and pop in the page numbers.

Sign me. On emails, use the signature feature so that every original email you send has your name, title, company, and contact information. Contacts will appreciate not having to dig out your card every time they want to find you.

Card me. *Never* say to anyone, "Um, my company doesn't give business cards to people on my level." If you don't have a business card, go to a local printer and get something classy made up with your home address and cell phone. Need a title? Try "consultant." Cards are inexpensive and worth every penny. Don't leave home without them—all it takes is one card in the right hands to *rock* your world.

I'VE HEARD SO MUCH ABOUT YOU. . . .

The Girls Who Call Us often ask, "How do I *know* what my Reputation is?" It's a great question but a tough one. It's not like you can drop $15.99 and get a Reputation report.

Unless you overhear people speaking about you, or you specifically ask them, you are not likely to know what they *reeeeaally* think of you or your work. But we've found that most of The Girls Who Call Us don't want to ask anyone how they are perceived because it seems too "needy." It's a tough call, but here's how we keep tabs on our own Reputation ratings.

- **If someone criticizes you, listen carefully—chances are the person who said it isn't the only one who thinks it.** Know, then, that in certain circles you have a reputation for being Difficult, a

(continued)

Slacker, or a Micromanager, and if you don't like those labels associated with a brand called [insert your name here], then avoid behaviors that can lead people to believe them. The fact is, if you have enemies and you can stomach it, *listen* to what they say about you.

- **Listen to every single word of your performance evaluation.** What you hear and read in your review is what your boss says about you. Correct problem areas, repeat behaviors that receive praise. Uh, duh.

- **Ask a trusted friend.** But realize that the way *she* sees you is most likely not representative of your general Reputation; your friend will be partial, and quite possibly not entirely honest.

- **Get a reliable spy.** The boss's secretary, someone in HR, people in the PR department, or an exec in the company who is *not* your boss will be in a good position to tell you what others are saying about you. Don't worry, you don't have to ask; they'll tell you during the course of a normal conversation. It's a good idea to be very nice to all of these folks, because they are also all in a position to wreak havoc on your Reputation if you rub them the wrong way.

Take Credit: It Pays to Be Discovered

You may think that hard work is its own reward, and so it is, but if you want actual recognition for it, then you'll have to do some more hard work to reap the rewards. Just like the special awards offered by credit card companies, be they frequent flyer miles or shopping points, you have to do the legwork to redeem them. Yes, sister, we have arrived at the ever-dreaded topic of self-promotion.

Conventional marketing wisdom dictates that people are seven times more likely to repeat something negative than something positive. So our rule of thumb is you need to put seven times more positive stuff out there in the world if you want to build a fabulous Reputation for yourself. And you *can* promote yourself without coming off like an obnoxious, bitchy blowhard. Here's the drill:

1. **Chat.** Tell people in a nonbraggy but enthusiastic way what you are up to. Be *positive,* like this: "I'm working on the most interesting project at the moment with Ms. Uppity Upper—we are conducting an entire inventory and creating a new database. The technology is incredible, and I'm learning a ton!" Note the "we." People will use your name when relaying the information to others, as in "Emily was telling me about the new inventory system," but because you said "we," your listener won't think you are clobbering him with your self-promotion club, plus you are associating yourself with Ms. Uppity and *her* Reputation for, say, Always Working with the Best and Brightest.

2. **Compound interest.** Every once in a while, drop a short, friendly email to lots of people with whom you have some personal relationship—even a tenuous one—and tell them what you are up to. Constantly give people in your life good reasons to talk about you by keeping them updated. Potential topics include special projects you are involved with that you think might be interesting to the recipient, professional development courses, travel plans, promotions, life changes (moving is always a good reason to reach out and touch someone), and the like.

3. **Make PR pals.** Make friends with people in public relations. Invite one out to lunch and offer to be her contact person in your division. Ask her if there is anything you can do to help the PR effort. If your PR people take a shine to you, they will give you a heads-up on juicy office activities and talk you up with the execs, plus they are out there in the world more than most of us and will mention your fabulousness out there too. If your office doesn't do PR, take a quick class and volunteer to do it; it could be your next big promotion!

4. **Press and release.** Learn how to write a press release (for instruction, go to lunareclipse.net/pressrelease.htm). There's a template in most word processing programs. It's not *that* hard. So if you have a new

job, won an award, or landed a big client, write a quick press release and send it to your alumni magazine. Go to thepaperboy.com and find the little dinky newspapers in your area by putting your city name in the search (free ones get read too), and send a release about yourself! They *will* print it—local papers are always looking for free, well-written space fillers—um, we mean stories. These articles will appear without a byline, so it doesn't look like self-promotion. Being known in your local community should never be underestimated—you have a natural and important loyalty connection with your neighbors, and it can open doors you wouldn't even think to knock on.

5. **Be the media.** Either make friends with the person who does your company newsletter or suggest that you start one yourself. It will give you access to members of the company that you normally have no business with and give you opportunities to promote activities in your own division and support your boss and colleagues in a terrific Backscratching sort of way. Type in "public relations" on about.com for an article on how to put together a newsletter.

6. **Designate yourself the awards person.** The world is full of prizes ripe for the picking. It's a huge pain in the ass to gather the information and package an entry for business awards, but your company will usually foot the bill (entrance fee) if you do the legwork. Even if it's not *your* work that you're submitting, you get credit for making it happen—but only *if* you win, because otherwise nobody cares. Go to your industry website and look for the awards tab. Join professional organizations—they have *loads* of award programs. Even rinky-dink awards count—enter for anything and everything. Uppities love to report that they are a winner, and you, dear, can make their dreams come true.

7. **Your friends are your best assets.** Tell your great friends to brag about you, and brag to your good friends. *They* won't take it the wrong way. Your friend, of course, will then tell everyone she knows because she likes you, she looks out for you, and your success makes her look good by association.

8. **Surround yourself with positive people.** Negative people spread negative stuff that other people *do* listen to. Cut off your Evil Network of Negativity at the knees by limiting exposure to toxic people in your life—even if they happen to be closely related to you.

9. **Find a mentor (or, as J calls her or him, a rabbi).** A mentor is an Uppity Upper in or outside your company whom you ask, formally or informally, to guide you along your career path. Most of our own mentor relationships were informal arrangements, but boy, we learned a ton, and those people *still* have nice things to say about us—as far as we know. Mentors are increasingly common in offices across the country. Figure out what it is you need or want to learn about to get you to the next level, and simply ask the person in your office you think best suited to teach you if she'd be willing to give you an hour a week to help you reach your goal. *Warning:* once someone is your mentor, you always have to treat her like a mentor. Even if you get more Uppity Upper than her someday, you still need to be very deferential, because *yes,* you *owe* her.

10. **Say nice things about your boss to everyone.** It *will* get back to her. Usually the boss will return the favor, unless she hates your guts— which still works, because *that* fact will get back to you faster than you can say "exit strategy."

11. **Get it in writing.** If someone—a client, a vendor, anyone but your mom—says something positive about your work, ask him for this tiny favor: "If it's not too much trouble, I would love it if you could jot me a quick note to keep in my annual review file!" Then you can walk around the office saying how nice it was that Mr. Client/Vendor/ Anyone-but-your-mom took the time to write this swell note to you. No, dear, this is not a move of desperation. If you truly gave someone good service, good enough for them to comment on, 99 percent of the time he will be delighted to return the favor with a note, plus you are complimenting him: you are saying that his opinion is influential. Come on, who doesn't like to hear that?

Not-So-Smart Cards

When you are trying to build credit, you *can* establish credit with just one card, which would *seem* to be the fully responsible thing to do—keeping things manageable and all. But, in fact, having only one credit card is *not* the best way to build a strong credit rating. You need to get all kinds of credit all over the place. The more cards you have and the more you use them and live up to your responsibilities with them, the stronger your overall credit rating.

It works the same way with your Reputation. While you should not try to be all things to all people, neither should you put all your eggs in one basket by trying to impress people in one single direction. Over the years, we've seen so many of The Girls Who Call Us try to build their Reputations on *one* virtue only—like honesty.

Honesty is definitely one of those concepts that falls into the too-much-of-a-good-thing-can-kill-you category. More girls have screwed themselves and destroyed their Reputations in the name of honesty than we could even begin to tell you. For example, if you give someone the honest truth, whether they asked for it or not, and it's *not* something they wanted to hear, which, honestly, it never is, you might get a Reputation for being Critical, Out of Line, Insensitive, Untrustworthy, and/or (our personal favorite) Negative.

J was once asked by a coworker for her "honest opinion" of a demanding and snotty letter the coworker wanted to send to her boss's boss detailing why she thought she should get promoted. J told her honestly: "You are nuts. This letter is *suicide*." Later, J found out that the coworker was telling people that J was "Aggressive" and "Insensitive" and had "Attacked" her.

Take our word for it—being worthy of trust is not the same thing as being brutally honest. Save your complete honesty for the mirror, and remember this: diplomacy is the best policy.

Another big Reputation that The Girls Who Call Us want is for being Smart. Smart is a killer, though. If *all* you are concentrating on is *convincing* people how damn smart you are, you might inadvertently be mounting up huge Reputational debt. Coworkers might brand you as a Know-It-All, Insecure, or Not A Team Player because you are trying so damn hard to prove that you are smart that you unconsciously trump coworkers right and left with your knowledge. Or perhaps you come off as Defensive as J used to, by taking direction as an insult to your intellect, frequently tossing off retorts like: "I know, I know, I know," "Of course I already knew that!" or "Duhhhh."

Being known for only one quality could leave the listener with more questions than answers about who you are and what you are like. Here are some other seemingly positive Reputations that we've seen women single-mindedly pursue, and how they can be misinterpreted:

If you try too hard to prove that you are:	They might see you as:
A Hard Worker	Works Too Much
	Kiss-Ass
	In Over Her Head
	Takes On Too Much
	Doesn't Know Her Limits
	No Fun
	Has No Life
	B-O-R-I-N-G
Passionate	Perfectionist
	Lacks Perspective
	Emotional
	Greedy
	Over the Top
	Humorless
Independent	Redoes the Work of Others
	Can't/Won't Delegate
	Not a Team Player
	Ruthless
Nice	A Pushover
	Mashed Tofu

Reputation Builders:
What You Want in Your Wallet

When we realized that people would form impressions of us in all of three seconds and repeat them to the universe, we decided to create a Gold-Card list that would keep us highly conscious of building a solid Reputation based on *a number* of positive things, including all the qualities listed in the previous section, that we want people to be able to say about us.

Ultimately, only you know who you are and the image that you want portrayed, but here are some of the items from our Gold-Card list that we have found are the most powerful, efficient builders of kick-ass Platinum Reputation Ratings. And honey, whoever builds up enough credit to secure a Platinum Reputation—Judy Woodruff and Condoleezza Rice come to mind—gets Career Carte Blanche.

Consistent. When it comes to the office, a foolish consistency is *NOT* the hobgoblin of little minds. Dependable consistency of mood, dress, performance, and respect for colleagues makes others comfortable and builds great Reputations. Dress well and create a look that fits in with your corporate culture; don't be changing your exterior image every forty-eight seconds—trust us, they won't think you "spontaneous" but rather Moody, Flaky, Indecisive. Consistently do solid work. Be consistent in your respect for *everybody.* Don't flatter your boss and then turn around and berate your colleagues, lest you get a Reputation for being a big fat Ass-Kisser. The key to consistency is knowing what your priorities are and sticking to them (see Chapter 11, "Y-O-U: The Ultimate Planning Machine").

In control. Get a grip on yourself. Never seem overwhelmed by the amount of things you have to do. Just do them. Don't broadcast your thoughts that maybe you *can't* get something done—even though commiserating is a common way we girls bond with each other. Have energy, but retain control of it. No manic giggling or public hysteria, please.

Organized. Present yourself as an organized human being. Keep your desk well organized, but never empty. Organize your thoughts before you speak (see Chapter 9, "Speaking of Talking") and ramble not. Show yourself to have an organized home life by seldom flying in the door late and leaving at a regular time—whatever time that is in your particular culture—on most nights. Prepare, prepare, prepare, and more importantly, *look* prepared. Show up *early* for those meetings, missy.

Polite. Mind your manners, mama. This is an *easy* credit. Say please, say thanks, look people in the eye, and *really* listen to what they are saying to you. Provide thoughtful commentary that demonstrates that you were in fact listening. Don't babble about things that are clearly not interesting to your audience. Don't repeat nasty gossip. Send thank-you notes, etc. If you don't know what's appropriate in the land of Civilized & Polite behavior—and hey, lots of people don't— pick up the latest edition of Emily Post or check out etiquettehell.com for fun and instructive victim-of-bad-manners stories.

Unflappable. When things don't go your way, take a step back; consider why certain decisions might have been made, and accept them without reacting all over the place. Don't be a pushover, though; pick your battles (see Chapter 14, "Held in Contempt").

Reliable. *Always* do what you say you are going to do *when* you say you are going to do it.

Flexible. Remain cheerful in the face of change, whether it's a change in direction, a change in responsibility, or a change in plans—even if it means the project you just finished is now irrelevant. Bitch about it all you want in the privacy of your bathroom mirror, but in public be the first on line to pitch in and help with the transition.

Generous. Take credit and share credit: "I worked very hard on that report, but I couldn't have done it without my amazing staff and the solid direction of my supervisor." OK, we know it sounds dorky. Do it anyway.

Supportive. Align your goals with those of your boss. Tell people what you learned from your boss, and lead them to believe you have a great relationship with her—even if there's some tension there (see Chapter 12, "Hail to the Chef").

Fun. Know how to laugh and tell a joke. J saved herself a world of trouble and made useful allies by knowing how and when to laugh at herself and make light of a tough situation with a well-placed joke. If you find yourself acting graveside grim, take a second to think of a funny spin on the same situation that is currently troubling you.

Intriguing. Demonstrate yourself to be a person with a life that you value and protect. Share only the most positive and interesting *high-lights*—no epic tales, please. If you are talking with someone about your personal life, know that in most cases his attention span will be about as long as one commercial break during *Monday Night Football*.

Solution-oriented. Don't freak if you make mistakes or encounter unforeseen obstacles. Solve the problem as efficiently as possible; look forward not back.

Graceful. Accept criticism. Whether you feel it is deserved or not, say: "Really? Wow. I had no idea. I wonder what I'm doing that gave that impression. It was certainly not my intent." Ask the critiquer for her advice for a specific to-do to remedy the situation. Immediately make adjustments to change that person's perception, and check back in with her later: "Hey, Doreen, remember that discussion? Well, I'm so grateful you brought that to my attention. Here's what I've done to correct the problem."

Diplomatic. Defer to and respect the expertise of others by asking for help and requesting advice, which shows you don't think you are a Know-It-All. Be wide open to the idea that you *can* learn something from someone else.

In the groove. Respond to the individual styles of each coworker and Uppity, and know how to adapt yourself according to the cues presented by your audience. So if your boss seems to value precision, and you notice that he nitpicks documents that have careless mistakes in them even if all the information is accurate, take the time to review your work and make it perfect. Skip the slipshod for that guy. *Warning:* don't expect other people to change their priorities to match *yours.*

Follow up. Follow up quickly: return phone calls, answer emails, and deliver requested information efficiently—and make it seem effortless. J was known for her fast turnaround and kept up the pace to hold on to her Speedy Gonzalez Reputation. It's a great Reputation, so don't be telling everyone and their grandmother about your horrific workload or that you were just too busy to get back to them. Use your 40 percent and return that call!

Powerful. Get known for knowing something. Build up knowledge areas that will get people saying: "Oh, you want to know about how to write pitch letters? Ask Marcelle, she's a whiz." It doesn't even have to be a work topic. One of The Girls Who Call Us was on *Jeopardy* because she knows so much trivia. When her coworkers have a question about any random thing under the sun, Wendy is their girl. The trick to this one is to allow people to "discover" your power by dropping a few clues and samples, rather than telling colleagues everything about yourself at once.

Security. Become sensitive to coworkers' ThreatThresholds by listening to what they say bugs them about other coworkers, and avoid making the same mistakes with that person. Strive not to threaten people by either showing them up or putting them down. Don't make excessive apologies or excuses for deficiencies you perceive in yourself (see Chapter 7, "Be Snow White & Deal with Your Dwarves").

Whatever you do, be aware of overcompensating—trying too hard to *prove* you are Smart, *prove* you are Dedicated, and *prove* you are the hardest most loyal worker since Lassie could have people labeling you as Insecure and/or Trying To Make Everyone Else Look Bad. Check yourself: if you feel you have something to prove, chances are you are trying way too hard. Lighten up, mama. It's just a job.

Looks *Can* Kill

Just like in the good old days, Reputations are mostly the stuff of appearances, not reality. Most of The Girls Who Call Us like to think that they are primarily judged on their abilities. But appearance does count. Big time. In fact, your entire Reputation can be based on what you wear, if people can't get past it and it's all they can seem to remember about you.

You know, she's the one with the . . .

- Big hair
- Cleavage
- Spandex addiction

Think of the way you look as your "packaging." What does your package say about you? Your look can help brand you in a good and memorable way *or* can be a distraction from the Reputation you want *or* may get you labeled with a Reputation you never dreamed of or wanted.

One of The Girls Who Call Us, Amanda, works as an on-air reporter. She loves clothes and shops for those that make her look expensive and powerful. Amanda is highly Ambitious and wants to show that she's Cutting-Edge. Both are good Reputations for someone in her line of work. So what's the problem?

The quality of her clothing and her sense of style are soooo far above those of her female supervisor that Amanda, who has the great misfortune of also being young and pretty, is actually threatening.

Amanda's packaging is too expensive for the culture she's in. She's like a Godiva alongside all the Goobers. Amanda's supervisor and coworkers are having a *real* hard time seeing Amanda's talent and dedication because they can't get past the feeling that Amanda in her Armani is trying to outshine them. From the supervisor's point of view, Amanda is Too Big for Her Britches and Doesn't Know Her Place—definitely not Reputations that are going to help Amanda get anywhere fast in that company, except perhaps out the door.

While Amanda is in the beginning phase of her career and still pretty low in the hierarchy, it would be better if she aimed for a Reputation like Team Player for the next few years and saved her Chloe for the weekend. By conforming a bit more to the culture, Amanda would not distract coworkers and superiors from her obvious talent, and they would be far more inclined to support her rather than block her.

What you present on the surface has a tremendous impact on the entire Reputation. Is it stupid? Yes. Is it real? Also yes.

HOW TO LOOK GOOD ON PAPER

Have you ever gotten a letter from a friend, and before you even looked at the return address, you knew *exactly* whom it was from because you could tell by the handwriting? Right. We call that the Visual Signature. It's a graphic clue that people associate with you.

Here are really *simple* things you can do at work that take only minutes but make a *big* difference in getting your name associated with great Gold-Card Reputations like Professional, Together, Organized, Savvy, and, yes, Smart.

(continued)

- **Develop a unique (but not froofy) document style**. Every company has a logo and a style sheet that it uses for all corporate communications. When you submit documents, create a template for yourself that has a header (see page 101 in the "What's in a Name" section), and always use the same typeface and point size for all of your documents to give yourself a signature "branded" look.

- **Get documents right**. Pick up *The Chicago Manual of Style* or Strunk and White's *The Elements of Style.* Know which words get boldfaced, underlined, or italicized. Learn how to turn documents into personal promotional pieces by using white space, bullets, and subheads to make every doc *highly* readable. You will be doing a huge favor for everyone who has to look at it—and making yourself look the über-professional.

- **Print it out and read it out loud.** We guarantee you will find something wrong with it—a missing word, bad syntax, verb-subject disagreements. Even if you are not a great grammarian, when you read it aloud it will *sound* wrong. If it's a super-duper important document, give it to someone *else* to read to see if it seems remotely like English to her. You don't want the general office buzz about you to be that you are so sloppy (or lazy) that you make mistakes no self-respecting tenth grader would allow on her English homework.

Even if you think that a document is "rough" and no one else but the recipient will see it, make it the best representation of you possible. (Hint: the briefer the content, the less likely you are to make an error.) Documents, even emails, that have stupid mistakes or are poorly conceived get passed around the office. And don't rely completely on spell-checkers. M was writing to a client once about a missed call and meant to write "sorry for any inconvenience." While running the spell-checker, she clearly wasn't paying attention and changed it to read "sorry for any incontinence." Read your document one last time *after* you spell-check!

Think of everything you write as a sample of how well you think and how much integrity you put into everything you do.

What You Don't Conceal You Reveal

Appearance, though, is more than how you look; it's how it *all* looks. We've learned the hard way that if you show them the dirt, your Reputation can be mud. From seemingly innocent and irrelevant conversational exchanges, many of The Girls Who Call Us have landed Reputations that have *nothing* to do with their abilities:

- **Big Drinker.** "Every Monday morning we look forward to Angela's weekend bingeing episodes . . . unbelievable!"

- **Incredibly Cheap.** "Beth spent nine hours tabulating who had the side of coleslaw."

- **Sleeps Around.** "Carol said that guy she was with was hung like a horse, and she hung from the ceiling! Last week it was a German gymnast, wasn't it?"

- **Slob.** "Donna had a week's worth of dirty thongs hanging from her NordicTrack, right in the middle of her kitchen!"

- **Irresponsible.** "Yeah, Flo told me she gets more final disconnection notices every month than she does paychecks."

- **Loser.** "God, that girl is *always* getting dumped. What the heck is *wrong* with Gracie, anyway?"

- **Obsessive-Compulsive.** "Hannah said she's late every day because she has to go back twenty times to see if she left the iron plugged in, if the stove was on, if the water was running . . ."

You get the idea here. Basically, all the unflattering specifics we inadvertently reveal can lead to only one place: the conclusion "This gal has Zero Discretion, which means she's not smart enough to keep her mouth shut, which means she can't be trusted, which means she will never be put in a position of trusted responsibility." All because we let our coworkers see our hangin' thongs . . .

The Damages: Over the Spending Limits

So what do you do if you find out that your Reputation isn't so hot, or if you *know* you've done something seriously brainless to damage it, like the time M bad-mouthed her boss to a staffer whom she later fired (big duh there)? Well, like defaulting on a loan, a serious blemish on your credit rating can stay on there a long time—seven years, to be precise.

First, give yourself a break. We *all* make mistakes. You *must* be patient with yourself while you dig yourself out. When your Reputation gets tarnished for whatever reason, we say plan each step according to The Big Sister Triple AAAs:

Appearance. After a huge gaffe—getting drunk at the office party, insulting the CEO's wife, telling the completely inappropriate personal story that has people thinking twice about you—make a noticeable change in your look. Get a different hairstyle and work on looking like you pulled it back together with a few new outfits, impeccable grooming, and a fresh makeup scheme.

Attitude. Don't do the walk of shame. Keep your head up and engage people—especially your detractors. This is considered Very Professional. Ask their advice about work-related matters. Act normal. People will eventually push the episode to the back of their minds if you don't do anything overt to remind them that it happened.

Ability. Enlist the help of someone within your company. Find someone you feel has influence and potential interest in you and ask her what kinds of things you can do to make a positive impression. Then do exactly what she tells you to do. Everyone likes to be solicited for their opinion, and in return for your trust this person will be likely to support you around the office in other ways and help you rebuild your Reputation.

Fresh Start

Sometimes a bankrupted Reputation—whether you defaulted on your loan or someone pulled an identity theft on you with malicious gossip or sabotage—can create too big a debt hole to climb out of gracefully. If you can't see a possible resolution, if you can't get someone to support you, it's time to declare Chapter 11 with yourself and move on to a fresh start. Know, however, that even if you move to a new job or industry, the Reputation and the story that caused it *can* follow you around. But no worries. You'll be prepared if it does.

If an unpleasant story or Reputation—accurate or not—follows you to your next job and someone questions you about it, don't get defensive and don't ignore it. Instead say:

- **"Oh God, everyone's heard that story.** It's a good one, and someday when we have time, I'll tell you aaall about it." But, of course, you never will.

- **"It was definitely one of those you-had-to-be-there situations.** You know how that goes: two sides to every story. But some of us have more discretion than to tell ours."

- **"It was an incredibly ugly political situation,** and I just decided to walk away from it."

And then, whatever you do, don't repeat the behavior that either got you into trouble in the first place or provoked another person to attack you. Keep your head up and don't let the past drag you down, sister.

be Snow White & deal with Your Dwarves

The behaviors that make you look small

Useful Terms: What We Mean When We Say . . .

Dwarfing Dopey behavior that Dwarfs who we are and what we do

JUST-ify When we unjustifiably Dwarf ourselves

ADD Affection Deficit Disorder

Self-slanderization Taking potshots at your sweet self for a cheap laugh

We've all had our office moments being Bashful, Happy, and Sneezy, not to mention Grumpy and Sleepy. But what we're talking about here are the Seven Poison-Apple Habits of Highly Ineffective Women. Overindulging in any one or combination of these behaviors can make worm's meat out of a woman in the fertile soil of Officepoliticus.

Snow White's Seven Dwarves are the Apologizer, the Duh, the Questioner, the Just-ifyer, the Overexplainer, the Complainer, and, grumpiest of them all, the Taker of It Personally.

While there are differences among each of the Dwarfish habits, they ultimately all sprout from the same places: self-doubt, fatigue, boredom, PMS (both of the office and menstrual varieties) impatience, defensiveness, and the absence of personal goals.

Keeping your Dwarves from trashing your Reputation is *not* about being perfect. In fact, when we are trying to be ideal little Snow Whites is when our Dwarves are most likely to raise their ugly little gnome heads and cause us to say or do something very Dopey.

If, as you read about the Dwarves, you recognize these behaviors in that "Oh my God, I do that all the time" way, please don't freak! It doesn't mean you do *everything* wrong. All it means is that you are just like the rest of us: perfectly imperfect.

Every woman we know has experienced periods where one or more of these Dwarves has completely taken over. When we first recognized our own supersized Dwarves, we were absolutely mortified and wanted to hide out in the forest for a few years. But then we realized that we are *way* bigger than our Dwarfish deficits, and we cut them down to size one by one. And Snow White, you can too.

Hi ho, hi ho, it's off to work we go . . .

♟ The Apologizer Dwarf

We're sorry, did you say something? We're sorry, was that intro just too long? We're sorry, does any reference to anything Disney and/or your childhood give you the creepy crawlies?

Saying "I'm sorry" to every animate and inanimate object in our path for every reason and absolutely no reason is one of the most ubiquitous Dwarfing behaviors of The Girls Who Call Us. We gals even apologize when someone *else* is wrong: "Sorry, would you mind getting off my foot?"

"I'm sorry" has become an all-occasion, autotext Girlogic response. Masquerading as good manners, the Apologizer Dwarf is a relentless Reputation killer. Remember, the most common and literal use of the word *sorry* is for accepting blame and expressing remorse. When you apologize endlessly, you may very well be undermining your own authority, or worse:

△ **You are apologizing for your own power and the position you busted your butt to get in the first place.** "I'm sorry, can you go fax this over to Joe Blow's office?" Don't apologize to people for asking them to do their job.

△ **You are begging forgiveness for daring to have your own point of view.** "I'm sorry, but I don't think that that's a good idea. . . ."

△ **You are accepting blame.** "I'm sorry I got a good raise and you got bupkes."

△ **You might be accepting responsibility for someone else's errors.** "I'm sorry, I probably didn't explain it right." With this type of apology, you are freeing someone else from the hot seat and putting yourself right in it.

△ **You might be perceived as making excuses.** "I'm sorry, I thought that my assistant would have brought you that report." Every time you make an excuse apology like this one, you are sending a signal that you ain't running the show and that you ain't in control.

Dwarfersize It! We recommend you go cold turkey. Habitwise, saying you're sorry is like smoking—if you smoke just one after you quit, you're liable to be back up to a pack a day in no time.

In a related thought: don't do that truly Dwarfish thing of accepting an apology by apologizing: "I'm sorry too."

Be conscious of how often (and when) you say "I'm sorry." Replace that sorry word with one of these Sorry Substitutes:

△ *"Excuse me, but . . ."*

△ *"I apologize for any inconvenience . . ."*

△ *"I regret that it didn't work out the way we thought . . ."*

If all of us gals don't stop apologizing all the time, we'll be sorry.

♟ The Duh Dwarf

"Alan Greenspan? He's that funny Jewish chef who throws around the matzoh balls on the Food Channel, right?"

What happens to many of The Girls Who Call Us is that they are so busy, busy, busy working and attending to the various other details of their lives—working out, catching up with friends, sending birthday cards (multitask, multitask, multitask)—that they don't stop long enough to do some basic things like read a newspaper.

If you don't know what's going on in the world, or who is who in it, you are going to run into trouble:

♟ **The world is changing all the time.** Businesses know that they must change to survive and grow. If you inadvertently show that your knowledge of the world is dated, it will be assumed that your skills are dated as well.

♟ **Leaders are decisive.** You become decisive by having strong opinions and the confidence not only to express them but to act on them. If you fail to share any opinions because you think others won't like them or agree with them or, worse, because you don't have any, you will find that you will miss the promotion train.

♟ **Employers are looking for evidence that you can think for yourself.** Honey, you can't fake that.

Dwarfersize It! Gather information—all kinds of it—and expose yourself to new concepts and experiences because it will teach you how to think and make you a more interesting human being. The more topics that you can converse on and give intelligent, thoughtful opinions on, the easier you will find it to speak to anyone.

Our Guy Spies tell us that it's easier for them because they can usually make their way around a conversation—especially with another man—by turning the discussion around to the sports news of the day. For men, sports provide fresh topics daily, and strong opinions are inherent to the subject matter: "Whaddya mean, the Red Sox suck?!"

In fact, if you don't know a hockey puck from Wolfgang Puck, we recommend that you include a little study of approximately what's going on in the world of sports. Even the President of the United States calls the winners of the World Series and Super Bowl. Know which teams made the playoffs, and be sure to know which team goes with which city, which team you prefer, and why.

Other than that, here are the quickest ways to get our opinionated selves up to speed:

♀ *Put yourself on a news diet.* Nibble your way to knowledge by following several stories in a number of news formats and perspectives—conservative, liberal, alternative, etc. Get the gist of the items and then give them some thought in the shower. If you can't graze away at current events throughout the day, at least give yourself a midnight snack of late-night news. With all these twenty-four-hour, news-only networks, there is *no* excuse for not keeping up with it at least on a weekly basis.

♀ *Surround yourself with smart people.* If you don't know any, get out there and meet some. Hint: try the library, a great bookstore, or a lecture series.

♀ *Listen to opinion leaders.* If you drive to work, skip Howard Stern and tune in to Don Imus (7 a.m. to 10 a.m.). Shock jock though he is, with a fondness for the word penis, *Imus in the Morning* airs the *best* interviews with senators, journalists, and other great minds of the moment. People with a strong viewpoint are compelling and Visible, which is why you should catch *The O'Reilly Factor* on the Fox News Channel. Bill O'Reilly has enough opinions for all of us, and he's utterly fearless in expressing every one of them. Tune in to National Public Radio for excellent reporting, diverse topics, strong interviews, and cultural commentary—all the stuff of great cocktail party conversation and impress-the-Uppities coffee-room talk.

Not knowing what's happening in the world, not having opinions about it all—or never expressing them—will render you invisible in your office. And that's not just our opinion. That's the fact, sugar shack.

☃ The Questioner Dwarf

"Why did you buy *yellow* legal pads?" "Who do you think you are?" "How am I supposed to do *that*?"

Back in school, we were praised for raising our hands with a good question. Questions were an appropriate way to express ourselves, and we could really never ask too many. But at work, when the Questioner Dwarf gets us in a choke hold, the results can be *lee-thal*.

☃ **Everyone thinks Nancy is not a team player because every time a decision is made, she throws up obstacles.** "But *how* can we *possibly* get it done by Friday the thirteenth? Do you really think we can *afford* to do this?"

☃ **Abigail comes off as a saboteur because she's always putting people on the spot by asking questions that they can't possibly answer.** "Do you have the numbers to *prove* that?" The perception is that Abigail is manipulating the situation to make herself look good by challenging the knowledge of others.

☃ **Coworkers think Eleanor is a self-centered, small thinker because she keeps asking about minutiae in high-level meetings.** "Should we staple the Kenney proposal, use paper clips, or hot-glue it?" If you reveal your obsession with small-picture details with too many questions, it will be difficult to get promoted to Uppity-ville.

  Dolly gets pegged as defensive because she challenges *every* decision. "Why would we do it that way?" Coworkers resent wasting their time explaining why the world is the way it is to demanding Dolly.

To ask, or not to ask? That *is* the question.

Dwarfersize It! Make sure you are listening, and then think before you speak:

  Ask yourself three questions before you ask anyone else anything. #1: "Do I *need* to ask this question?" #2: "What will I *gain* by asking?" #3: "Is the *timing* good?"

  Only ask questions in meetings that other people can easily answer and which will make them look good. "So, Ms. Marketing Director, how many more names did you add to the subscriber list this month?" Ask only if you *know* that the numbers are fabulous. If you have other questions, ask privately.

  If you see a problem, don't point it out until you've figured out the solution. Then don't ask a question—make a statement, baby. "We need to take a serious look at the circulation figures in light of the recent dip in the economy. I recommend that we take such-and-such an action."

  Rather than throw out those questions that are burning behind your lips, keep your mouth shut, take notes, and go away and think about it. Reframe your thoughts as statements in an email that starts with: "Here are my reflections on our discussion today. #1: We will need to know what resources will be available for the Patwell project. #2: Blah, blah."

  Unless a meeting's agenda is specifically about process, don't ask questions involving execution logistics. When the decision has been made, think through all your need-to-know questions and write a very concise email to the person who can answer them.

⚇ The Just-ifier Dwarf

"I'm *just* a mess!" "I *just* can't get my act together!" "I'm *just* a flake!"

Many of The Girls Who Call Us Dwarf themselves and their achievements by JUST-ifying. They don't want to come on too strong or look presumptuous or too self-important, so they put themselves as far down as they possibly can by using the deprecating word *just* to describe themselves, like so: "I'm *just* a girl. . . ."

Many of us use the coy JUST-ifyer Dwarf to appear humble, which we think is attractive, or possibly to get the other person to say nice things about us, which is manipulative. Here follow the most common unjust Girlogic Just-ifications.

Just Plain Ignorant

We're not sure why women do this, but for some reason, many pretend to be airheads. These types of JUST-ifications indicate not only that you don't know about a subject, but also that you don't believe yourself smart enough to learn about it.

⚇ *" I just don't* have a strategic bone in my whole body. . . ."

⚇ *" Oh, I'm just stupid about* politics. I *just* can't remember who is who and which party believes what. It *just* confuses me. . . ."

⚇ *" Oh, I just couldn't be bothered* to understand all that fiscal reporting and boring tax mumbo-jumbo."

We promise, no one will *ever* be impressed by your bragging about how much you don't know. When it comes down to choosing between two people for the promotion to a better place, the one who is clearly the confident leader and doesn't advertise her defects will be the one who gets it.

Dwarfersize It! Resist the urge to broadcast your ignorance. If you want to learn something, research it: go Google, girlie. Better still, find someone knowledgeable, express your sincere desire to know more, and ask her to mentor you. People are flattered when you ask for help, and that mentor, proud of her brilliant protégé, will probably support you in other ways around the office.

Just Insulting

One of The Girls Who Call Us, Karen, a teddy bear manufacturing project manager, is incessantly insulting herself to make people laugh. She is the queen of self-slanderization. Humor is a powerful tool for building relationships and defusing tense situations, but too many of us girls get in the habit of making ourselves the big ol' butt of every joke.

- *"Oh, I'm just a total wreck! Can you believe I'm just such a spaz?"*
- *"I'm just a loser. Just can't shake this arm fat! I just can't stick to any diet that doesn't include Cherry Garcia."*
- *"My life is just one bad joke after another. I'm just an accident waiting to happen."*

A little self-deprecation is OK and shows that you don't take yourself too seriously. Too much, though, is exhausting for your listeners. After a while they are likely to tire of saying, "Come on, you know that's *just* not true," and quite possibly they will feel resentful of an approach that seems to be fishing for compliments. It's *just* not funny.

Dwarfersize It! Catch yourself before you make a negative comment about yourself by thinking: "Would I say this about my best friend?" If you wouldn't, *don't* say it about yourself—no matter how funny you think it is. Think of advertising: you just don't slam your brand, unless you are Joan Rivers and self-slanderization *is* your brand. Find *other* ways to be funny. Read, watch, and listen to smart humor. Learn some jokes and relate funny stories. Try humorsearch.com. Catch something on Comedy Central every week. Thinking funny is a habit you can pick up. Exposing your brain to brilliant comedy will make you funnier—about more things than *just* yourself.

Just Too Humble

A little conscious humility can be worthwhile when you strategically decide to make someone else, like your boss, feel more important—"I *just* couldn't have done it without your guidance"—and the JUST-ifier is a handy little pal to have around. But when the Dwarf gets too big, it will overshadow your achievements and skills.

> *"Oh, I just got lucky.* Anyone could win a Pulitzer . . ."

> *"Oh, it was just a little thing really.* Being made SVP is not such a big deal."

> *"I just happened to be in the right place at the right time,* and things *just* fell into place."

When you JUST-ify your accomplishments, you are not giving yourself credit for the work, the time, or the know-how it took to achieve them. And guess what, sister—no one else will either.

Dwarfersize It! If someone praises something about you or something you've done, don't Dwarfishly deflect the praise. Keep your head up; no aw-shucks toe kicks. Smile and say: "Thank you very much." True humility is found in simplicity.

ALLOW ME TO INTRODUCE MY INSECURITIES

How many times have you introduced yourself or been in a conversation and the topic turns to careers, and you Dwarf yourself in the first ten seconds with statements like "I'm *just* a secretary" or "I *just* have a nothing job"?

M used to tell people she "just worked for a little food publication." M didn't bother to say she was managing editor. Most people would say, "Wow. Writing about restaurants must be so great!" M would bat away their interest: "Oh, you know, it's *just* a job." They would say, "Oh," and start looking over her shoulder for someone more interesting to talk to.

The JUST-ifier Dwarf makes it so much harder for others to communicate with you. It puts them on the spot, and they feel *obligated* to say something nice: "Um, er. Uh . . . well, the world needs ditchdiggers too." JUST-ifying yourself can make people just want to steer clear of your general vicinity.

Dwarfersize It! When you are introduced to people, make it your goal to impress *them,* not diminish *yourself.* So in any business context, such as a trade show or convention or conference:

- **If you have a great title, use it**. It's *not* obnoxious bragging to let people know what you've achieved. So it's *not* "Hi, I'm Rebecca from Pinky Inc.", but rather "Hi, I'm Becky, the senior marketing director of Pinky Inc."

- **If you have a generic title, add a few impressive specifics about your company.** "Hi, I'm Rebecca from Pinky Inc., the largest rhubarb-extract cosmetics company in Texas."

- **If someone else introduces you but doesn't say your title,** which happens far more frequently to women than guys, stick out that hand for a solid shake and say: "Yes. Hi, I'm the assistant production coordinator of Pinky Inc."

- **Use the "in charge of" tag to extend and expand upon your title.** No one is going to sue you if you don't use your exact title: "Hi.

(continued)

♟ The Overexplainer Dwarf

"OK, the first thing is this, and then, you know, then there was that, the other, and the third thing, and then, of course, the whoobity-boobity, and finally the ibbity-boppitty-boo. Do you know what I'm saying? Lemme explain myself. The first thing is . . ."

Wea culpa, wea culpa, wea culpa. Perhaps there were never two women in all of womendom more guilty of overexplaining than yours truly. This chat-chat-chatty little Overexplaining Dwarf got us in more hot water in more ways than you can cook an egg, and frankly, we're not so hard-boiled that we don't still occasionally run on at the mouth.

The Overexplainer Dwarf is a hard habit to crack. Leigh, a hospital administrator, calls her tendency to overexplain a "Confession Complex." She will go into epic detail about what she *didn't* get done in a day, and then expound at length on *why* she didn't do it.

The horrible part about Leigh's Confession Complex is that *nobody* would have asked her in the first place about what she didn't get done—she *volunteers* to Dwarf herself and point out her liabilities. Leigh feels guilt about not meeting her own goals and compulsively confesses her shortcomings to anyone and everyone—including her boss. Leigh does *not* feel forgiven or otherwise relieved of guilt after an overexplained confession; she invariably feels worse for having blabbed.

Virtually all of The Girls Who Call Us Dwarf themselves by overexplaining, and like Leigh, they actually *know* it, but they have not figured out *why* they do it, or why it might not be such a good idea. Those of us who overexplain do so in reaction to any number of insecurities:

Louisa thinks she's not being heard. "They're not paying any attention to me."

Charlotte fears she is being misunderstood and/or misinterpreted. "They are not getting my meaning."

Alice keeps framing and reframing the same thought in order to make it sound more official. "I bumble through the first time, then restate it trying to use bigger, better words that make me look smarter."

Julia doesn't usually know what she's trying to say until she's halfway through her point. "I'm working it through my head as I'm speaking and usually have no idea where—or when—it will end."

Laura thinks that people don't believe her, so she keeps explaining her case to make it more credible. "I feel like I have to justify everything exactly."

Emily is afraid that if she is direct and concise, she will be perceived as rude. "I really just hate having to tell people what to do, so I soften it by beating around the bush."

Ida just likes to hear the sound of her own voice. "Me, me, me, me, meeeeee."

LET'S EXPLAIN SOMETHING HERE

Many of The Girls Who Call Us become utterly dumbfounded when they discover that their tendency to overexplain has given them a less-than-desirable Reputation:

- **Micromanaging control freak.** Gives way too much detail.

- **Insecure.** Completely lacking in confidence and authority.

- **Boring.** Tediously redundant.

- **Stupid.** Hint: the more you say, the more likely you are to contradict yourself and say something duh-duh-dumb.

- **Condescending.** Has zero trust in anyone *else's* ability.

- **Egotistical big mouth.** Just keeps talking to listen to the sound of her own voice.

- **Defensive.** Excuse maker who keeps talking and talking to justify every action or inaction.

And on, and on, and on. Never anon.

Dwarfersize It! Don't explain anything to anyone unless you are directly questioned; no unsolicited confessions please!

   If you must explain something, give the bottom line first. Plan on saying only what you have to.

   Always ask, "Any questions?" If the answer is no, don't give more details.

   Know exactly what your summary statement is. Stop talking after you've made it.

   Be comfortable with silence. Do not start babbling if someone is unresponsive. Don't give in and start reexplaining; let them hang in silence and just look at them till *they* feel awkward. M likes to sing Springsteen lyrics in her head to keep herself from opening up her mouth to reexplain herself while waiting it out. J starts thinking about what fabulous restaurant she wants to hit next.

♟ The Complainer Dwarf

The Complainer Dwarf is an insidious one. Most of The Girls Who Call Us don't recognize when they are on a doozy of a whine fest, but they're quick to crook their finger at others as moaners. The Complainer habitually projects her inner dissatisfaction onto everyone and everything else and seldom realizes it when she has crossed the line into becoming a problem herself.

Complaining is an *easy* habit to fall into. It's a reason to speak when you have nothing to say: "Damn, it's hot in here. Are you hot?" A coupla good complaints can provide a convenient excuse: "Well, of course I couldn't hit the deadline! Sally didn't hold up her end, the light in here is terrible, I have a cold that I got from Martha, and my dog ate the project, *and* you don't pay me enough."

We complain to let off steam, to get sympathy, and sometimes just because it's fun to indulge in a good old-fashioned bee-yach session. But when the Complaining Dwarf takes up a permanent residence, we grumble and rumble every time we open our mouths.

When she was young(er), M—who fancied herself an optimistic, upbeat sorta gal—thought that if she complained about how hard she was working, someone would take notice and/or care. But her negativity about work got so out of hand that she didn't limit her griping to colleagues—she complained to *everyone* in her life. M made the choice to work long hours and made everyone else pay the price by having to listen to her bitch about it. Finally M was mortified into consciousness when a family member took her by the shoulders and said: "Enough already!"

It's best not to let the Complainer Dwarf rule your speaking and thinking habits for too long because:

Kim got her way by complaining but eventually got tuned out, then thrown out. "No, we definitely don't want Kim on the project. She's judgmental and completely inflexible."

Wilhelmine complained so much that she became a target of other people's complaining. "Have you ever seen such a whiner in your life?"

Elizabeth complained about so many of her coworkers, everyone thought her untrustworthy. "Does that woman ever say a nice word about anybody?"

Francisca's complaining gave her a Reputation for being manipulative. "That one bitches and bitches until she gets her way."

Nobody believes *anything* Antoinette says because she complains with such exaggeration, she inevitably contradicts herself. "She always says she has no money, but then she goes out and gets a full-carat diamond for her belly piercing."

Dwarfersize It! The key to diminishing your Complainer Dwarf is consciousness.

Be aware of the complaining you do. Take a Post-it pad around with you for a full day and give yourself a bitch mark every time you complain. If that paper has more than three marks on it, keep doing this exercise to diminish this Dwarf before someone takes Y-O-U by the shoulders and says, "Enough already!"

Just about anything you say that's negative can be perceived as a complaint. Make the first thing out of your mouth a positive statement. We both had to do this. When we felt inclined to let our first statements be negative—"I'm *so* tired!" "This copy machine *always* jams up just when I need it!"—we forced ourselves to say something positive: "Great blouse! Where did you get that?" "I saw the *best* movie over the weekend." Now being positive is second nature. We can't complain, honey, can't complain.

♟ The Taker-of-It-Personally Dwarf

"What did she mean by *that*?" "Did you see the way his eyes were boring through my brain?" "What could I *possibly* have done wrong here?"

We don't know any woman who hasn't let this paranoid Taker-of-It-Personally Dwarf cause her to waste a ton of time and energy second-guessing herself, jumping to conclusions, and torturing herself with imaginary emotional scenarios. In fact, our Guy Spies report that the tendency to take things personally is their number one complaint about working with women. "Women take things way too personally, and they think that everyone is out to get them," reports John, a cable channel program director. "The stupid thing is that paranoid behavior won't get them anywhere."

Lots of The Girls Who Call Us complain that guys *never* seem to take things as hard or as personally as we do. According to our Guy Spies, generally speaking, they don't. Guys are far more likely to compartmentalize, so when they leave the office playground and go home, world order is restored—and they either brag about how well they did or deflect the blame: "Of *course* it was totally George's fault." Guys might not be happy with what happened, but they are far more likely to take the hit, move on, and think about the next play than we are.

Not us. Oh no, no, *nooo*. When there is a conflict, misfired communication, or other disappointment, we hang on to it, take it home, and examine it for hours wondering just what it was *we* did to make George such a jerk. Can you imagine if those guys could read our minds and see the way we absolutely anguish inside when we take it personally? What a hideous thought.

Our friend Sandra, a general manager at a pharmaceutical consulting company, confessed that she would be in the middle of a business conversation with a guy, and then he would suddenly end it by saying, "Gotta go. Bye." Sandra would sit around for hours trying to figure out what she had said wrong to spoil what seemed to be a nice conversation. When she couldn't take the wondering anymore, she would fabricate reasons to call him back, to make sure everything was still OK.

The Taker-of-It-Personally Dwarf transports us off Planet Reality over to Patheticville—population: one.

The sad part of all this is that most of us women have Taker-of-It-Personally Dwarves of titanic proportions because we *care* so damn much. We are emotionally invested in the work we do. We put so much of ourselves—heart, soul, backbone, and busted ass—into our jobs that we lose perspective. We don't think, "Oh well, tomorrow is another day. Win some, lose some." No way. We girls are far more likely to think: "Today it's the Big Show, the Super Bowl of my career—and everything is riding on [insert immediate issue here]."

Here are some of the other reasons we Take It Personally:

Our expectations of others are too high. Lots of us expect people to care as much as we do. So whenever they don't react the way *we* would or the way we expect them to, we can't comprehend their actions, and we Take It Personally.

Many of us have Affection Deficit Disorder (ADD). It seems essential to be liked by our coworkers and Uppities. Our egos can need so much reassuring that no matter how much we accomplished *yesterday* or how well it was received, we need a seemingly steady stream of praise from people *today* to ensure that they still like us and won't fire us Just Like That.

Sometimes we take things personally because it *is* personal. Guy Spy Greg, a VP, confessed: "The people who really know me *know* that I can be full of crap. Most of the time when I'm being a jerk, I'm doing it to elicit a reaction. I have been told that people who don't know me well cry sometimes when I do that." Does he care? No. So there it is, ladies—vindication. Sometimes it definitely *is* personal.

Dwarfersize It! Here's the bad news. If you tend to be oversensitive and take things personally, there's not really any way not to. *However*, it's what you do next that counts—how you control your reaction. The good news is that as you grow in your position and have more confidence, you will be more able to roll with the punches, whether they are actually personal or not.

- *Evaluate yourself first.* "Am I tired? When was the last time I ate? Am I burned out? Am I about to get my period?" Try to see if your oversensitivity is actually something out of whack with you before you *assume* it's a personal attack. If you determine it is or might be Y-O-U, sleep, eat, get some recreation, or medicate accordingly before you allow yourself to react to the situation.

- *Consider the source, and look for patterns.* We have some clients who *never* call us to tell us they liked the work we submitted, or even that they received it. Eventually, we find out that they loved it. Chances are they treat *every* vendor the same way. So if someone is *always* slow to respond, if she's *always* a backstabber, don't assume it's personal or that you caused her rudeness in some way. Say to yourself: "This behavior is consistent for *her*. It's *not* about *me*."

- *Cultivate a little apathy.* A wise Guy Spy, a shrink, taught us the million-dollar lesson: learn to say, "So what?" These two little words have saved us more time and more aggravation than you could ever imagine. So what if it *is* personal? So what if you got it wrong? So what if you screwed up? You know, if you can say these words to yourself, you *won't* become a mediocre human being—you will become a realistic human being. If you can honestly say that you did your best—or as good as you could do given the circumstances—then all of it becomes a shoulder-shrugging "So what?" And if you didn't do your best, or made a bad call, so what? The world won't end. You'll do it better next time. You can't control it all, and if the worst-case scenario is that you lose your job, lose a friend, or damage your Reputation—so what? That's why God invented the concept of tomorrow.

Get a plan, man. (See Chapter 11, "Y-O-U: The Ultimate Planning Machine.") If you know what your focus is, if you know what your life is about at any given moment, then it's far more likely that you will have more perspective on a situation that you might otherwise have taken personally. If an event or person doesn't create a direct obstacle to you reaching your specific stated goal, then say to yourself: "This noise is just a distraction from getting what I want and what's important to me right now." Fuhgeddaboudit.

Get a hobby, Holly. If you have something that you *love* going on *outside* of work—not just another have-to, like food shopping—invest in it. M plays the flute, likes to knit, and she gets them both in daily—two rows, two songs, ten to twenty minutes—no matter what. J likes to cook, work out, and build her shoe and handbag collection. We've noticed that people who just *live* for ski trips don't take problems at work nearly as personally. They just turn it off, tune it out, and think about hitting the slopes. When you have a life and other activities that are meaningful to you beyond your job, the job itself takes on less significance. It becomes the means to your lifestyle, not the lifestyle itself. If all you do is work, and work is your top priority, you will tend to define yourself by what happens there and begin to lose perspective when office turbulence shakes your world.

Don't react, distract. Resist the urge to react. Sit on your hands if you have to. Don't send that email. Don't pick up that phone. If you can't focus on another work project because you are too freaked to concentrate, find something to make you laugh. No joke. Go to headlinehumor.com and look at the "Funny Signs" section. You *will* laugh. As far as we're concerned, laughter is the most appropriate reaction to just about all the stuff we've ever bothered to take personally—even when it didn't seem at all funny at the time.

Try not to worry so much if it is personal or waste your time wondering why, because with some people, it's nothing you did—maybe they just don't like the sound of your voice. And so what?

Chapter 8

Who
to Trust?

What Monica Lewinsky learned the hard way

No one.

Chapter 9

Speaking
of Talking

In order to be seen, you must be heard

Useful Terms: What We Mean When We Say . . .

Transactional Talk The main language spoken in business; characterized by a clear lack of embellishments and tangents

Hihowareya? The question almost everybody asks but virtually no one wants to hear the *real* answer to

Talkus Interruptus Just as you are about to reach the climax of your speech, someone else barges in

If you've never seen Disney's *The Little Mermaid*, stop reading here and go rent the DVD. We can wait. Why? Because there's an important message in it for us girls, and no, it's not that we should wear seashell bras.

Ariel, the mermaid, gives her voice to Ursula, the multitentacled sea witch, in exchange for a set of legs—a rather nice set too. Great gams or not, without her voice, Ariel *can't* get what she wants, in this case a prince. When her voice finally does find its way back to her, guess what? You got it: she gets her prince. How often have we all had those speechless Ariel moments in the office? "I wish I had said blabbity blah!" "Why did I just sit there like an idiot?" "Eric *never* lets me get a word in edgewise."

Our voice, what we say, and how we say it are our secret weapons.

We have to take all our raw natural chatting ability and turn it into an arsenal of powerful talking skills.

Pandora's Chatterbox

We became highly Visible in our respective offices by our ability to Chat & Hum, but when it came time to get down to business, we didn't quite realize that it called for a whole other mode of talking. As a result, we were *constantly* using too many damn words.

The excessive verbiage was really brought home to M by a co-worker who would routinely ask her how her baby was. M would launch into accounts of diaper count, rashes, and daily regurgitations. One day the guy—who, btw, didn't have kids—cut M off and said: "You know, I'm just being nice. Can't you just say, 'She's great! Thanks for asking'?"

How horrifying. M learned right then and there that in the office "Hihowareya?" is *NOT* an invitation to have an *actual* conversation but is just a transactional exchange between captive employees. That guy did M a huge favor. She had *no* idea that she was boring anyone who had the courtesy to ask about her baby to tears with details they could care less about. Since then, when anyone other than a family member inquires about her kids, M says: "They're fantastic. Thanks for asking."

Talking Points of View

So many of The Girls Who Call Us complain that people don't listen to them in the office, that they are not being heard, that they feel inse-cure while speaking to groups, and that they are intimidated in certain one-on-one situations. We used to have the exact same gripes. But through sticking our foot in our mouths so often we had permanent scuff marks on our tongues, and through extensive interviewing of our Guy Spies, we discovered that most business communication consists of what we now call Transactional Talk.

The point of Transactional Talk is to get to the bottom line quickly and directly, no fuss, no muss, no special sauce, lettuce, cheese, pickles, onions, or sesame-seed bun—just the two all-beef patties.

To master Transactional Talking, think of yourself as a TV commercial. You have *thirty seconds* to get your message across clearly, be appealing, and be memorable:

- **If you lack focus, you don't get buy-in on your concept.** "Hey, Larry, did you hear an actual point in what Sally was saying, or is it just me?"

- **If you are underrehearsed and don't seem polished, you'll get dismissed.** "Who invited the paper-shuffling 'uuuuuhhhh, uuuuumm' girl to the meeting?"

- **If you are so overrehearsed that you seem inhuman, they can't relate to you.** "Does that woman ever even blink?"

- **If you distract the viewers, they miss your point but remember the distraction:** "Oh, she's the one with that hideous Boston accent . . . what was she talking about anyway? Was it caahs?"

Chat & Hum to build relationships, but use Transactional Talk to conduct business. For example, before and after the meeting, feel free to be Chatty Cathy, but the second someone whips out that agenda, it's all Transactional Talk—give the meat, not the garnish.

Anticipate to Participate

All those professional people who make it look soooo damn easy to come across as clear thinkers are soooo *not* winging it. They know exactly what their agenda is at all times. They prepare. They plan. They write it down and practice it. They *really* do rehearse well in advance—not like we used to in the car or subway on the way to the meeting.

We royally screwed ourselves on several occasions by not taking the time to *totally* prepare for a meeting. 'Fess up! How many times have you gone to a meeting and not been entirely sure what the topic du jour was? After a particularly bad showing once, where J babbled through a presentation to her staff at the Big Important Media Company, her boss actually said: "Hon, you were not that good. In fact, you sucked. Let me do it next time." And he did.

Don't get locked out of important meetings because you're not a good Transactional Talker. Take some of your 60/40 time—it really could count either as *work* work or advertising time—and reduce all that bubbled-over passion you have about a topic into a couple of strongly positioned Big Bullets:

- **"Here's the situation."** Shoot to sum it up in three sentences.

- **"Here are three possible ways to resolve it."** People like Options!

- **"Here is my recommendation."** State *briefly* why it's a damn good idea. Uh, three points would be good.

Whether you want to ask for a raise, are pitching yourself for a promotion, or have an idea to sell, do your brainstorming on paper and boil it down to just those three Big Bullets. You will be *ah-maazed* what this technique can do for you.

When we began to think and write and speak in Transactional Talk Bullets, it completely changed how people viewed us. Suddenly more people were asking our advice, we were invited to more meetings, and people actually praised us for our clarity! Us, the Chatty Cathies! M even got a big promotion to VP after a great board presentation: she sounded like a player, so the board made her one.

PODIUM PANIC

Public speaking. It can reduce even the most articulate and competent of us to babbling like the proverbial village idiot. We *know*: we've done our fair share of blathering and bumbling on the dais.

When we were young(er) and we saw people speaking to groups so effortlessly, we figured that since we can talk to anyone at any time, we would be naturals. We found out the hard way that there are no naturals. But there *are* things you can do to appear like one (even if you are making your first public appearance):

- **Know that you are going to be incredibly nervous.** Prepare, prepare, prepare.

- **Spend some time envisioning your audience.** Practice looking up from your notes and then back down; when you are stressed this simple action is more difficult than advanced origami.

- **Never look people directly in the eye when giving a presentation.** You might freeze and begin sucking oxygen like crazy. Uhh-hhh . . . ummmm . . .

- **Time bends on the podium.** Have you ever heard someone drone on and on about nothing for a half hour? They thought they were speaking for five minutes. The flip side is that if you don't know what you are going to say, three minutes can be an eternity. If possible, take off your watch and lay it down next to your notes so you can surreptitiously time yourself, but never actually look at your watch on your wrist—it says you are boring yourself!

- **Bring a bottle of water.** Expect your mouth to become as dry as the martini you promised yourself as a reward for surviving the whole ordeal.

- **Take a class in public speaking or media training.** It will be the best money you, or better still your company, ever spent. Media trainers will teach you how to get your message across convincingly, how to stay focused and collected, and what *not* to

(continued)

do by showing you fun videos of people completely embarrassing themselves in a public speaking venue.

- **Pick up a karaoke machine.** You can get cool little tabletop versions for about $35 on sale. Turn the mike to the maximum echo so you will never be stunned at the sound of your amplified voice. You can also record yourself. Do it! Be brave. Practice, record, listen, refine, and learn, ladies.

Public speaking is like learning to play the flute. You need to study the techniques, listen to and observe the masters, be able to read notes, and practice as frequently as possible if you want to make beautiful music; otherwise, all you'll manage to do is blow it.

The Dirty Talk Dozen

Once you know exactly what your Big Bullets are, then you have to control as many of those random Dwarfish speaking habits as you can. Here are the Down and Dirty Dozen Commandments of Transactional Talk:

1. **Thou shall represent relevant interest to the audience.** You never see a tampon commercial during the Super Bowl. So if a meeting is about strategizing ways to get new clients, this is not the time to bring up your impassioned thoughts on vacation days.
2. **Thou shall use the power of pronouns.** Say "we" and "us" as often as possible, because your company is one big happy family, of which you are a proud, well-adjusted member. Shortly after M got that VP title, she was chastised for saying "the company" instead of "our company." Thank God M didn't say "my company."
3. **Thou shall not show thy self-interest.** Don't spin your Big Bullets so it looks as if the only party that benefits is Y-O-U—even if it's true.
4. **Thou shall not request a do-over or editorialize thy presentation.**

Don't pull a Tanya Harding: "Oopsie! Can I start over, please?" or "What I'm *trying* to say, and, uh, well, failing miserably at, is, uh . . ."

5. **Thou shall monitor thy tempo.** Don't get so nervous that you talk like an auctioneer. Speaking too fast signals that you are out of control and not prepared.

6. **Thou shall stick to the facts.** Don't say "most" or "the majority" or "tons" when you can say "four out of five." Support your recommendations with statistics and sources, as opposed to emotional supposition. So it's *NOT* "We should advertise on radio because people looooove radio" but rather "We should choose radio because according to *Ad Age,* it delivers a fifty percent higher response rate than print." Get those quotable facts and figgers!

7. **Thou shall not digress or otherwise lose focus.** Stick to your Big Bullets faithfully; on-the-spot improvising could put you in a tight situation and cause you to lose the precision of your point.

8. **Thou shall modulate thy tone.** No monotone droning—note the similarity to the word *monotonous.* But don't speak with so much wild variation that you sound like you're about to bust out into a show tune.

9. **Thou shall spin positively.** Nobody likes fire and brimstone and prophecies of doom. Even if you must present the downside, make sure your recommendation represents the upside of the downside.

10. **Thou shall bring a handout.** People like to doodle on these or use them to play buzzword bingo while they're not listening to you. Plus it gets your name attached to your ideas.

11. **Thou shall avoid defensiveness at all costs.** Say bye-bye to your expectations. Your job is to give good Transactional Talk—if they don't buy in to your idea, it doesn't mean you didn't do a great job selling it. So if your idea gets shot down right there and then in the meeting, don't Take It Personally. Go back to Chapter 7, "Be Snow White & Deal with Your Dwarves."

12. **Thou shall mind thy grammar.** Consistently careless grammar and

mispronounced words will give you a Reputation as a Dumb Broad. You *ne-vahh* want to make listeners feel embarrassed for you.

Closing Time

Once you've made your point, *stop* talking! Whatever you do, don't say, "Um, that's it"—as if apologizing that you have nothing more to say.

Right before you make your last point, say, "And in closing . . ." or "And finally . . ." Be sure that your last word is punctuated with a falling inflection, to ensure your thought doesn't come out sounding like a question. Then, ask a question: "Any questions?" This will signal that your presentation is finished, and it will allow you to keep the floor for a few extra moments of airtime as you expertly field the queries.

Soft Sappy Selling

You'll *never* see a commercial that throws into question the desirability of the product: "Why don't you think about giving us a try? Do you think you might? Huh?"

Hell no! Advertising is about making bold declarative statements that *sell:* "Try us! You'll like us!"

Many of The Girls Who Call Us float their thoughts out as questions rather than statements. It's not Transactional Talk, it's Tentative Talk.

- Don't say: "Should we consider . . . ? " Just say: "We should . . ."
- Don't say: "Do you think we could . . . ? " Just say: "I want to . . ."
- Don't say: "Why don't we think about . . . ? " Just say: "Let's . . ."

Remember: everything you say and the way you say it send messages to your audience. When you pose the majority of your thoughts as questions, you are communicating that you are about as decisive as a bulimic in a bakery. Also, keep in mind that when you ask a question, you are *inviting* someone else to speak—and they just might.

Girl Interrupted

We now interrupt that last thought to insert this one. Your whole life your mama told you to wait your turn and that interrupting was R-U-D-E. And you know, it really is R-U-D-E, but at certain times it's essential.

Interrupting is about grabbing prime airtime. The more airtime a coworker snaps up in a meeting, the more Visibility that person has and the more it is perceived as a "win," which is why you'll notice that it's mostly those winning-obsessed guys doing the majority of the interrupting. There's not enough time to play nice and make sure that everyone gets a turn. People *will* interrupt as soon as they see the first logical opening, like when you ask a question or sound like a pipsqueak.

Learning the art of interrupting wasn't too hard for us—after all, we're both from New York. But many of The Girls Who Call Us have asked for Talkus Interruptus advice. Here you go, sister:

- **Expect to be interrupted.** If you don't, you will likely become a speechless mermaid out of water, and later spend way too much time thinking of all the brilliant comebacks you think you should have splashed around.

- **Keep going as if you hadn't heard.** Raise your volume slightly; if necessary, say, "Excuse me," but utter no Dwarfish apology. Continue with your original point. When J was interrupted in a meeting, she never even stopped to acknowledge that someone else had opened his mouth; she just kept right on talking.

- **Don't let that pitch get wild.** Our voices tend to zoom higher when we get aggravated. Keep the tenor on the low end of the spectrum.

Stand down if your boss interrupts. Even commercials are preempted when the president makes his State of the Union address.

Cut them off at the impasse. When you interrupt someone, say (loudly): "I have two important points to make." This handy phrase deters people from jumping in on you so quickly without looking like R-U-D-E clods. As long as you are *fast* in making your points, people will respect the boundary you so cleverly constructed.

Contributions, not clutter. You must make a valid point when you interrupt someone. If you change the topic or say something irrelevant, you've just taken up prime airtime to annoy people.

Offer your thoughts, not theirs. Finishing someone's sentence, which too many of The Girls Who Call Us do *too* frequently, is the worst form of interruption. Bite that tongue before someone bites your head off!

Watch *The NewsHour with Jim Lehrer* or *The O'Reilly Factor* to see different professional interrupters' styles. It's a hoot: those people are stompin' the heck out of others' comments to get the maximum airtime. But the two things you will *never* hear them say are "As I was saying before I was so rudely interrupted . . ." and "I'm sorry for interrupting, but . . ."

Is Your But Too Big?

We used to have the biggest Buts in the business: *every* single time we had to say something unpleasant, or make a simple request, we would use a Big But Beginner (BBB) before we made our point: "You're not going to like this, *but* . . ."

Basically, when you use a BBB, you are making the following public service announcement: "*Attention!* Please disregard what I am about to say." Don't let any of these BBBs weigh you down:

   I'm sorry but . . . *"I just did something terribly, terribly wrong."*

   You will probably think this is a dumb idea but . . . *"Because you are smart, and I am a moron."*

   I hate to contradict you, but . . . *"I am going to anyway."*

   I'm sorry you feel that way, but . . . *"I am about to close my mind entirely to your absurd opinion."*

   You're not going to like this, but . . . *"Let me tell you what I think and how you will feel about it."*

   No offense, but . . . *"I'm about to offend you."*

   I'm no expert, but . . . *"So my opinion has noooo value whatsoever."*

   I hope you don't mind, but . . . *"I just did something I knew would annoy the crap out of you."*

   I doubt you'll agree with me, but . . . *Why* put that thought in their head?

   You'll probably say no, but . . . *Why* answer for them?

   I know you are busy, but . . . *"Could you please, please, possibly, when you have a moment of time, spend it listening to the likes of my pathetic, slacking, shiftless self?"*

Even if you think you are using your Buts to soften the blow or be polite, 99 percent of the time people will perceive you as manipulative. Think about what you want to say before you open your mouth. See if you were going to start with one of these Big But Beginners. If so, plan to chop off the first half of your thought, and just make your point. If you must say something as a preface to your thought, ask: "Do you have a minute?" and if the answer is positive, proceed with your thought. Don't wait another day—trim down your big Buts starting right now. No ifs, ands, or Buts.

Unhappily Ever After

We must confess that while we've whipped our big Buts into shape, we still struggle to control the urge to add on Codependent Endings— habitual, throwaway add-ons that clutter up our thoughts and send a subliminal vibe to the listener that we *must* have their approval and/or validation. These Codependent Endings beg for permission for you to have the thoughts you think:

- " . . . ya know what I mean?"
- " . . . okay?"
- " . . . wasn't it?"
- " . . . are you following me?"
- " . . . does that make sense?" We love this one, because we are telling the listener that we're not entirely sure we are, or can be, making sense. Or, worse still, we are saying that we think the listener is too dense to understand our simple statement.
- " . . . ya know?"
- " . . . right?"
- " . . . but what do I know?"

For precise Transactional Talking, drop these unhappy Codependent Endings. Does that make sense?

Dropping the Hints

Most of us girls are big hinters. It's classic. "I dropped fifty-five hints to my boyfriend that I wanted to go to the Sonoma Mission Inn for my birthday, and he got me a slow cooker instead. What's wrong with him? Can't he take a hint?" The answer, honey, is no.

Most of us generally don't like it when people say no, so rather than issue a direct Transactional request, we'll hint around, hoping someone will get the message. Problem is, no one at work has *time* to pick up hints, especially not the boss. Most of the time, even a big, in-your-face hint isn't going to get you what you want. Also, what we gals might see as being polite and unpresumptuous a guy might see as a manipulation. Just come right out and ask for what you want or need. Practice dropping your hinting habits:

Don't hint: "I've been clocking in twelve-hour days for over a year now."
Just say: "It's time to talk about a raise."

Don't hint: "I've been working really hard lately, I'm kinda burned out."
Just say: "I would like to take a personal day."

Don't hint: "Gee, the carpeting in *that* room might upset my allergies, and I really need a little more space for my books."
Just say: "I've earned that corner office and I want it!"

Ask and ye might receive; hint and for sure you won't.

Oxygen Suckers

Frequently, when we're on the phone with The Girls Who Call Us, they are at work and sending instant messages and emails during the conversation. As a result, they periodically lose their train of thought. And it's so *obvious.*

All that multitasking means we're forced to listen to a whole bunch of Oxygen Suckers:

"Ummm . . . uhhhh . . ." Long *um*s and *uh*s automatically transmit the idea that your brain has stopped functioning.

   "Like . . ." Like, you like, should really, like, stop saying, *like,* like so much, because, like, people don't, like, like it.

   "Well, ya knoooooooow . . ." Winner for the most-frequently-said O_2 Sucker when we are not listening at all.

   "Mmmmmmmmmmmmmmmmm . . ." Means "I've been contemplating the rip in my stocking and I have absolutely no idea what you just said."

   "Wellllllllllllllllllllllllllllll . . ." Means "I have no idea what *I* just said."

Make sure your vocal cords aren't vibrating while you're not actually speaking. Oxygen Suckers show that either you are not paying attention or you can't, ummmm, errrr, uhhhh, think fast enough. Extra silence is better than, like, fillers. The best way to avoid the Oxygen Suckers? Pay attention.

Wimpy, Wimpy, Wimpy

Lots of The Girls Who Call Us also use Wimpy Words (WWs) and Puny Phrases (PPs). Think of a commercial; would you buy something if the pitch included "*Maybe* you could try it" or "*Hopefully* you will like it"? No way.

Steer clear of these common WWs & PPs:

   "Maybe we *could* . . ." Just say: "*We should . . .*"

   "*Hopefully,* we can . . ." Just say: *"We will." Hope* implies wishing; *will* implies doing.

   "I *think that* we should . . ." Just say: *"We should . . ."* If challenged on this for being bossy, simply say: "Fred, I'm giving you an *opinion,* not an order."

   "If it's *OK* with you . . ." Just say: *"I want to . . ."*

- **"I'll *try* to . . ."** Just say: *"I will . . ."* Once you've said it, there is no out; you will do it.

- **"I *kind of* thought . . ."** Well, do you think it or not?

- **"I *sort of* wanted . . ."** Well, do you want it or not?

- **"I have a *little* (or *tiny* or *teensy*) problem . . ."** If it's so minuscule, why can't you solve it yourself?

- **"I have one *small* comment to add . . ."** You might as well say that your thought is so insignificant it isn't worth the time to say it, let alone listen to it. Instead say: *"I have one quick comment to add,"* and be as good as your word.

Your Volume Speaks Volumes

When you are watching *Everybody Loves Raymond,* notice how the commercial breaks are even louder than the already loud show. Commercials are designed that way to get your attention. Transactional Talk calls for the same strategy.

When your voice is too soft in Transactional Talk, you invite yourself to be a Girl Interrupted. Not only that, but others will perceive you as either ineffectual, passive-aggressive (getting attention by making people work hard to hear you), or completely lacking in conviction and/or a spine.

This has never been a particular problem of ours because we are used to having conversations in the NYC subway. But so many of The Girls Who Call Us sound so sweet and gentle with that low volume that it's easy to see how they become verbal road kill.

Transactional Talking should be just slightly louder than conversational tones. If you are a soft talker, kick it up a notch. Practice being heard in loud places—go with a girlfriend to Old Navy, where the music will blast you out of your socks, and have a chat. Be a barfly and practice speaking up till the guy next to you doesn't have to lean over into your lap to hear you. Also, we highly recommend taking an acting class or joining up with your community playhouse—there's great Chat & Hum potential *and* you'll learn how to be heard clear to the back of the house.

If you tend to control your volume because your voice is so high-pitched that you get shrill, on behalf of Corporate America we thank you. If, like us, you are apt to blast people out of the room, remember to tone it down, sister. For a great bunch of tips on controlling your voice, go to vocalcoach.com. Register for free, and then go to the tips section and scroll down to the info for your particular concern, such as "too soft-spoken" or "a deeper, more authoritative voice."

Closing Remarks

You don't have to speak perfectly, work perfectly, and get it all right all the time. Remember that if you rant, rave, and ramble today, let it go and stand tall tomorrow, no matter what.

Chapter 10

some
Body

Your body speaks louder than your words

Useful Terms: What We Mean When We Say . . .
Body Words What your body spells out about you behind your back
Body Read How people read your Body Words
Mona Lisa Face A look more impossible to read than *Beowulf*
Broadcasting Babes Women newscasters; those who never forget the
camera is rolling and recording their every move

Once we went to a wedding of a mutual colleague. Ahh, the beautiful bride on the happiest day of her life! Too bad she looked as if her corset was laced tighter than Scarlett O'Hara's. All day she looked *paaaaained,* so while her mouth was saying, "I do," her face was saying, "Do I *have* to?"

We're quite sure that she had *no* idea that despite the designer dress, the perfect makeup, and the string quartet, she looked about as joyful as a person waiting on line at the post office on December 23.

Bet you want to know how quickly she got that divorce, huh? She didn't. It's five years later and she just had her second kid. Turns out she *did* like the groom after all. Well, you never would have known it to look at her wincing down that aisle.

In cases of mixed messages, the audience will be far more likely to believe what your body is silently saying than anything coming out of your mouth. We've seen some women in action in the office, and while they might have actually been on the ball, they *looked* like they were totally out in left field by doing completely senseless things like making mustaches with the ends of their hair.

Certainly we've done our fair share of brainless fidgeting. When we first started in our Big Jobs, we didn't realize that no matter how sophisticated our speech, our Body Words were babbling baby-talk blather as we swiveled merrily around in the conference room chairs: "Whee! Don't take us *too* seriously!" After being talked down to enough, we had to teach our bodies to chill out and grow up.

Broadcasting Babes

We began to closely watch the Body Words of other women in our offices—those whose bodies said the most inappropriate things ("Hug me!") and those whose bodies said the most powerful things ("Fear me"). But the single most instructional tool for taming our twitching, swishing, and squirming was watching women newscasters—with no sound.

You've got to try this. Turn on your local news with a woman broadcaster and hit the mute button. You'll see that Ms. Local Newscaster from WDUH in Buffalo is all smiley and her eyebrows are jumping up and down. When we did this, we were laughing at how stiff some of these newswomen look. But then we started thinking about how *we* must look when we speak and are swiveling our chairs like oscillating fans. Even the *worst* newscasters don't do *that*. Not so funny.

Now, turn on CNN or Fox News and watch those Broadcasting Babes with the sound down. They *don't* look ridiculous at all, except for maybe some of that lip gloss. Compare what they do to what *you* do when you are speaking. Those newswomen watch their Body Words and maximize their physical vocabulary for maximum credibility. The only difference between lots of the local newscasters and the national Broadcasting Babes is that the network newscasters are better at controlling their body messaging and looking completely comfortable while they do it.

Great Broadcasting Babes have been *trained* to be conscious of their bodies every single second those cameras are rolling. And *we've* all got to think about it the same way, because virtually every minute you are in the office, those cameras *are* rolling—and, God help us, recording. So here's our Body Word Rule: if you don't see the Broadcasting Babes do it on the nightly news, don't do it in the office.

In this chapter we're going to do a quick head-to-toe makeover to make you conscious of the Body Words you use and what they might be saying about you behind your back. All of the tics and tricks we cover are either things we've seen other women do or things we've done ourselves—we'll only cop to the least embarrassing.

Don't Get Ahead of Yourself

Women often tilt their heads to show they are listening. The Body Read, though, is that we are either puzzled (huh?) or we agree (yup, yup, yup)—even when we don't.

Watch the Broadcast Babes; they *never* tilt their heads. Nor do they talk with their chin down in that shy little girly way. When you lower your chin, your volume drops, and you can't look people straight in the eye (unless you can see through your lids, that is).

Keep that head straight up, and keep that chin up if you want to be heard. The skinny on chinny: chin down says shy and tentative, chin up says, "I dare ya."

Land of Nod

In a related head trip, there's nodding. Perhaps we girls picked up the autonod from watching our mothers all those years pretending to listen to us whine by nodding, nodding, nodding: "Mmmm, yeah . . .

that's nice, dear," while they stirred the spaghetti sauce. It's outta hand, though: we've seen entire conference rooms full of women all looking like their necks need shock absorbers.

Keep your head straight, like you've got a flagpole running straight up through your body. If you nod simply to be polite while someone is speaking and to show that you are listening, it gets automatically translated by everyone who sees you do it into the idea that you completely agree with the point being made, and you just might not. It's a classic mixed message. Don't feel the need to encourage the speaker with the big bopper head routine, either.

Hair Say

We've all seen them. The women with long hair who study the ends with such fierce concentration, you would think they were searching for the Meaning of Life. The message this hairy habit sends is "I find my split ends more interesting than you." The Body Read on this eye-avoidance technique is passive-aggressive, active nonlistening.

Then there are the hair chewers and suckers. The Body Read: immature, insecure, little-girl manipulative. Neither of us has ever been a hair chewer, but we do have our own stupid hair tricks. M runs her fingers through the hair on the top of her head all day long while she's thinking. We've seen lots of other women do the hair hoe, too. What they don't realize is that the Body Read is exasperation. So they are sending out frustration signals, even when they are not feeling that way.

J is a hair adjuster: reclip, retwist, refasten. It's a little busy activity that she does when she's uncomfortable or bored. But if you redo your do every two seconds, it's a distraction to anyone who might actually want to listen to what you have to say. Hands off the hair, honey. Can you imagine Greta Van Susteren yanking up her ponytail in the middle of interviewing the former director of the CIA?

Scalping Tickets

Attention all scalp pickers: the Body Read on that one is *gross!* Knock it off. For all you scalp scratchers, the Body Read on even the tiniest little scratch to the head is that you are confused in some way: "Huhhhh?"

If your head is itchy, we have two words and an ampersand for you: Head & Shoulders. It happens to the best of us, but hit the hygiene aisle as soon as you start to flake out. Don't have a dandruff storm on your shoulders, or worse, the black desk blotter snow-globe effect.

While we're in the shampoo aisle, keep that hair consistently clean—not clean one day, slimesville the third day. And if you dye your tresses, the skunk effect is a stinky idea. M is still trying to get J to just go natural, but J has a deep-rooted fear of roots. Bottom line: this stuff counts because if you don't look like you take care of yourself, it won't look like you can take care of business either.

Face Facts

Think about your face as a storefront. Would you go into a store with dirty windows? What if it was really tacky or otherwise frightening? The answer is no way, Tammy Faye.

Those newscasters are always nicely made up, but most of them are not overdone—lip gloss notwithstanding—and their faces appear as neutral and pleasant as their makeup. If you *really* don't know how to put on makeup, call a Mary Kay lady or hit a department store for a quick lesson. It's free.

Tweeze what needs tweezing, squeeze what needs squeezing, but never, *ever* do them sitting at your desk in plain view. You will *never* see Katie Couric torturing herself with her eyelash curler. You are supposed to be getting work done, sweetheart, not getting done up.

The Eyes Have It

Your eyes are power tools—you can use them to attract people (wink wink), dis them (the big eye roll), seduce them (Bette Davis eyes), and on and on. But eye contact is tricky: the second you become self-conscious, your eyes start darting around like a hummingbird seemingly able to alight anywhere but on the other person's ocular orbs.

Can you imagine if newscasters didn't look straight into the camera or were looking down to the left? You would think, "What the hell is distracting her from talking to *me,* the all-powerful viewer? What is she *hiding*?" Looking straight into the camera is hard; it takes practice. It's the same exact thing with looking straight into people's eyes, and it's absolutely essential—'cause if you go all lazy-eyed, people will think you are *lying* or otherwise fishy.

The Body Read on looking a person in the eye is strength, confidence, and respect—for yourself and them. Aren't those all qualities you want to be known for? Consciously working on eye spying is well worth the time and potential anxiety you invest in it.

J had a serious problem meeting people's eyes, and she was told by senior managers in several jobs that she *must* make eye contact for effective communication. To break the eye avoidance habit, J started looking *everyone* in the eye. As a result, she began to connect faces with names, and it transformed her. Once she even heard a secretary mention it: "She knew *my* name! She's sooo cool."

M *still* has some difficulty with the eye thing when she is super-duper nervous (uh, a lot) or hasn't had enough sleep (insomniac). But because M *knows* that she has this particular bad body grammar, she uses the old look-them-*between*-the-eyes trick we mentioned back in Chapter 4, "Hiring Hell." Try it on a friend. Look high on the bridge of her nose and ask her if you are looking her in the eye. She'll say aye, absolutely.

The Evil Eyes

Speaking of tricks, there's the Gaze Glaze: when someone stares into your eyes with such intensity that it seems like they are barely blinking. It's a form of intimidation that seems to challenge your very right to breathe.

If someone eye-locks you in a Gaze Glaze, *don't* look at your shoes, which you will instinctively want to do. Instead, look *above* his eyebrows, forehead, or hairline. Works like a charm—he will be unnerved, wondering what blob you see on his head that is drawing your attention. Try it and watch him drop *his* gaze to the dirt.

Also, be on the lookout for people who either talk down to you (literally) while you are seated at your desk or someone taller who catches you in the hallway to discuss something important. It's a body language power struggle, and when someone is looking down at you, he's in the dominant position psychologically. When the discussion is significant, get the coworker to sit down and get him at eye level. If you are in an exec's office, never choose to sit on the couch if a chair is available; you will sink too low, disappear into the Naugahyde, and put yourself at a considerable disadvantage eye-level-wise.

Be mindful that you don't inadvertently look down (literally, that is) on your superiors. We guarantee that they will start to become uncomfortable, if not agitated. If your boss is seated in her office and you've got something to say that will take longer than five seconds, ask her if she has a minute and take a seat.

Don't believe this eye level stuff is a power struggle? What do *you* think happened to Tom and Nicole's marriage?

Don't Smile When Your Heart Is Breaking

Smiling rules. We're big smilers and have seen the magic of teeth to transform a biting situation into a kiss-and-make-up one. The Body Read on a well-placed flash of the pearly whites says that you are open, approachable, and pleasant. When all hell is breaking loose, a *confident* smile says you're in control.

But there are definitely times when smiling is inappropriate. When you watch the seasoned newscasters, note how they don't sport a "hi, Mom" smile when delivering news of a serious nature. Nor do they give one of those nervous little "heh heh" smiles—ever. A smile says you are happy, but naturally there will be times in the office when you are *not* happy, and if you smile your way through them, you will be sending a mixed message. If you are angry and you know it, don't clap your hands.

If you are the type who smiles through tears or when you are angry, as if to apologize for your more inconvenient emotions, you need to work on your Mona Lisa Face—there is no telling what her look actually means. Practice your Mona Lisa mug in the mirror: grimace a little, and don't grin at all. Once you've got it down, try it out a *few* times in the office; if you can get people to say, "Why the sour look?" you've got it. Pull out old Mona the next time you've got a beef and you want there to be *no* mistake about just how raw you feel about it.

Chew on This

Lucy, a COO of an Internet store, used to nibble a pencil round and round like an ear of corn during meetings, and then, invariably, she would leave it behind on the table like some sort of territorial dropping. We can tell you, nobody ever wanted to touch these things—even just to throw them away.

The Body Read on chewing and other nervous mouth maneuvers like inner cheek chewing (cud), lip biting (till it bleeds), and lip corner tonguing (the face you make when you are trying to untie a stubborn knot) can run the gamut from hiding something to frustration, anger, anxiety, loneliness, and boredom.

After we told Lucy that her unconscious chewing thing was bizarre and a topic of office conversation, she bought a Costco-size container of Twizzlers to work out her oral angst. For meetings, we taught her our secret tongue tamer: push your tongue against the inside of your top teeth and hold it there. It requires some concentration to keep it in place, so it will keep your mouth from other oral acrobatics. Warning: don't space out entirely on the topic du jour while you are contemplating your tongue.

WAITING TO INHALE

Breathing, so easy. Breathe in, breathe out. No problem. Except when you are anxious or nervous and don't realize that you are not breathing at all. (Gasp, sputter, sputter.) Before you go to say something important or pick up that phone, catch your breath and watch out for other bad breathing Body Reads:

- **Sighing expresses exasperation, exhaustion, and boredom.** Don't do it—you will remind people of their forlorn mothers.

- **Yawning.** This can be a physical response to anxiety but the Body Read is boredom or fatigue. Unfortunately, when M is nervous or uncomfortable, her brain sends her a signal to yawn. I'm sorry, Marcelle, are we boring you?

- **Out of breath means out of control.** It signals something is wrong. Stop and take a deep calming breath to make sure that your voice will sound calm and in control when you open your mouth.

- **A forced-air "huh" or harrumph is a cousin to the sigh but huffier.** This is the female equivalent to that low, airy, passive-aggressive, whistlelike sound guys blow that says: "I am *sooo* sick of this shit."

We, like the rest of America, are yoga converts. While we've found that it won't help us lose the weight that all our yoga-head friends promised us it would, all that concentrating on breathing and stillness is fabulous training for breathless fidgety girls like us.

Oh, and as long as we're breathing deeply, eat mints, and brush

(continued)

your teeth after lunch. J knows one woman who was so oblivious of her bad postlunch breath that her officemates started making up halitosis songs. And what rhymes with *halitosis? Psychosis. Neurosis.* Not a pretty ditty.

Glad Handing

Hands can utter the biggest Body Word profanities, hands down. Almost anytime you touch your face, you are either distracting listeners from what you are saying, or showing doubt that you believe—or understand—what someone else is saying to you. Newscasters never rub their foreheads, smooth their eyebrows, or feel around for upper-lip peach fuzz while on camera.

Here are the Body Reads on other empty slights of hands:

Nail or cuticle tearing: out-of-control anxiety or cannibal. You might as well be trimming your toenails on the conference table. As for cuticle pushing, the Body Read is that you're bored out of your skull. To stop doing this, get a weekly manicure.

Manicure studying: narcissistic and/or unimaginative. Are your nails really *that* fascinating?

Hand sitting: trying too hard or has to pee. While this may keep your hands from doing all manner of other fidgety things, it can also make you look like a mental patient—people who literally sit on their hands also tend to be "rockers."

Pointing and poking: powerful and threatening. Save pointing at someone's chest or poking him in the shoulder for when you need to come on strong.

Scratching: murderous or suicidal. We once had a boss who was an unconscious scratcher. She clawed at her neck till it was red; she dug her nails into her forearms till it looked like she had track marks. It gave us the creepy crawlies to watch.

♀ **Finger smelling:** eeewww. No matter *what* you think you got your hands into, don't smell your digits in front of *anyone.*

Booby Traps

We love our cleavage. Is that so wrong? Now that we've got *that* off our chests, it is with deep regret that we have to tell you to put 'em away and keep them on the shelf till you get home.

It's terrible, but true. If you overreveal your perky little sisters at work, you will be exposed to gossip and ridicule. Flaunting "the Girls," as J calls them, will never work in your favor: guys will think you manipulative (or worse, that you *want* them) and other women will find it irritating and threatening.

It's OK to wear clothes and undergarments that flatter the Girls (no pun intended), but you just can't flaunt, flounce, or fondle, even unconsciously.

♀ **When you are fingering that necklace, resist the urge to give the Girls a fond little stroke.** People, particularly guys, will notice.

♀ **Do not stare at anyone's boobs and especially not your own.** A guy actually caught J admiring the Girls and said: "You checkin' out those big fancy tits of yours?"

♀ **Don't stick a pen into your cleavage.** The Girls are not a pocket protector.

♀ **No matter what your size, wear a bra at all times.** None of that distracting peekaboo nipple stuff through the sheer blouse. Make sure the bra fits too. That "back fat" bra has *got* to go. High beams, jiggling, and sagging are all distractions from you, the work you are doing, and the Reputation you would give your left tit to have.

⚔ **Do not draw attention to the Girls by pointing out or talking about your bra.** "Huh! I just unsnapped."

When dealing with certain male coworkers, you might have noticed that frequently their gaze falls somewhere south of your clavicles. We've both had entire discussions with male coworkers where not once did their eyes find their way to the general vicinity of our faces.

We hate this one, and so do The Girls Who Call Us. We used to think it was some type of psych-out tactic to distract or perhaps diminish us, but our Guy Spies have told us that it's simply because they can't help themselves. Fair enough. We understand. Still, it's annoying to deal with, so here are our thoughts on avoiding it:

⚔ **Lower your head to meet his gaze and bring his eyes up.** Sometimes it helps to say something to snap them out of it: "What were you just thinking about, Randy? You disappeared there for a minute or two."

⚔ **Stop talking.** After he notices the silence, he will look up at you to see what happened. When this occurs, pick up where you left off. Repeat as necessary.

⚔ **If it's anyone you want to embarrass,** say: "My ears are on my head."

Belly Baddies

We just like the word *belly*, so we *had* to mention it here. Here are some tummy topics:

⚔ **Never show that belly.** No cropped shirts, no showing off the new navel ring. The Body Read for bare bellies is S-E-X. So if you show tummy skin, it will look like an invitation to come on in.

⚔ **Stand up straight and suck it in.** Really, most of us do it. The Body Read on bad posture is indifferent, insecure, lazy, sloppy. Conversely, the Body Read on good posture is confidence, poise, and efficiency.

However, the Body Read on an *overly* erect, rigid posture is uptight, impossible, and unapproachable.

Wiggle Room

Take a sec and think of all the random mindless physical activities you do while sitting at your desk. Are you a ring twister, necklace chewer, binder-clip clicker, earring spinner, stocking puller, nail biter, chair spinner? All of this stuff is pass-the-Valium anxiety fidgeting, and if you do it at your desk, you are bound to do it in the conference room. All that twitching and tinkering will distract your audience from your message. Tone it down, girl. Think about Greta.

Stand and Deliver

When you are standing around having a hallway Chat, realize that when you sway like you're on the *Titanic*, you might just be sinking your Reputation.

- **Stand tall.** No rocking, no shifting weight dramatically and sinking into your hip. A little shifting is OK; big shifting is, um, shifty, and you will seem uncomfortable or, worse, like you are hiding something. The less movement you make, the more confidence others perceive in you.

- **If you cross your arms in front of you, the Body Read is, of course, defensive.** Give yourself a prop when roaming the halls. An empty coffee mug is good to keep from hugging yourself or putting your hands on your hips—which indicates anger.

- **Standing with the bottom of your foot against a wall is O-U-T.** Body Read: unstable or *very* available. Don't do this one unless you are wearing fishnet stockings in Hell's Kitchen or you're on a reeeallly long line to get Springsteen tickets.

Return Your Seat to Its Full Upright Position

Most corporate business is conducted while seated. And, you know, sitting is hard work. We used to think that sitting Indian style, lounging with our feet up on the desk, or adopting some similar floppy pose made us seem cool and approachable. Which it did, but what we didn't realize for far too long is that it made us a little *too* approachable: "Oh, the coast is clear, it's *just* Jocelyn."

Although we thought of ourselves as pros, we didn't sit like executives, so all too often we were not treated as such. So much for personal style. When you take a seat:

- **Sit as far back in the chair as you can.** Body Read: powerful, grounded, confident. Don't hang off the edge, as some do to make their thighs look smaller; it will make you look off balance and tentative.

- **Keep those feet flat on the floor.** Even though people might not be able to see your feet, if you are doing something weird with your footsies down there, it will snake up your legs, twist your torso, and before you know it you'll be chewing on the ends of your hair.

- **Shoulders back, chin up.** Lean into the table if you want to make a power point.

- **If someone is trying to intimidate you, you might get the urge to go fetal.** Don't let your shoulders slump, your spine go flaccid, and your legs start to curl up like one of those party blowers. Put your feet on the floor and apply pressure, like you are going to push up to a standing position. Get rooted and hold on to your seat, girl.

She's Got Legs (Does She Know How to Use 'Em?)

Walk the walk, baby. People you don't deal with directly will most likely form an impression of you as you walk on by to the ladies' room, head out to lunch, or run to make a copy.

You can actually make yourself Visible and create the beginnings of a positive Reputation just by the way you walk. So do it: get up and walk around your office a few times a day. Invent some urgent errands. Whoopsie! Don't you need to go to the supply room (again) to get binder clips? We thought so. Here's how to do it:

- **Walk with determined energy.** Every little walkabout should appear as if you are on an important mission—even if it's just to get coffee. You are a busy, productive person. J observed a woman who was always speeding around the office: "Where was she going exactly? Should I be going there?" When J picked up her own pace, people actually commented to her that she must be "very busy these days." Oh yes.

- **No tiptoeing.** You want people to know you are coming. The point is to walk as if you don't know that people are observing you—but doing whatever you can to make sure they do. However, clomping like a pachyderm, as M used to do, is appropriate only if you're a big boss. Otherwise it's just disruptive—and take it from M, people *will* tell you so.

- **Think about payday or S-E-X.** You want your walking face to look eager and self-satisfied—never angry or goofy.

- **Heads up!** Remember the old book-on-the-head school of modeling? It's still valid. When you look at the floor it signals sadness, distraction, defeat.

Acknowledge, don't avoid. When you pass someone in the hall, *look* at him, smile, and say, "Hello, Joe Schmoe!" But don't break stride unless Schmoe does first—*you* are far too busy.

 Stride right. Longer steps say you are on the *move*. Dainty, dinky steps say you are afraid to go too far.

 Be sensible. If you have heels that hobble you, don't wear 'em, or else the next office newsletter will read: "Dumb Account Exec Gimps Self with Own Shoes."

Footloose and Smelly-Free

Sandals. Need we say more? Make sure those tootsies are tidy or keep them locked up in the pump house. Puh-leeze, for J's sake, no toe or heel overhang—it does *not* make your foot look more petite to wear a sandal two sizes too small! Toe overhang is the equivalent of too-tight-bra back fat.

Table Hopping

Where you put your body counts. Even if you never say a word in a meeting, people will remember that you were there, front and center, if you sit in the right place.

We used to think that if we sat right next to the Most Uppity Upper in the room, we would look important in the minds of the other people: "Wow, she's the boss's right-hand girl." But if you sit right next to the Uppity, you might feel pit-stain self-conscious if you actually have to speak.

When you sit *that* close, you can feel the Uppity breathing on you. You might imagine that he's staring at the pores in your nose or your clumping mascara when it's your turn to speak. So you start sweating and then panic about him seeing your forehead bead up with "Oh, shit!" dew. Then you try to make eye contact with the boss and lose your train of thought 'cause you are distracted by the size of the pores in *his* nose.

If possible, sit almost, but not directly, across the table from the exec. If you sit directly opposite, you might get the line–of–fire eye lock—it's not pretty. Sit to the side of the person in the line of fire, so you can easily see and be seen by the boss, but not so close that you can smell the onion bagel he had for breakfast.

THE WHOLE KIT AND CANOODLING

Sexual tension, like muscle tension, needs to be iced or medicated or you might just pull something.

If you want to dress all Sexy Mama at work, go for it. We did . . . for a while, anyway. But *know* that if you dress all hottie, you will be inviting advances, lurid looks, and eye rolls from those nice ladies in the midcalf-length skirts. In some office cultures, Sexy Mamas can have a grim credibility problem; in others, they will fit right in; in still others, they provide the daily amusement.

No matter what you wear, being young and healthy it's likely that you will have a close encounter where some sexual tension thang begins to build up between you and a colleague. While this can be great fun and can certainly make going to the office every day a little more thrilling, it's a dangerous game if you want to be taken seriously or value your privacy.

You want to make sure that you've thought through your goals and the ramifications in the office if the sexual tension explodes one night into a sticky situation by the copy machine. Do you want to add a whole layer of complication in your work life: between the wondering, the what-ifs, and the worrying, it *will* be difficult to concentrate on your J-O-B. Which is to say nothing of the breeze you will feel as the rumor mill cranks up and blows right up your skirt.

Do what you will, darling. Hey, some of The Girls Who Call Us are now married to guys they ran into by the Xerox, but know that there

(continued)

are repercussions from not being conscious of when your Body Words could be considered porn. If you want to play with fire but not get burned, it's best to keep the heat on a low simmer, keep some distance, and avoid fanning the flames of office affairs.

Pound for Pound

No matter what you think of your body—and let's face it, which of us who sits for a living *loves* her body?—always talk about how *good* you feel. Don't point out the pounds you need to lose, don't blab about your flab. No one wants to hear it.

Besides, coworkers might not even notice your flaws, but the second you point them out, well, there it is: your chubba-lubba thighs laid out on the conference table for all the office to take a poke at. Suddenly you are known not as "that great, smart girl from HR" but as "that chunky girl who can't stop talking about how her thighs rub." Not a good plan, man.

Chapter **11**

Y-O-U:
the Ultimate
Planning Machine

How to get where you want to go

Useful Terms: What We Mean When We Say . . .
DestQuest A head trip through your fantasies
The Girl Guilt Tipping Point The point at which you've gone too far and have
to keep going because you feel too guilty and
stupid not to
The Fear Factor The thing that keeps you from moving even one inch in any
particular direction

When it comes to that surreal movie called *Thelma & Her Career,* you have a choice between only two roles to play: either you are the driver or you are the passenger—who may or may not have *any* say *whatsoever* in where you are headed.

Now, there is but a single factor that determines if you are steering or simply being taken for a ride: the presence or absence of a Strategic Plan. Trust us. That's how it works. We've *seen* this movie.

Personally, we resisted the very notion of creating any major plans for our lives. When we were young(er) ingenue types, we thought that planning was the mortal enemy of spontaneity. From our perspective, people who planned seemed rigid, uncreative, and uptight. And you know what that spells: B-O-R-I-N-G.

We were free spirits. Whee! Problem was, we were floating around aimlessly. There we were, out there in the big world trying to get somewhere, but we had no road map, no strategy, and, clearly, no clue. The details from those early years are pretty blurry, probably because we spent most of our time riding in the backseat doing 180 MPH—destination *nowhere*.

But we do remember this with painful clarity: no one was more surprised than we were when things didn't exactly work out the way we *didn't* plan.

Ultimately, this is a book about choice. If you think that planning is a big snoozola and you just want to sit back, relax, and be a passenger, be our guest and skip to the next chapter, but remember this: the driver is *never* the one who gets carsick.

We Got a Fast Car if You Want a Ticket to Anywhere

After our first stabs at planning, we wanted to slit our wrists. Like all other planning converts, we would spend an inordinate amount of time religiously creating priority lists and filling out our day planners. Invariably some distraction, some conflict, or some good opportunity would arise, and the whole shebang got tossed out the window. Most of the time, all we achieved with these complicated planning scenarios was humongoid feelings of failure over not getting our overdue expense reports done between 1:16 and 2:32 on January 9, or the tenth, or the eleventh . . .

After several years of trying to block out every nanosecond of the day in planners, Palm Pilots, and the rest of the "solutions" proffered by the gazillion-dollar-per-year personal management industry, we finally said, "Enough already!"

We came up with a simple planning paradigm that wouldn't drive us crazy. It goes like this: figure out the Destination, get directions, and start driving.

Slide right in. We'll take you out for a spin and show you how this baby works.

Take a Head Trip

Think about MapQuest. What's the first thing you need to do if you want directions? Yup. Select your Destination. You *gotta* know where you want to go before you can figure out how to get there.

So how do you figure out what your Destination should be or if you are already headed toward the right one for you in your career? It's as easy as losing your keys: you pull over for a pit stop and think about it.

Go to Wal-Mart right now and drop a buck fifty on a little notebook. Not some fancy-schmancy writer's journal that you won't use till you find just the right pen—we want something down and dirty here. M uses cloth-bound marble composition notebooks so she can't tear out the pages. J uses an index-card-size bound spiral notebook that fits in her purse because she likes to do her thinking in taxis. On the cover write one word that no one will understand but us girls: *DestQuest.*

What we want you to do is write out your *fantasies* as fast and as furiously as you can without thinking too long about any of them; then put the notebook away. Find ten to twenty minutes at least a couple of times a week to do this. M stirs up her fantasies on paper almost every day before she's even half awake, while the coffee is dripping; J does it leaning on her purse bouncing in the back of a cab between appointments. Clearly, you don't need to wait until your brain is fully functional; in fact, it's probably better to do it when you are a little spaced out and your subconscious feels free enough to go out for a little joyriding.

Your DestQuest is not a logging of your days, but rather a logging of your longings. There's no room in your DestQuest for pros and cons—money (or lack thereof), time, age, practicality, and reality are *not* factors to be considered, so leave 'em out.

Write down what you like, what you don't like, what you are good at, what you suck at, what you think you would like to be good at, what thoughts make you want to hurl a brick at someone's head. The point of this exercise is to force you to spend time thinking your own thoughts without being influenced by a thousand naysaying voices in your head, not to mention the choir of your Evil Network of Negativity, which only knows one song: "But . . . but . . . but . . . you *can't* do *that!*"

Include any and all random fantasies:

- **Job fantasies.** Include occupations (wanna be a firefighter?), money (big cashola?), environment (entrepreneurial?), your desire to see your supervisor run over by a truck and eaten by wild dogs. As the song says, *anything* goes. Specifically, you are looking to fill in this blank: "I can't believe I get *paid* to [insert fantasy activity] all day."

- **Lifestyle fantasies.** Quiet life in the country? Telecommuting? Family? Part time? Retirement by age forty? Travel? Jet set? Starting your own business? The goal with this one is to ask yourself: "How would I live if money were a nonissue?" Tick-tock—listen to your clock, princess. Ask yourself, "What does my ideal week/month/year look like?"

- **Short-term desires.** What is the *one* thing you want most out of today? What would make this week a memorable one? Here's one: what's the one thing you could get done or achieve at work that would make you feel like a goddess?

- **S-E-X fantasies.** What the hell, why not? Hey, it worked for Madonna.

You must take stock of what your dreams are if you ever want to begin to attain them. We know so many women who just don't even take the time to define how they want to live and simply sit around hoping that things will improve. We want to put you in the *daily* habit of thinking about What You Want Most from your job, your life, and each day. Honey, you *need* to give those self-interest muscles a good regular workout or you can't *possibly* know what you want in the next five minutes, let alone five years from now. So many of The Girls Who Call Us never stop choochin' along long enough to consider if they even *like* the jobs they are in, let alone whether they love them.

We really want you to *write* out these thoughts, though. Trust us—so many great ideas are lost for-evah because we don't capture them fast enough or they get smothered under piles of to-do lists and the other insignificant flotsam and jetsam of our day-to-day logistics.

Keep your DestQuest book for about a month without reading it, then go back and start leafing through. We promise that you will hardly remember even writing that stuff, let alone that you had thoughts like *those!* Do this for a year, and you might just realize how little you know about the random thoughts you think.

When you look over your notes, pay careful attention to themes that repeat. Herein lie your Personal Destination Points: where you want to go now or next. For example, if the one about your supervisor and the wild dogs shows up five times, it's time to start looking for a new gig. Where items in your notebook echo, slash them with a neon highlighter, 'cause that's where you are headed, sistergirl.

Focus on the Destination, Not the Journey

So many of The Girls Who Call Us who've tried the DestQuest have been so stunned by observing the consistent themes in their fantasies that they became highly motivated to drive toward Destinations they once thought unreachable. Few make huge dramatic life changes overnight, mind you, but over time our friends took the steps they needed to to get from where they were to where they wanted to be. Check it out:

⚭ **When Tracey started thinking about what it was she** *really* **wanted her life to look like, she left her job as an administrative assistant** at a prestigious publishing firm and went to culinary school. She's now on the road to becoming a pastry chef, something she hadn't considered till she started checking in with herself about what she *might* want.

⚭ **Patti discovered she wanted three things, badly:** to move out of Brooklyn, to work fewer hours, and to have less job stress. Patti was an over-caseloaded DA in the Manhattan district attorney's office. She moved to Albany, found a job with a state regulatory agency, and now works 26.25 hours per week, from 8:15 to 1:30. Nice-looking hours, no?

⚭ **Sue, a marketing exec at a major cosmetics firm, decided to walk away from a chunka-hunka-cash salary** because she realized her entire career had been about "making a whole bunch of white men wealthy." Now she does marketing for a nonprofit that's run by a woman entrepreneur.

⚭ **France blew off her big-$$$ job as a full-time chemist** to become a full-time violin teacher. She now has a sizeable roster of students, plays in a chamber orchestra, and has put her music in the center of her life—a fantasy she had since high school but could ignore no longer in the DestQuest process.

⚭ **Our favorite DestQuest success, though, is our agent,** Alička, who worked for a literary agent in New York City but came to the bold conclusion that she wanted her *own* agency. Today she runs the Alička Pistek Literary Agency.

Will they all live happily ever after? Who knows? But so far, so good. Each of these women is happier and feels more in control than before—even those who are making far fewer $$$ each year. If you were to talk to any of them, they would tell you that they didn't think their current lives were possible when they first exposed those ideal fantasies. They would tell you that there were too many reasons *not* to make the choices they ultimately did make. Yet they did it. We did it. And you can too.

You *Can* Get There from Here

We used to think that in order to reach any Destination, we had to know every single inch of the road we would need to follow and every turn we would need to travel to get there. If we didn't know the *exact* route, we didn't even put the key in the ignition to see if we could get whatever idea it is we had to turn over and start up. It took us years to discover that we didn't need to know the whole way to begin moving in the right direction.

We also found that when we *did* attempt to map out every detail, we were merely defining every obstacle. When we could see in black and white the tremendous distance we were thinking of traveling, we became *afraid* that it was just too damn far; frankly, we weren't *sure* we could make it.

People who know us personally are generally inclined to think that the two of us are pretty fearless. And, compared to many, we are. Yet it was most definitely Fear, Fear, Fear, and more Fear that kept us from personally committing to our big dreams ten years before we ultimately did. Many of The Girls Who Call Us have had an even tougher time than we did getting mobilized when stunned by the Fear Factor.

But Fear doesn't keep us safe from anything, really. We eventually discovered that Time is completely indifferent to whether or not we're happy and on the road to wherever it is we think we want to go—it will pass just as surely.

What we do these days is take the Fear Factor out of the picture entirely with our Three-Step Rule. It works like this: we take any given Destination (also known as a goal), rough out *only* what we think are the first three steps in the right direction, and focus exclusively on them until all three are completed. It doesn't even matter if they are actually the *right* steps as long as we're consistently doing *anything* to drive in what we think is the right direction toward our Destination. When we've taken those three steps, we've got momentum—the power to keep moving and keep trying.

We designed the Three-Step Rule to yield the two qualities that the most kick-ass driving directions have: they are *simple* and *specific*. With our Three-Step Rule, each step becomes its own Destination, and if that Destination seems a bit too far to reach within twenty minutes a day, it gets broken down into a series of steps, which then become their own Destinations, and so on. The whole thing telescopes down, so the Three-Step Rule helps us plot our way to closer and closer Destination Points until we are taking the road as it comes, one measly milestone at a time.

If we don't know the first three steps, then—duh—our first step is to figure out what the first three steps are.

The Three-Step Rule works. Here's why:

Each Destination is a small fraction of the entire distance it takes to reach any goal, so the expectation that any one step will take you terribly far evaporates. "What the hell, I'll call my uncle Sylvester and see if he knows anyone I can talk to about becoming a speech pathologist." With the Three-Step Rule, you complete the step, arrive at the desired subgoal, let go of any expectation of what might come of it, and move directly on to the next step.

We used to sit around waiting for some earth-shattering response after taking one tiny step like sending a pitch letter, but we trained ourselves to get it done, *forget* it, and move on down the road to the next step. When you are driving somewhere, you don't stop after the first mile and admire your progress or wait for someone else to pick you up and drive you the rest of the way, do you? Same deal.

You won't feel overwhelmed. In the beginning, you want to devote just twenty minutes a day or less toward any given step, so even though the step might not be the most urgent thing on your plate, it will only take twenty minutes, so you *can* make it a priority, fit it in, and get it D-O-N-E. It's kinda like your 401(k) plan: you'll never miss the tiny time investment, but over time, you are amassing one jumbo egg for your future nest.

♟ **The plan is continuously being revised and updated based on your current reality.** Once you've completed the first three steps, whatever they are or wherever they take you, you figure out the next three based on where you *now* find yourself. Frequently we've found that nailing those first three steps opens new paths that might look so attractive, we begin fantasizing in another direction.

♟ **These ministeps are accessible, and every one that you reach will give you more confidence that you can reach the next, and the next, and the next.** After a little while, you will realize that you've invested so much time that you've reached what we call the Girl Guilt Tipping Point—the moment at which you *know* you won't back out because you've gone too far. The Three-Step Rule actually puts to work all that guilt you've got going on over there.

Having a manageable set of directions that maps out three easy-to-follow steps is taking-off-those-pantyhose liberating. It will allow you to think there *is* a possibility that you're headed for something more or something better and that Y-O-U, your own sweet little self, can get you there—'cause you got the keys, baby.

Two Authors in Search of a Contract

If you follow the Three-Step Rule, you will make things happen for yourself, and you *won't* have those days where, before you know it, David Letterman is doing his late-night thing and you realize you *never* got to do the one thing you needed to get done for *you*. That used to happen to us *all* the time. But no more, sistergirl.

The book you now hold in your hands is the result of a DestQuest idea that J had for a girls' guide to office politics that she let loose on the phone one day with M, who had been kicking around writing-a-book fantasies since she was nine years old.

And we're telling you, if we had not applied the Three-Step Rule, you'd be doing something else right now. Neither of us had ever published a book. We both had clients and unfinished projects and weren't sure if any potential advance on the book would cover our living expenses while we actually produced the book. All pretty compelling reasons to seriously postpone—as in forever—thinking about working on the project, but the Three-Step Rule won the day.

Here's how we saw it:

Step one: get in touch with our friend Alička the book agent and see if she thought there was any merit to and market for the idea. She did. Time: twenty minutes, most of that chatting about assorted personal blah-blahs.

Step two: get a sample book proposal. Alička emailed one. Time: two minutes.

Step three: start writing our proposal one section at a time. Time: twenty minutes a day till we reached the Girl Guilt Tipping Point and we were so involved in the project that it began taking more and more of our time. Within two months, we had a seventy-five-page book proposal that more than one publishing house reported was "one of the best book proposals we've ever seen!" Who knew?

Did we know what we were doing? No. Did we care that we didn't know? No. We knew what we wanted, quickly figured out what seemed to be the logical first three steps, drove it twenty minutes a day, reached the Girl Guilt Tipping Point by investing too much time to turn back, and here we are.

Don't get us wrong—lots of these steps were B-O-R-I-N-G. On

any given day, we could have thought of dozens of more exciting and pleasurable diversions than making those phone calls and staring at the computer. But we've found that we can keep ourselves motivated and focused by the vision of looking back over our shoulder at the tedious, seemingly endless road we traveled to see that we've logged a lot of miles and arrived at where we most wanted to be: behind the steering wheel.

The fact is that writing a book was just one of the first three steps in a larger fantasy we've both been brewing for about four years: to never, *ever* have to utter the phrase "my boss" again.

But even if the proposal for *this* book had been a big fat flop and no publisher would touch it with a ten-foot dipstick, we would have had the satisfaction of knowing that we gave it a shot, the experience of doing it, and the knowledge that next time it would be easier to do with the lessons learned this go-round. Had this journey wound up at a dead end, we would have not dwelled long at the comfort station. Driving is all about moving, and that's exactly what we would have done: moved on directly to the next Destination.

DON'T TELL THEM WHERE YOU'RE HEADED TILL YOU'RE HALFWAY THERE

Lots of business books out there will tell you to broadcast a new goal as soon as you set one. The point is not only to get support but also to give you an audience that will shame you if you don't follow through. *Bad plan!*

First of all, shame sucks. Second of all, if you don't in fact follow through, you *will* look like a Flake Who Can't Get It Done. But more importantly, your idea and your confidence might get *crushed* under the weight of endless leaden opinions. We've killed more good ideas by allowing them to be sampled and trampled before they were big enough to live and breathe independently. Remember: you don't take that puppy away from its mother until it's at least eight weeks old if you want it to have a healthy shot at survival.

(continued)

Our rule is, don't tell anyone about your plans unless you specifically need to enlist that person to help you reach your goal. As we were working on the book proposal, we didn't tell a soul—not our clients, not our friends, not our extended families, not our ex-colleagues who called to brag about *their* exciting promotions and achievements—what *we* were working on until the proposal was finished and in the hands of our agent.

Once we had created something concrete, it was impossible for people to be negative about it. When we finished that book proposal, we had accomplished something, to which everyone in our lives could *only* say: "Wow. Good for you!" *Then* we broadcast it to *everyone* in the universe. It didn't matter that we didn't have a deal, 'cause we'd made something *real*. That in and of itself was the achievement.

We *know* how hard it is to keep a new plan under wraps, particularly when you are excited and feel the need for feedback, praise, validation, or whatever. But believe us: shut up and trust yourself, 'cause backseat drivers suck too.

Be Driven by What's Inside

Having goals, a plan, a vision for your life will help you from getting distracted by anything in the office that does not somehow figure into your priorities. You'll be far less likely to take slights or unfortunate episodes personally because they have no impact on where you are headed.

If you know what you want *specifically,* it can give you courage to take a risky road that could turn out to be an amazing short cut. While M was working at *Food Arts,* the original backers pulled out, and it looked doubtful that the magazine would find a buyer, as it had only been published three times up to that point. Logic and, of course, the Fear Factor could have pushed M out the door waving her resumé, but M *loved* the founding editors, the magazine, and the work. M's fantasy was to keep working *there*—despite the obvious fact that there no longer seemed to be any *there* there.

Long story short: M stayed on, worked for free, taught herself how to put together a magazine, and after three months, just as M was seriously running out of money to live on, the magazine was sold. M suddenly found her name printed in the third position down from the top of the masthead as managing editor—with only six months' experience in publishing, three of which were essentially on a volunteer basis. Because M knew very specifically what she wanted, she took the completely illogical step of working her butt off for free for a summer, and that choice put her in the right place at the right time to be hired for a job that in virtually any other scenario would have taken her a *minimum* of five years to attain.

Here's a roundup of other ways that having a Strategic Plan can help you order your priorities:

Å **A plan will keep you from getting stuck in a paycheck rut or from becoming a Job Snob.** When you drive somewhere, there are times when just because of the way the roads are laid out, you have to travel backward in order to go forward. This is perhaps one of the hardest things to do careerwise: walk away from the great job title or the big paycheck to go back to school, or take a less prestigious position in order to get the experience you need to do something else.

But if you have a compelling vision of your goal, *know* what those three steps are, and *know* exactly why you are settling for less money or a lesser position or moving into a smaller apartment with a roommate to reduce expenses, you can easily make those choices. You will *know* you are doing it because those sacrifices make sense to you and short-term losses are nothing compared to the long-term gains in getting the career and lifestyle you want.

Å **A plan gives you the courage to boldly go where Conventional Wisdom fears to tread.** One of The Girls Who Call Us, Amber, was let go from a major cable station after a difference of opinion with her direct supervisor. She worked in her DestQuest book to figure out where she wanted to go next, but her recurring fantasy was to return to that *same* company. She couldn't let it go. So she got in touch with one of the channel's Most Uppity Uppers and told him how much she had *loved* working there, and requested a meeting with him to discuss the possibilities of her return. He took the meeting . . . and he offered Amber a different and perhaps even better job. Here's the question— would you *ever* think to call a company that had *fired* you to ask for a job? Amber gets our vote for our Ballsy Move of the Year.

Having a plan enables you to prioritize: to *choose* which aspect, professional or personal, will take precedence at any given time. Until she was thirty-five years old, J was microfocused on her career. At this milestone birthday, she desperately wanted to leave her job, as she felt there was no opportunity for her to climb higher. But, increasingly, her DestQuest revealed her desire for a husband and a coupla *bambini.* J reasoned that the amount of energy that it would take to look for another job, land the job, and start the job would take over her life and that any guy would get lost in the job shuffle—that is, if she had the time to meet one at all.

Having changed the orientation of her goal from professional to personal, J amended her strategy accordingly. She stayed in the hateful job but left the office on time *every* night, which she achieved by doing only what was asked of her rather than going out of her way to overdeliver. She also passed on high-visibility business trips and projects. J spent her newfound time going to every party she was invited to, working the phones to get set up, and going on dates. She took time to go to the gym so she would feel and look good. She met E within six months of changing her goals and initiating this particular Three-Step Plan. Six months later, J and E moved in together. Six months later, the wedding. One year later, little E was born. *Voilà!* Insta-family.

Your plan makes it easy to say no and let it go. If you know your goal is To Work Fewer Days Per Week and you are offered a job promotion to manage people that will *add* hours to your week and involve more travel that will likely tap into your weekend time as well, do you take it? If you didn't know your objective or if your fantasy was to Make Bigger Bucks, of course you would. But in this case: no way, man.

No matter how hard you worked to earn that promotion, nor how much more the promotion would pay, nor how many people would tell you that you would be *crazy* not to take advantage of such a great opportunity, you can walk away knowing that it was the right choice for you. We, personally, would tell you that you would be insane to take it unless you could see with incredible clarity how this step would take you toward your more-time-for-you goal within a reasonable time frame—say, do it for a year and then take a year off. We *guarantee* that taking a job that requires *more* time when your heart tells you that what you want most is to work *less* will make you miserable once you pass the initial honeymoon phase of it.

A plan will help you determine when it's strategically appropriate to let everything else go and not worry about pissing people off. You will not waste any precious time worrying about the fact that your colleague is mad at you, that your boyfriend got you a clock radio for your birthday, or that your in-box is jammed with unopened mail. Even though those things might be bugging the crap out of you, you *know* that they are detours and not in the direct path to your goal. It's perfectly OK to let all hell break loose around you in order to meet your objectives. You will focus on completing all three steps toward your current goal. Then *maybe*, if you feel like these things are important steps toward another goal (say, Dealing with Crap that Bugs Me So I Can Focus on Planning the Rest of My Life), you will, in your own good time, turn your attention to your colleague's pettiness, your boyfriend's lack of romance, and your clutter issues.

The Three-Step Rule can also help you on a micro level. When you get in the habit of asking yourself: "What is my fantasy outcome for this [insert event type here]?" you'll be more productive on a day-to-day basis. One of The Girls Who Call Us, Sheila, a newbie VP of merchandising for a retailer, had a depressingly dismal experience speaking in a board meeting. She babbled hopelessly, and just as she was getting to her actual point, her boss, embarrassed for her, interrupted her. So the next time Sheila had to make a presentation, her goal was to Get It Right, and she worked out a three-step plan specifically for the meeting: (1) write up the exact points that need to be made, (2) sit up tall at the table to be more Visible and have more stature, and (3) speak confidently, loudly, and get to the point quickly. Knowing precisely what her goals were for the meeting gave Sheila *tons* of confidence, and she was much better prepared than the last time. In fact, Sheila reported that it was the best presentation she'd ever made.

Personally, we swear by the Three-Step Rule and seldom leave home without knowing our goals and having some kind of map that directs us how to reach them. We're talking not just about the big long life journeys we'd like to take but also about our personal objectives for a given day or a given meeting. By consistently devoting ourselves to our DestQuest notes and whipping out three steps for each goal we define, we've become the ultimate planning machines. It's *how* our rubber meets the road.

Day Tripper

The Three-Step Rule provides you with your directions, but we also recommend creating an itinerary to give each day structure. When armed with your three-step plan and a good itinerary, you won't confuse busywork (i.e., driving in circles) with productivity (i.e., logging miles that get you somewhere).

To create a realistic and efficient day trip itinerary:

Block in everything that your boss needs you to accomplish for the day. The main function of every job is to make the boss happy. Put her directives on your itinerary first. See Chapter 12, "Hail to the Chef."

Review *all* your to-dos. Select those things that are the *most important* in terms of reaching at least one of your objectives from your three-step plan; remember, it should take you only twenty minutes. So if your goal is to move up in your company, focus your attention on projects that bring in or save money for the company. If your goal is to walk out the door and go home and have a life, do everything you *must* do first and then make yourself leave even if you still have work on your plate. The rest will wait till tomorrow.

Estimate the drive time. *Double* the amount of time you estimate it will take for *each* task or project you need to accomplish. We say double your original time estimate because (1) Girlogic makes most of us overly optimistic about how quickly we can accomplish a given task, and (2) you want to build in cushion around every to-do to allow for emergencies, contingencies, and Chatting & Humming.

Plan in efficiencies. Once you know what you want to accomplish, order your itinerary so you do the least amount of backtracking. Plan to tackle emails in one stretch, rather than hopping off the email exit every hour. Same with phone calls, snail mail, and other administrative issues. Limit the time you have for these activities, but do them every day—the one-day-a-week thing for all that never seems to happen and *boom,* big pile up.

Don't overcommit. No matter how fast you go, there are only so many miles you can cover in a day. Cramming your itinerary with more to-dos than you could ever reasonably accomplish is an accident waiting to happen. Delegate as many administrative tasks as you can to subordinates or willing coworkers.

Finally, you must put your mental and physical health somewhere on the itinerary *every* day. Listen up—you *won't* get ahead in your career by wearing your tires threadbare. If you're not in the habit of taking the time to care for yourself, make that a goal for a while until it becomes as second nature as buckling up. Seriously, there is no excuse for skipping lunch, eating crap food, ignoring your significant other, and never getting to the dentist. Not one. Be sure to give yourself a break from time to time or you are going to be a wreck.

MAKING GOOD TIME ON THE PAY DIRT ROADS

During those times when we've needed to be superefficient so we had time to Chat & Hum and complete a step of our plan, we applied these rules. If you can keep your mind on them while you are driving through your day, you'll find you'll make more progress and get more done than ever before:

- **Have tunnel vision.** The shortest distance between two points is always a straight line. If you want to get some project done, turn off that instant-messaging program, don't answer the phone, shut off the email. When you *must* move a project forward, think about yourself as being in a tunnel—you move one way, there are no exits, and your radio and your cell phone are useless. Keep driving the effort through till you come out the other side.

- **Don't pick up hitchhikers.** People who are not so interested in driving (i.e., working) will try to hitch a free ride with you. Generally, these are *not* people who will be ultimately willing to return the favor. Roll down the window and give the guy some quickie directions if you must, but don't pick him up and do *his* job unless you see a damn good reason for doing so—like you're pretty sure this dude is on the fast track and will remember your help down the road.

- **No standing and idling.** When you are at work, there should be no idle time. Limit your personal calls during work hours unless you are specifically Chatting & Humming to maintain a relationship. You should always be moving: 60 percent of the time doing the productive business at hand and 40 percent moving specifically and strategically to create turn-off career Options in case you are suddenly confronted with a dead end.

(continued)

- **Coast to save gas.** Coasting is great on the downhills. If you've met your goals for the day and have been productive, don't launch into another major project or jump the gun on tomorrow's load. It will just wear you out. Do some brainless task like straightening up your desk or organizing your computer files and enjoy the ride.

- **Don't spin your wheels.** If you are stuck in the mud, revving the engine will not get you out of your rut, but only dig you in deeper. If you can't get a project off the ground, get help. Speak to your boss about getting the resources you need. Don't wait until you've had a deadline blowout to ask for help and support.

- **Stop sign.** No matter how fast you are going, you see one of these, you stop. A stop sign could be your boss telling you that the project is suddenly on hold or no longer a priority. *Always* be prepared to slam on the brakes without freaking out or looking back. A stop sign could also be that you get sick or have some other personal issue—a birth or a death in the family. These types of things are your actual Life, so no matter what is going on at work or with your plans, you must come to a full and complete stop and allow your personal issues to take priority. No job will ever be so important that you can't attend to your personal Life.

- **Turn signals.** You *must* communicate. Let people in your department know what you are up to so you don't duplicate efforts. If you don't, you might just get rear-ended.

Chapter 12

Hail
to the Chef

How to move the Big Cheese

Useful Terms: What We Mean When We Say . . .
The Big Cheese The person you report to; may or may not be stinky cheese
The Whine List Should never be served to any Big Cheese
Waiter There to serve; is best when silently observing, but is never dumb

Unless you are blessed with either a good-egg manager or a Teflon ego, understanding how to behave with a boss and how not to take her inscrutable behavior personally can be a dicey business. God knows, when we first started out we had only the *vaguest* idea how the whole boss deal worked. The one thing we knew for sure was that we did not want to come off as suck-ups.

It wasn't until we *became* bosses that we began to *get* it and realized that we had been expending too much energy in the wrong direction when dealing with our bosses—trying too hard, taking things personally, being frustrated, misreading situations, missing opportunities to shine. Back then, we made everything ever so much harder on our hardworking, overthinking selves than it had to be.

Ultimately, though, we discovered that the care and feeding of bosses is not as mysterious as we once thought. Everything we ever needed to know about handling the Big Cheese we learned in restaurants.

Bet you can't wait to hear this one. Well, be patient. A lot of what follows is about waiting—on the Big Cheese's table.

No Matter What Business You're In, You're in the Hospitality Industry

Picture this: you own a chic café. It's cool. It's gorgeous. It is your creation, a reflection of all your soul, all your training, all your experience. You are passionate about it, and you've named it Ma Kareera.

You are not only the genius chef and owner of Ma Kareera but also the hostess dying to make a great impression and the waiter with a vested interest in giving amazing service.

The Big Cheese is your area's most powerful restaurant reviewer. One scathing review (the soup was colder than the Chardonnay!) and Ma Kareera could be out of business. One glowing review (the Chardonnay soup was ingenious!) and you are *set* and on your way to a cookbook contract.

When serving the Big Cheese, your goal is to make him feel as important as he thinks he is, without melting and oozing all over him. You want him to respect what you can bring to the table, and marvel at how effortlessly you serve him.

Be the Hostess with the Mostest

Think about this. You walk into a nice restaurant. You wait there at the hostess stand. Nobody comes to greet you. You shift your weight from leg to leg. You cross your arms. Still nada. None of the staff even looks up—or, worse, they look right at you and *ignore* you. You start thinking, "What the hell am I going to spend my money *here* for?"

OK, that right there is *exactly* how the Big Cheese feels when you don't greet and attend to her when she wants greeting and attention. How many minutes does it take you in the restaurant to start to get *steamed*—about five to heat up and seven to come to a rolling boil?

If you are one of those who thinks your boss is an irrational hothead, well, chances are good she's not any more of one than you would be in her Ferragamos. See how that works?

How often have you remarked on how great the service was in a restaurant? Or how miserable service pretty much wrecked what otherwise would have been a perfectly good meal? No matter how great the work you do is, if your attitude stinks and your service is sloppy or inconsistent, the Big Cheese is going to have a major meltdown. Ever been burned with hot cheese? Not pretty. Usually leaves a nasty scar.

Serving vs. Self-Serving

One of The Girls Who Call Us, Madeline, a media buyer, has a terrible relationship with her boss and says she just doesn't understand it because she is a good worker. "I have been totally honest and up-front with my boss," explains Madeline. "I confront him a lot because he doesn't admit when he is wrong and he *never* apologizes. It makes me *too* angry."

Now, imagine Madeline is the waiter for *your* table and she snidely tells *you* that you've made a terrible choice and *no one* orders lobster bisque with creamed corn. Would you apologize or admit you were wrong? No way, sweetcakes. You would walk out. What Madeline doesn't realize is that while she might be good at her job, her hospitality is suckola.

You are responsible for your relationship with your boss. And if you're not happy with your boss, we'd lay odds on the fact that she's not too thrilled with you either. It's probably *not* that your boss is a jerk or that she dislikes you personally. It's far more likely that you need to examine your personal customer service policy.

Bad service comes in all flavors. Have you ever sat in a restaurant and not been able to find the waiter who is being *paid* to serve you? How about the waiter who says, "Sorry, not my table" when you ask for a little more butter? Then, of course, there's the waiter who is so anxious to please, he's practically sitting in your lap. Don't you just want to slap these people?

Right. Now let's translate that to your relationship with your boss.

Taking Orders from the Big Cheese

A boss's job is to give orders; yours is to take them. If you want a smooth and successful relationship with the Big Cheese—or at least one you can live with—you have to give the same kind of amazing service you expect from great professional waiters when *you* are the boss sitting at a table in an expensive restaurant.

Here are twenty-one ways to please the Cheese:

1. **Don't keep the Big Cheese waiting.** When the boss calls a meeting, be on time.
2. **Don't show up unprepared.** That's like those aggravating waiters who realize that they forgot to bring a pen just when you are ready to order.
3. **Know the menu.** Know what needs to be done in your department, and be prepared to give the boss the menu of what's cooking whenever she asks for it: "The Kirk campaign is in its final round of proofs, the Huber slogan still needs to be written, and the Sickle copy is still waiting for client approval."
4. **Never tell the boss what to order!** You may, however, *influence* the Big Cheese by making knowledgeable suggestions: "I suggest that we include that tasty data we found in this year's forecast for the purposes of comparison. Does that sound good to you?"
5. **Engage in personal chitchat *only* if the boss invites it.** Never view the boss's friendliness as an invitation to pull up a chair and start a gabfest. Always turn the conversation back to her: "Yes, I do take the train into the city. It's a lovely ride. Do you find it difficult to find parking for your Mercedes?" Hint: do not tell your boss anything you wouldn't tell a complete stranger.

6. **Never make the boss feel that she is wasting *your* precious time.** So you *never* say: "Are we *done* here? I really have a lot of *other* stuff to do. I do have a *life,* you know, and I'd like to . . . blah, blah." You have all the time in the world to wait on the Big Cheese, and you cannot rush *her.*

7. **Patiently answer your boss's questions, no matter how ignorant— and never make him *feel* ignorant.** "Great question. Our company makes money by selling stuff." Keep the answer simple and direct and don't editorialize.

8. **Never interrupt when the Big Cheese is ordering.** Never say: "Do you *really* think that's a good idea?"

9. **Don't keep reconfirming the boss's order.** "Are you positively, absolutely *sure* it's OK with you if I go on that sales call?"

10. **When the boss is finished ordering, ask only the questions you *really* need to know in order to serve her correctly.** "How would you like me to prepare that document, in Excel or PowerPoint?"

11. **Commend the Big Cheese for her decision with a snappy, not sappy, opinion.** "Excellent choice."

12. **Never tell your boss that you think she can't afford her order.** Make sure the boss knows what things cost by providing price lists so that she is aware of how big her bill could get. But *don't* say: "My God! Do you *know* how much that will cost? You can't waste that much!" Just take the order.

13. **Never leave the boss's table until you are sure she is finished ordering.** "Is there anything else I can get for you?"

14. **Be flexible.** If your boss decides to change his order, that's perfectly fine with you. So it's *not:* "Are you crazy? I just *finished* calling all of our vendors to tell them the deal is *off.* You *can't* change your mind now!" The correct answer is: "No problem, I'll get right on that." If the Big Cheese wants butter—even if it's not in your job description to fetch it—fetch it. It won't kill you to make the copies, keep a visitor busy, or man the switchboard for a morning.

15. **Let the boss know what's cooking.** Generally speaking, you want to

let the boss know what you are up to, rather than having him wonder—especially when he's out of town. Pithy, slightly vague emails are great for this, as in: "I contacted Mr. Johnston, and he's happy to file the claim for us." Plus, updates send a subliminal message to the Big Cheese: "I'm on it. Stuff is getting done, and I'm working for you, O chief fondue."

16. **Don't deliver bad news without simultaneously presenting a buffet of palatable solutions.** "Unfortunately, the new back-end system won't be up and running until Tuesday. But we *will* be able to run the site on the old servers through the weekend, or we can use the Servers R Us cohosting service instead. Which would you prefer?"

17. **Drop inside information to your boss as subtly as a napkin.** So it's "I heard from Joe in accounting that the CEO is thinking of clamping down on business-class travel," not "Well, *I* know what the CEO wants and *no one* can fly first class, not even youuuu!"

18. **Accept praise graciously.** If the Big Cheese tells you how much he enjoyed what you dished up, *don't* say, "Oh, it was nothing," or "It could have been better." If he said it was good, it *was* good—validate his opinion, don't contradict it. Say: "Thank you so much. I'm glad you enjoyed it."

19. **Don't hover.** You cannot stand over the boss while he's digesting. After you hand him a memo to review, *don't* be lurking around saying: "Do you like it? Huh? What do you think?" Just because he never *says* he likes it doesn't mean he doesn't think it's dee-lish.

20. **Do NOT touch the boss.** J once thought she was doing her boss a favor by straightening his tie before he went to a meeting. He slapped her hand and said, "Please don't *ever* touch me."

21. **No matter how R-U-D-E, gruff, picky, or indecisive the boss may be, you are the professional waiter.** Stand neutral and nonreactive, patiently waiting to serve.

WHINE DOES NOT GO WITH CHEESE!

No Big Cheese *ever* wants to hear about your whines.

What the Big Cheese *does* want is a thirst-quenching cocktail that will help her get a happy buzz.

THE WHINE LIST

I can't . . .

I wouldn't . . .

I don't have time . . .

Shouldn't we . . .

I demand . . .

It's not my fault . . .

Unfixable . . .

I don't think it's a good idea . . .

It will never work . . .

I would love to, but . . .

I surely will, but first I must . . .

COCKTAILS

that Complement Cheese

Thank you!

Great idea!

Can do!

Will do!

Sure. No problem!

I'll get right on that!

Do As I Think, Not As I Say . . .

One of the frequent complaints from The Girls Who Call Us is that they feel that their bosses expect them to be psychic. We sympathize; it took us *forever* to realize that we didn't always have to wait to be told every single thing. We learned not only to put our focus on *our* immediate to-dos but also to anticipate what the Big Cheese would need to do *her* job.

There's nothing supernatural about it. It's just like those waiters who *seem* to be mind readers. You're sitting there thinking, "Gee, I'd like some more water," and before you even turn your head to look for her, there she is, filling your half-empty glass. Great waiters are *watching* the glasses from a distance; they keep tabs on certain things going on at the table. They read all the signals, so they know when they need to ask, "Would you like more water?" or when they can just go ahead and top you. They are invisibly *Visible*. This is exactly the illusion you should create for your boss.

For example, our friend Ginger, an executive assistant at an environmental engineering firm, has a boss who is constantly misplacing his paperwork. Ginger keeps copies of *everything* right where she can grab them, and the second she hears her boss say, "I can't seem to find . . ." Ginger has the exact proposal he was looking for, ready to drop into his lap, so he's not late for his meeting. See? Magical, but not mystical.

Timed to Perfection

You need to adjust to the Big Cheese's needs and speeds. In Ma Kareera the timing of the meal is nearly as important as the quality of the cuisine.

Figure out the points during the day when your boss might be looking for you, or when she needs to be left alone to dig into her work. Most of us are crabby right before lunch, for example, and backed up after, so avoid making requests or asking questions during those times of day. What day of the week does the Big Cheese crave the challenge of tackling a porterhouse-size problem? For most people, it's not Monday morning and it's not Friday afternoon.

Does your boss like to linger over a discussion, as one of J's bosses did? Then do as J did and sit and listen to his droning no matter what you've got on *your* plate. Does the Big Cheese need to get in and out in a hurry? Think fast food: speak fast and write short. Be constantly on top of the pace of things, and just because you brought out the drinks on time, that doesn't mean you can wait ninety-five years to bring out the salad course. Keep up with Cheese, please. You're on her clock.

Don't bring the boss any dishes too soon. Bring them when he *expects* them. If you finish a project too early and turn it in, he then has time to pick it apart and make you redo it. You don't, however, want to make every project you work on à la last minute either. Do the work, then keep it on the back burner. That way, if he asks for it prematurely, *voilà*—it's well done.

If you are going to blow a deadline, don't wait until the project has reached a complete crisis. You *can't* go into your boss's office at five o'clock on Friday and tell him that the brochures that were supposed to be delivered to the trade show over the weekend won't even be printed until the following Tuesday. As soon as you know a deadline is in trouble, make it known: "To hit the deadline on the Greenky account, we are going to need more resources than we originally projected," NOT "I'm freaking out! There is *nooo* way to get this done! I'm gonna *diiie*!"

Don't make excuses. Just promote the future benefit to him in exchange for his patience now.

When the Shiitake Hits the Fan

Think of yourself as the ultimate waiter: "A fly in your soup! That's outrageous!" Share the fury of the Big Cheese. Do *not* say you don't see the fly! Take full responsibility for resolving the problem but none of the blame for causing it.

Appease the Cheese like so: "I apologize for this, and I promise I will find out *how* that happened and make sure it never happens again! Is there anything I can do to make up for this terrible oversight? A brandy, perhaps?"

Be Discreet for the Elites

People love to criticize the critics. You *will* hear other people slamming the work or the style of the Big Cheese. Do *not* agree with anything negative that someone says about the Big Cheese, and don't elaborate with your own stinky stories.

If you take not one other piece of advice from this book, take this: *never, ever, ever say one bad word about your boss to anyone. Ever.* Your friends don't really want to hear it anyway, and your colleagues can't wait to repeat it. It's a hard habit to break, particularly because boss bashing is more contagious than chicken pox.

Among our very *worst* job faux pas was boss blasting. It's *such* a cliché! We actually believed that *everybody* bitches about work and their boss. Well, take it from us—not the people who move up in companies.

It's not that we sliced up *every* Big Cheese. We've had bosses we absolutely *worshiped,* who taught us more skills and gave us more insights into corporate psychology than we ever thought we could learn from one person. But in those jobs where we had bosses we thought were major turkeys, we roasted them but good. Later, we invariably found that it was precisely those moments of indiscretion that ultimately got *us* skewered. And we've heard about the same phenomenon over and over again from The Girls Who Call Us.

Suzanne, a media buyer, went to a boss once with a bereavement-leave request for an out-of-town funeral. Suzanne had used up her allotment of personal and vacation days, and because the deceased wasn't a blood relative, the boss denied her the extra time off. Suzanne was incensed and talked about the boss's incredible insensitivity to everyone in the office. Two months later, this same boss told Suzanne he was moving on to a new position, and added (nastily): "I have strongly recommended that you *not* be promoted into my place." He continued on with more vicious comments before he left, and Suzanne just couldn't understand why. Later it came out: word had gotten back to him that Suzanne had bad-mouthed him.

What you might see as idle kitchen gossip about your boss, she might see as a cleaver in the back. You are dead meat if it gets back to her—which is as inevitable as dirty dishes. Keep your hands clean.

What Moves the Big Cheese

It's not easy being the boss. The Cheese truly does stand alone. When you are the boss, subordinates tend to leave you out of social events and ignore your role as a human being because you are the "authority fig-ure"—not one of the gang.

So many of The Girls Who Call Us have those fear-of-ass-kissing issues and avoid opportunities to express praise. But most bosses can see through sycophants as easily as they can a Pyrex pie plate. If you are not a Brown-Nose Betty, you won't be mistaken for one. Sincerity shows.

Providing great service means making a person feel welcome and recognizing special occasions. Know, for example, when the boss's birthday is, and don't blow it off. If you have a great relationship with the Big Cheese, go ahead and leave a little vase of flowers on her desk or a book you think that she'll devour. If your relationship with your boss is rocky and you get the urge to improve the dynamic, don't ig-nore his birthday—acknowledge it with a cigar or something equally simple.

We're not talking showering gifties and glory all the time here. An appropriate gesture at an appropriate time will be long remembered.

M *still* keeps a pretty paperweight on her desk that was given to her along with a touching note of appreciation by a great, hardworking editor she managed three companies ago.

Don't be afraid to drop a little praise, either. Not just a comment about the nice tie or the nice shoes, but something *heartfelt* about the work, the leadership. Try: "Hey, you handled that really well," or (our favorite compliment) "I'm learning so much from you." Trust us— many may never show it, but everybody wants to feel genuinely appreciated, even Le Grand Fromage.

All Fired Up

Your job is to serve the Big Cheese. If you are a R-U-D-E and surly waiter, you will get F-I-R-E-D. It's that simple. A boss is not going to *tolerate* being treated like that by a *waiter.* It's a matter of self-respect.

We can't tell you how shocked we've been at the behavior of some of the people we've managed, or at some of the stories of The Girls Who Call Us who got fired and freak out at the injustice of it all when it sounds to us like *they* were 100 percent responsible for their own un-doing.

Once J was at a political convention interviewing celebrities. She told a subordinate to go conduct an interview with a nonceleb while J herself interviewed Aretha Franklin, who was standing right there. The guy flat-out refused because he wanted more Aretha exposure. "No," said this suicidal subordinate. "I won't do that." Bad move. Later that day, J called him in and practically sang: "You are *sooooo* fired." And that was that. Dissing your boss in front of the queen of R-E-S-P-E-C-T— ding ding! There goes the Irony Alarm! A leader *cannot* allow herself to be publicly challenged. So many of The Girls Who Call Us don't get this part. They think, "Well, I was just angry and acted out. I'll apologize and we'll move on." Nuh-uh. It's called flagrant insubordination. Do it and you are probably doomed.

No Shirt, No Shoes, No Service

We're not saying that you *always* hafta suck it up. Hey, if you're fed up, you're fed up. If the Big Cheese is clearly way out of line *and you are prepared to leave your job* to defend yourself and hold on to your self-respect, go for it. When you feel you *must* go and take a hunk out of the Big Cheese:

Do it in private. Do not contradict your boss in public, even if she pins blame on you that you don't deserve. Wait until you can confront her in private; let your feelings be known and make a specific recommendation about how you would like to see this type of incident handled in the future, but don't demand an apology.

Present your side calmly. If you disagree with a decision that the Big Cheese makes, you can go in her office and discuss it. *But* if it becomes a power struggle, 99 percent of the time you will not win. To avoid the power issue, present your information in a way that suggests that you accept her decision but that you have more information that you think will benefit her. If she will not listen, drop it. For more on confrontation techniques, see Chapter 14, "Held in Contempt."

The Waiter's Revenge

You can eat only so much crow. If the Big Cheese is unusually cruel or critical or is otherwise abusing his power, it might be time to consider calling *his* boss. However, girlfriend, you *have* to know that you should go above your boss's head *only* when you have *nothing* to lose—we're talking tossing in your apron here.

Expect that high-level execs will send you *right* back down to the original problem person and have you work it out with her. That's what good managers *should* do. However, your boss *will* know that you've gone "over her head," and unless she is willing to admit she was wrong, she will never trust you again, and the relationship will deteriorate from there.

If you see no alternative but to go over the boss's head:

Address the issue with your boss first. Assuming this gets you approximately nowhere, have your facts completely documented and dated before you go to *her* boss.

Unless your problem with your boss is legal in nature, such as sexual harrassment, the human resource department will not be helpful. If you go to HR, chances are that unless they already know the manager is a problem and are working on getting him out, you have now identified yourself as a problem. The folks from HR are really not on your side unless the Most Uppity Uppers want them to be.

Think about your alternatives. Have a plan. Know what you are trying to achieve. Do you want a transfer to a different division? Do you want to report an abuse? What's your Plan B if this blows up in your face? For example, if the execs make it clear that they can't resolve this problem with your boss for you, be prepared to request an exit package—meaning severance, unemployment, and possibly continuance of health insurance benefits. J once got a delicious severance package when she went above her new boss's head to complain about the revolving-door management of her division: she had had three bosses in four years. The execs at that company could not promise that the situation would stabilize, so J resigned, and when she did, she got a golden parachute because she had the presence of mind to ask for one right then and there.

Clear off your computer beforehand. If you go above your boss's head, be prepared to vacate the building. Sounds extreme, we know, but we've seen it happen more than once: an employee goes to complain to upper management or the board of directors and *never* returns to her desk. Copy your contact file and remove anything personal from your workstation—just in case. If the management thinks you are upset enough at your boss, you might just get a personal escort out of the building.

If you have strong allies in the upper echelons of the company who value your talent *more* than they value your boss, you might— repeat, *might*—win. Most of the time, however, if you go above your boss's head, either you will lose your job or it will become intolerable. That's just the way the biscotti crumbles.

No matter what happens, remember this: Ma Kareera is *your* restaurant. *You* are the boss of your own life. Have confidence in your work, take pride in the service you provide and your professionalism, and if that doesn't please The Big Cheese, don't let it eat you up alive—just make plans to take your pots and pans elsewhere.

RECIPE FOR A RAISE

You can't expect the Big Cheese to remember everything you've accomplished in a year. Whether or not your company conducts formal reviews, tallying up the cost of all those moments of faithful service will be extremely valuable when it's time for the Big Cheese to pay his bill and throw some more dough your way.

A company might keep a detailed record of every time you screwed up something, but we guarantee that no one but you will keep a file of all the good stuff you got done and how much you contribute.

So what we want you to do is to create a spreadsheet called the Tab. Take ten minutes every Friday at 4:50 to outline what you worked on during the week. Include all activities, like meetings you ran or clients you contacted, and the results. Fold in any dollar amounts of business you brought in or how much you slashed from a budget. Quickly type up whatever you did, even if you think it's redundant or insignificant. Also include positive feedback you've received on your work from within or outside the company.

(continued)

Your Tab file has three functions:

- **It will serve as documentation** if someone challenges your contributions and/or tries to put you on probation.

- **It will be incredibly useful for doing the annual resumé update** and preparing for a job interview.

- **Seeing all you get done in a year will give you confidence** to ask for a promotion or more money, take a vacation day, or, for some of you, to look for a position where you feel your skills will be more appreciated and better compensated.

If you feel you deserve a raise or promotion, don't wait until the annual review—by then the management has already figured it all out. Assuming the timing is good—the company is healthy and your boss is happy—go into your boss's office and say: "I know that performance reviews won't be held for another two months, but I'd like to discuss my compensation package with you for next year, before it's all set in stone." This is the only way to indicate to your boss that the companywide 3 percent salary increase isn't going to make you happy.

Once you have a discussion date set, you will want to create a bulleted list of all the development areas in which you've contributed and improved. For ideas, go to the about.com "career planning A–Z" section, scroll down to the "Performance Reviews" link, then scroll down to the "How to Do an Employee Appraisal" link, then scroll way down to "Discussion Topics" for phrases like "Handling pressure and uncertainty" and "Adjusting work plans to meet changing company needs." Then take your tab file, find specific examples of your work from the past year, and list them under each of the development area bullets. You can either give this one-page summary to your boss or use it for talking points during your meeting.

When it's time to talk cashola, express your desired increase in terms of percentages (as in 10 percent) instead of dollars (as in $10K) because it sounds smaller. When negotiating for a higher salary, *never* give a range; if you say, "A 6 or 8 percent bump would make me happy," they will surely give you the lower number.

(continued)

Threatening to leave if you don't get your requested increase is an ultimatum; it's a power play that most bosses are not willing to lose. It's a big, big risk: it could pay off, but it might not, at which point you will either (a) get fired or (b) have to make good on the threat and vamoose.

Unless you are actually willing to leave the job if you don't get the raise you requested, don't threaten to. Even if you think you *will* quit, don't mention it, because it will only make your boss, who probably can't authorize the raise herself anyhow, defensive and unwilling to fight for you.

Chapter 13

Ugly Stepsisters
vs. Sistahood

The taming of the shrews

Useful Terms: What We Mean When We Say . . .

Ugly Stepsisters Those who indulge in bullying behavior and disrespect other women

Wicked Stepmother What an Ugly Stepsister can turn into when she is promoted; we all know what happens to her in the end, though . . . heh heh heh

Girl A four-letter word

Bitch A five-letter word that is not synonymous with the four-letter word above

OK, just between us girls, what's one of the most upsetting problems most of us have ever had at work? Right. It's us girls.

The situations that most frequently sent the two of us for a crying squall in the stall over the years, and those that The Girls Who Call Us are the *most* emotional about, invariably involve vicious and/or utterly incomprehensible behavior from other women. So much for all that Yadda Yadda Sisterhood stuff.

We have had the honor to work with some of the greatest human beings on earth who happened to be women, but we wouldn't be doing our jobs here if we didn't haul out our dirt on some of the more frightening ways that women undercut themselves *and each other* at work—possibly without even realizing it.

As one of our Guy Spies put it: "Guys will stick together, just 'cause they're guys. Women, though, treat each other badly. It's a paradox. I guess women are other women's natural enemies."

He's only half right. We can be our own worst enemies, too.

Think about all those Ugly Stepsisters, Evil Queens, and Wicked Stepmothers that present completely absurd pictures of the jealousy-driven meanness of women. These are the two-dimensional stereotypes we should *all* be fighting against. Alas, far too frequently we don't. Instead we fight each other and prove the point.

Ugly Is As U-G-L-Y Does

We know so many women who will proclaim that they are "just not competitive" in one breath and then proceed to verbally rip another woman to shreds in the next. Hello?!? That *is* competition. And from where we sit, it's not a friendly little competition either. It's big. It's fat. And it's U-G-L-Y.

Do you think that Cinderella's Ugly Stepsisters *knew* they were mean and ugly? Probably not. After all, look at their role model—the Wicked Stepmother. We've come to the conclusion that so many women simply don't realize when they are being seriously hideous, and just how awful it makes them look—not to mention the job it does on the rest of us.

Lock this thought in your pretty little head: *anytime* you engage in behavior that makes someone else look bad, it's U-G-L-Y, and it's competition in its lowest form: foul play.

Here are the top eighteen Ugly tactics women employ to put down other women, along with how they justify their actions—if they bother to—to themselves. We would guess that many of these behaviors are ingrained habits and that many women don't recognize that this is *not* how big girls play the gamola.

1. **Reputation bashing.** Gossiping and deliberately cramming in as much nasty innuendo (intended to eat away at the victim's credibility) as possible. The justification: "We were just talking!"

2. **Paranoia provoking.** Cackling, sniggering, the big hairy eyeball, the up-and-down appraising look of disgust, eye rolling, or elbowing a coworker as the victim walks by. The justification: "We were just having fun."

3. **Public condescension.** Speaking (loudly) to another woman as if she were utterly incapable of understanding the simplest of instructions. The justification: "I was just trying to be clear."

4. **Marginalizing.** Forcing another woman to do excessive busywork and never allowing her to do any meaningful projects. The justification: "She just doesn't get anything right."

5. **Spying.** Asking other colleagues to report on the woman's behavior, insinuating that the woman needs to be watched. The justification: "I need to keep an eye on that one." *Uh, in this case we would recommend simply telling the other woman directly what your concerns are.*

6. **Freezer burning.** Going out of the way to avoid speaking to, or even looking at a woman, making the freeze-out obvious to all onlookers, and never offering a word of explanation for the sudden cold front. The justification: "I just don't want to deal with that bitch."

7. **Petty picking.** Constantly pointing out minor faults in every aspect of the victim's work, approach, style, or voice. The justification: "She just drives me crazy."

8. **The silencing of the ma'ams.** Deliberately locking a subordinate female out of meetings, ignoring all emails and suggestions. This trick is designed to keep the victim's Visibility as low as possible. The justification: "She just doesn't know her place."

9. **Fishing and dishing.** Trolling for dirt. Asking lots of personal questions about another woman for the express purpose of repeating the worst of it to officemates or Uppities to make the office Cinderella look bad. The justification: "She just had it coming to her."

10. **Getting in with the in crowd.** Choosing to believe the absolute worst about another woman after hearing a bit of malicious gossip, in order

to be accepted by the gossiper. The justification: "I'm just going by what I heard."

11. **Taxing with misrepresentation.** Getting only half the story after an incident, *assuming* the woman in question was operating with the worst intent, then bad-mouthing her right and left without ever having attempted to ask the woman directly about her side of the story or her motives. The justification: "I just knew she was a phony."

12. **Rudeness.** Giving clipped one-word answers, using a nasty tone of voice, not saying thank you, or never offering any other common courtesy. The justification: "She just doesn't deserve it."

13. **Oscillating.** Being friendly one minute, rude, insulting, and dismissive the next. The justification: "I don't know what you are talking about. I wasn't bitchy."

14. **Blindsiding.** Coming out full force, without any respect or attempt to be otherwise rational, and screaming at another woman in a way that you *know* would never happen in the same situation with a male colleague. The justification: "I was just really angry."

15. **Two-facing.** Being quite pleasant or even posing as a friend to another woman's face and then complaining bitterly about her behavior and her work to others, especially managers, without ever even once having *mentioned* the issue directly to the other woman. The justification: "I have no problem with her personally—I like her. I just have a big problem with her work."

16. **CC-Riding.** Sending a series of emails and/or other written correspondence to a woman expressing "concern" about the quality of her work and cc-ing the woman's superior. Frequently the content of the email is full of intangible criticism that can't be substantiated. The justification: "I just want her to know what I'm thinking." *Uh . . . in this case, just tell her privately what you are thinking, or email her without cc'ing her superiors.*

17. **Setting up for an upset.** Intentionally setting a woman up for failure by creating impossible deadlines or not providing the information or

the resources she needs to succeed. The justification: "I just wanted to take her down a peg."

18. **Credit stealing.** Think Sigourney Weaver in the movie *Working Girl.* The justification: "If it weren't for me, she couldn't have come up with that idea."

There's a name for all this stuff: it's called psychological bullying or emotional abuse. Wanna know how prevalent it is? Check out the oft-quoted U.S. Hostile Workplace Survey conducted by the Workplace Bullying and Trauma Institute (bullyinginstitute.org), which says that *50* percent of all women are bullies and that women bullies target *other women* 84 percent of the time. Men target women 69 percent of the time. That's a *lot* of Zoloft.

Furthermore, the documented results of continued exposure to this kind of covert abuse include depression, chronic anxiety, and post-traumatic stress disorder. These conditions lead to issues that affect the company's bottom line, such as high absenteeism and low motivation. Big girls do cry.

Be Prepared for the Boy Scouters

We think the absolute worst Ugly Stepsister behavior is Boy Scouting. This is done by women who absolutely *will not* or *cannot* accept another female as an authority figure or by women who manipulate situations to curry favor with the good ol' boys.

We've both had firsthand experience inheriting a staff and then being given a hard time by female subordinates who, we are quite sure, never would have tried to pull similar stunts with us if our names were Mark and Joseph. But when we began to do a little research, we were positively *mortified* to find statistics like this one from an Oxygen Media poll: 65 percent of women *resent* women who either are in power or act like they are.

Boy Scouters do things like intentionally misunderstand directions given by a she-boss, blatantly disobey direct orders, challenge and attempt to verbally bully their she-boss, bad-mouth her, and, arms folded, make The Face (you know the one) in every conversational exchange. The truly stupid thing about this is that we've seen more talented women sabotage *themselves* and lose jobs they loved because they would not or could not accept direction from another woman and did nothing but hassle their female bosses.

Speaking of stupid, sometimes the Boy Scouter will be perfectly respectful to her she-boss's face and then run right over her to the nearest Tom or Harry with a dick.

J once hired a woman named Nora, who was always very agreeable to J and nodded a lot at J's every directive. Eventually, however, J found out that each time she asked Nora to do anything, Nora would nod vigorously, then run right to J's boss—a man. Nora was trying to make herself more Visible to J's boss by making sure that J's instructions were OK with him, but in doing so she completely undermined J's authority. Boo, hiss. What's worse, it amused the crap out of J's boss.

But Boy Scouting isn't subordinate-only behavior. There seem to be some women who will do *anything* to make themselves look better in the eyes of the guys. For example, J had a meeting once with a woman named Helen, who was essentially on the same seniority level as J but in a different division. At the beginning of the meeting, J said: "My boss can't make it because he's in with Steinbeck [the male CEO of the company]." After their meeting, Helen called J's boss, John, and said: "Do you *knowwwww* that *your subordinate* refers to the CEO *of this company* by his *last* name?" Helen took the opportunity to attack J's professionalism.

Helen never spoke to J about her gripe. Instead, Helen used the incident as an excuse to make herself Visible to The Man. In the end, J didn't look bad at all, and she and her boss had a good laugh about the whole mess because Helen was *always* looking for a reason to call a male executive in the company to discuss the lack of professionalism of one female manager or another.

The Cinderella Complexities

You know, some people are just bullies who don't discriminate—any man, woman, or small animal will do. They are negative and mean, and we suppose their purpose on the planet is to keep things interesting for the rest of us. But when it comes to the majority of abusive women in the office, we believe it's not a permanent affliction but rather a chronic ailment that flares up from time to time, one that can be immediately remedied by a reliable cure-all: consciousness.

We don't care about the whys of bullying, of the mean-girl phenomenon, of women's inhumanity to women, of same-sex cruelty, or of, as we obviously like to call it, being an Ugly Stepsister. We just want every single woman reading this book to make sure that she's *not* doing it.

Need motivation? Well, first of all, those Ugly Stepsisters *never* get the prince, but if that's not enough for ya, try this: if you mistreat a female colleague, you might be doing some pretty wicked things to your own sweet self.

♟ **If you act out with your female boss, you *will not* win.** You *will* get fired or at the very least set yourself up for a world of hurt. Need we say more? There's a word for making trouble for your boss, arguing, disobeying, being rude, or otherwise hassling her—it's called insubordination. The she-boss will have no choice but to put you on probation or fire you—no matter how long you've been there.

♟ **Generally speaking, publicly not supporting people is a losing strategy.** It might keep coworkers from wanting to deal with you on projects or personally, and it will definitely put them on alert to watch their step around you. Plus, if you constantly pick away at someone or overtly freeze them out, you will get a Reputation for being Negative, Bitchy, Small-Minded, and/or Annoying.

♟ **Gossips and snitches are not trusted.** If you betray confidences or otherwise rat out your female colleagues, the execs might be grateful for the gossip, but then each of those Uppities knows beyond a doubt that *you* can't be trusted worth a damn.

♟ **When you're engaged in overt Ugly Stepsistering (eye rolling, whispering, etc.), *everyone* in the office *sees* it.** It's not a good image—very third grade. That kind of childish behavior won't exactly make you look like management material. This behavior keeps the worst offenders down and working in the hallway for the rest of their days.

♟ **If you have two faces, one of them will invariably get smacked.** If you are caught lying or gossiping to gain favor, it will contradict any positive image you've otherwise projected to upper management. Even if your work is superior, if you are snagged in anything that whiffs of sabotage or character assassination, savvy execs will come to regard you as a manipulative phony.

♟ **You're probably not as subtle as you think you are.** Seasoned executives always see the cracks in even the most perfectly manicured manipulations.

♟ **You can get fired or sued for harassment.** Emotionally abusive behavior and outright sabotage can damage people, and if a person can *prove* it, it's off to court you go.

♟ **You might be limiting your own Options.** Chances are the person being derailed or disparaged is talented and smart—a common trait of those targeted by bullies because they are perceived as a threat. By cultivating *positive* relationships with these types, you could be doing yourself a huge favor. Very smart, talented people have a way of rising to positions of power, and one of them might eventually be in a position to help or hire Y-O-U. Think long-term.

Cat Scratch Backlash

Ladies, we have *got* to learn to stick together. Whether you know it or not, or think you care or not, women are still getting a raw deal.

Women *still* don't make as much as men. Don't kid yourself—facts are facts: according to the U.S. Department of Labor, white women earn about 73 cents to each dollar earned by a guy—and if you're black or Hispanic, you only earn 52 cents on the boy buck. Sorry, sisters! Additionally, only 1 percent of Fortune 500 chief execs shave their legs, and women hold only 79 of the 535 seats in the House and Senate.

So what does this have to do with you? Tons. Darling, we live in a world with a Costco/Sam's club group-buying-power mentality: the more people you bring together under a united cause, the better deal it is for everyone.

If we help each other rise to positions of influence in our society and all give other women a hand up rather than a kick down, we will be taken more seriously and have more power to address the needs that are significant to us: more job-sharing options for people with kids, more pay equity, better possibilities for quality-of-family-life options like telecommuting, and eliminating the dubious distinction of having women as the largest group of the "working poor."

Maybe any of those things aren't relevant to you at the moment, but trust us, honey, at some point they probably will be. And even if they never are, at the very least we need to get in the habit of treating each other better, because just like in the fairy tales, the Ugly Stepsister ends up losing her power, and her day-to-day existence is filled with bitterness and frustration.

Speaking of bitter, get a load of real quotes from some of The Girls Who Call Us, all of whom are around or under thirty years old:

"Women who have succeeded have *clawed* their way to the top and *refuse* to share."

"I think *men* are better to work with because they aren't as competitive with you."

"Women are passive-aggressive—they do it to me, so I do it back to them."

♟
△ **"Women are *viciously* competitive.** They don't hold each other up, they step on each other."

♟
△ **"A female boss is totally competitive with you** and won't help you up. She'll push you down. All she sees is a young, bright, intelligent woman who could usurp her job."

This is what the youngest of our number are saying about their female brethren. Note the repetition of the word *competitive*. Unfortunately, we've got *scads* of quotes just like these, and some that are worse—way worse.

But it's not just what we say about ourselves among ourselves, either. Seriously. One look at the bookshelf and you'll see charming titles like *Woman's Inhumanity to Women,* a 536-page treatise on how women are so horrible to each other (in a nutshell, it's your mother's fault). You'd think we are all addicted to attacking other women. Oh, and it's on TV too. Don'tcha just *love* the me-owww portrayal of women on "reality" shows? Sweet, huh?

Then there are happy headlines on the newsstand, like this one from the *National Enquirer:* "Catfight: Battle of the Network News Gals—Who's Stabbing Who in the Back?" Even when the news is good, it's bad. When Pat Heim and Susan Murphy's book *In the Company of Women: Turning Workplace Conflict into Powerful Alliances* came out, the story was advertised in the teasers on *Good Morning America* as "Corporate Catfighting: Do Working Women Keep Each Other Down at the Office?" And on and on.

Honey, we are ruining our Reputation as an entire *gender.*

Sisters in the Hood

If you truly feel you've had a disproportionate amount of negative experience with other women at work, you need to get out there and balance it with some good ones.

Join a women's professional organization like the American Business Women's Association (abwahq.org) or the National Association for Female Executives (nafe.com) and we *promise* you will meet the most generous, talented, and supportive professionals you could ever hope to meet.

If you don't know which organization to join, the best thing to do is ask women in your company which organizations they find worthwhile. It's a perfect excuse to Chat & Hum with an exec. Also, if you join one of the organizations a colleague tells you about, then you will know at least one other person when you show up at your first annual meeting. If you want to research some on your own, seekingsuccess .com has an extensive list of organizations divided by industry ("Associations" link) and catalystwomen.org is also worth a visit for good links to professional women's associations.

Now, consider this: according to poll results from careerwomen .com, 64 percent of women reported that their most important career mentors have been male. Can we fix that, please?

Look for a female mentor in or outside your company. Become a mentor to a younger or less experienced woman. Make it a point, mama. To learn about mentoring, go to womentor.com or sba.gov/ womeninbusiness/wnet.html. For info on coaching, start with coachu.com. Learn more about mentoring, internships, the future, and facts about women in the workforce—go to dol.gov/wb and click on the "By Topic" link to find easy access to info on government initiatives and statistics.

In general, try to tap into the positive female influences in your life—in person. To really do it, you need to commit some time to it, and we recommend you make it a regularly scheduled event. Otherwise it's six months later and the "let's get together sometime" still hasn't happened.

M drinks a ton of coffee and works out with Francine five mornings a week. Francine comes at 7:30, and by 9:15 they are both at their desks working. M meets with Wendy and Lee Ann, two fabulous former colleagues, on the first Wednesday of every month for lunch.

They keep it to one hour, so it's a very manageable commitment during their respective workdays. She also gets together with fourteen to twenty local businesswomen once a month on a Friday night from seven to nine.

J has Girls' Night Out with six to eight women every week, which she swears is vital for her sanity. "I get a friggin' night out, a good meal at a restaurant, and a chance to sit face-to-face and hear what's on the minds of other working women and the buzz in NYC. For a few hours a week, what could be more important to me?" Good question. Think about it.

Watch Her Back, Don't Stab It

We want you to consider making it a goal to be your sister's keeper in your office. Here's how to become a woman of substance who refuses to abuse:

- **Avoid negative generalizations about your fair gender.** There is a word for lumping all members of a sex under a single insult—it's called sexism, mama. Anytime you are tempted to woman-bash, think of the great women in your life—your mom, your best friend, and that gal you see at the gym who told you the other day that you look like you lost weight.

- **Before you act or react, ask yourself: "Would I do this to a man?"** If you wouldn't do it unto him, *don't* do it unto her.

- **Whenever possible, come to another woman's defense.** In general, make the choice to say the supportive thing about another woman rather than the destructive thing. Keep your negative opinions for bad restaurants, awful movies, and the horrible state of television (unless you work for a network).

- **Don't form your alliances on the basis of Ugly Stepsisterism.** Most of us have been seduced by those dangerous women in the office. We gravitate toward them because they lure us in with gossip and the pretense of being nice, not to mention the hope that we will no longer be the topic du jour. But if you fall for it and align yourself with non-productive energy, you will be perceived as an Ugly Stepsister your-self. In a similar vein, don't try to gain favor with an Uppity female colleague by being party to harassment, spying, or manipulation of another female coworker. If asked, say: "I just can't do that." You might lose your job, but you'll keep your integrity.

Girl is a four-letter word. We can call you girls. You can call us girls. But there are times when using the word *girl* is definitely akin to a racial slur that Dwarfs all women. You would never hear someone say, "Give it to the boy in the mailroom," yet how many times have you heard or said, "Give it to the girl at the front desk"—even if the "girl" is in her forties? Don't refer to any professional woman as a girl to a third party (although when addressing her directly, it's cool to say: "You *go,* girl"). If you hear a man referring to a professional woman as a "girl," call him on it: "Oh, you mean the *woman* at the front desk?"

Don't form your opinion of another woman based exclusively on what you've heard through gossip. You never know if it's just the old Ugly Stepsister routine.

When a woman announces her pregnancy or marriage or promotion, be positive. A woman M worked with, upon hearing the news the M was expecting her first child, said: "Good, now you'll get fat." No congratulations. How Ugly was that? Be as supportive as your best Jogbra. Be a sport and say congratulations. In fact, the two of us use that word as often as possible, even if it's just congratulations on a job well done.

Give other women the benefit of the doubt. If you've had a problem with another woman, don't automatically assume that she did some-thing conniving, underhanded, or otherwise backstabby. Get your information firsthand, not secondhand, then hear her out; don't freeze her out.

Put yourself in her uncomfortable glass slippers. No one's life is *that* easy, and certainly no one is perfect. Read *The Bitch in the House,* edited by Cathi Hanauer, and remember, you have no idea what a female coworker struggles with personally. If you feel the urge to cut a woman down because she pissed you off, assume her life sucks and try to cut her some slack instead. It will keep you from automatically sliding into ugliness.

Treat female bosses with R-E-S-P-E-C-T (even pretend respect). Even if you think your she-boss is not qualified or competent and that you could do her job better than she does, remember that the number one function of *your* job is to support her. If you can't even pretend, it's time for you to go boss shopping.

If you are in a position to hire people, make sure that you hire the best, most qualified candidate. We've known women who won't hire other women because of previous bad experience with women. We don't suggest that you hire a woman *because* she's a woman, but don't do the opposite either. Keep your mind open.

If you recognize that you feel threatened in some way by a woman in your office, go see a therapist. Just because you might *feel* threatened doesn't mean the woman is intentionally trying to make you look bad. If you're too short on cash for a shrink, pick up a notebook and try to write out what you find about her that is specifically threatening, and how you can be positive and productive in dealing with it. We swear by paper therapy.

Do good work. Focus less on the intrigue of it all and more on production.

In short: be a Big Sister, sister—not an Ugly one.

DITCH THE BITCH

Let's bitch a moment, shall we? We both love the word *bitch* and find it a very useful and fun-to-say word—in the *verb* form. As a noun, however, the word *bitch* is primarily used to shut up, shut down, dismiss, and marginalize women who do anything that couldn't otherwise be categorized as "nice."

Look around. Virtually any of the hard-nosed, successful businesswomen we can think of have been given the ever-so-facile bitch label at one time or another—or always: Martha Stewart, Madonna, Barbara Walters, Diane Sawyer, Martha Stewart, Vera Wang, Donna Karan, Jennifer Lopez, Hillary Clinton, and, of course, Martha Stewart. Notice that the bigger the success, the bigger the Bitch Reputation.

And you know, maybe all these women *have* had their bitchy episodes. Which of us hasn't? But when was the last time you heard Bill Gates, Peter Jennings, or Newt Gingrich called a bitch? Uh, only never. It works like this:

- If *he* does it, he's an **aggressive go-getter**; if *she* does the same thing, she's a pushy bitch.

- If *he* does it, he's a **strategic thinker**; if *she* does it, she's a manipulative bitch.

- If *he* does it, he's **passionate**; if *she* does it, she's an emotional bitch.

- If *he* does it, he's a **leader**; if *she* does it, she's a bossy bitch.

- If *he* does it, he's **great on the details**; if *she* does it, she's an uptight bitch.

Before you dismiss another woman as being a bitch, ask yourself how you'd characterize that action if a man did the very same thing.

If someone calls you a bitch, say: "You know, I'm just not going to accept that from you. I'm not a bitch, I'm a [fill in the blank] doing my job, thank you very much."

And, finally, if someone accuses you of being bitchy, ask her to

(continued)

be more specific: "Do you mean bitchy as in rude? Bitchy as in assertive? Bitchy as in mean? Bitchy as in threatening? Tell me, what *exactly* do you mean?" Chances are, she won't know what she meant. You'll give the accuser something good to bitch about for a while.

Like Her or Not, Here She Comes

Until every working woman becomes aware of and resolves not to indulge in competitive Ugly Stepsister behavior, odds are that somewhere along the line you will be in Cinderella's fragile slippers. You must know that the worst thing about it is not the damage that the abusive woman can inflict on you, but what you can do to *yourself* when you react to her behavior.

Here are fourteen ways to watch your step:

1. **Examine thyself.** Think first: is there anything you might have done to provoke the ugliness? Are you being arrogant, dismissive, or unkind? If so, stop it and spend the two seconds it takes to smile and be kind to the offender, and see if that resolves it. We're not advocating becoming everybody's new best friend—we're saying be respectful to one and all.

2. **Don't sink to her level.** Take the high road, mama, and don't return ugliness with ugliness. Either let it pass or confront her in a dignified, nonemotional way with your observations. They call that Being Professional. (See Chapter 14, "Held in Contempt.")

3. **Do *not* tell your boss that you are unwilling or unable to work with someone he asks you to work with.** No matter how evil you think some colleague is, you *must* work with her if the Big Cheese says so. If you fight it or say you simply can't work with her, it will only make *you* look uncooperative.

4. **Be civil.** We know so many women who feel the need to communicate in every possible language, body and otherwise, that there is some

other woman in the room that they can't tolerate. This only makes *you* look bad. Don't take The Tone. Don't fold those arms, and whaddevah you do, don't make The Face.

5. **Use humor.** We've both gotten pretty good at disarming people with unanticipated humor. It's a great diversionary tactic, but it takes practice. Just try to think of something that's funny or ironic about the situation, and make the observation with a smile. *Warning:* don't slip down into sarcasm—it's U-G-L-Y territory. Also, too many women have a one-track approach to getting a laugh: self-deprecation. But all that does is Dwarf them and make the Ugly Stepsister feel superior. Don't do it. You won't respect yourself in the morning.

6. **Be decisive.** If a mean-spirited subordinate is your direct report and her behavior is seriously hideous, boot her out as soon as possible. She will only cause you grief and impact the performance and morale of your entire team. Do not bother trying to save her from herself. Tell her what you want and what you expect, and if you don't get it, start documenting what you said and what she did (or didn't or wouldn't do). Put her on probation to show her you mean business, and if that doesn't solve it: sayonara, sistah.

7. **You never know just how Ugly things might get. Document everything you can.** Save offending emails; write down what you heard, date it, and keep it in a file in case the bully (either a boss or a subordinate) is effective in cindering your image and you find yourself in the unfortunate position of needing to defend yourself.

8. **Don't desperately try to make your Ugly Stepsister like you by bonding with her.** Be pleasant, be nice, but say *nothing* revealing about yourself. Many of us feel that sharing every detail about our lives automatically guarantees a quality relationship. It's how we girls bond with each other. For most of us, our first instinct will be to try to heal the relationship by reaching out and making ourselves even more vulnerable by confessing some shortcoming. Aaagh—don't do that! Alternatively, we'll relate some personal difficulty we may be experiencing, in order to gain sympathy. Aaagh—don't do

that either! It will only make it worse. If you even *suspect* another woman of having Ugly tendencies, don't bond! Get comfortable with the fact that some women just won't like you. You *can't* win 'em all, nor should you try to.

9. **Do not engage with this person in a "Why are you always picking on me?" discussion.** It will only make you look weak and vulnerable and give her an opening to really lay into you.

10. **Do not withhold information or in any way try to make this person's job harder.** Passive-aggression is not a good tool for defense. It's Ugly.

11. **Don't overexplain.** Bullies make us defensive. It's incredibly hard not to feel the urge to justify ourselves and overexplain. Silence, however, does not indicate guilt, it indicates strength. Resist the urge to defend or explain yourself to this person or to anyone else involved with the Ugly Stepsister's shenanigans. (See Chapter 7, "Be Snow White & Deal with Your Dwarves.") The only person you ever need to explain anything to is your boss. If the bruiser *is* your boss, see "I'll Get You My Pretty and Your Little Dog Too" on page 229.

12. **Don't complain to others about the mean coworker's treatment of you.** Again, it makes you appear vulnerable, and it also propagates the ugliness around the office faster than a guy can fall asleep after a six-pack and sex.

13. **Know who you are and what you're good at.** Don't argue with running criticism; if you do, you're feeding into that Ugly Stepsister's Evil Network of Negativity. Instead, wrap yourself in positive energy from friends who tell you how perfectly fabulous you are, indulge in activities that make you feel fab, and treat yourself to a pricy pedi— we've found a foot rub works wonders on the soul.

14. **Don't Take It Personally.** Easy to say, tough to do. It will definitely be hard not to Take It Personally, but silence is key in this situation. Be polite, say hello, but keep it at that. Don't hash and rehash things, either with the Ugly Stepsister or in your own head. Read "The Taker-of-It-Personally Dwarf" (on page 134) 150 times and follow its most excellent advice.

If you are feeling particularly courageous, you can point out to your personal piranha that she is indeed being U-G-L-Y. How? Just say, "You know, I've got a question for you: would you ever have done that to Bob in accounts receivable?"

M did this once. After returning from her *honeymoon* to find a nasty note from a female office manager on her desk *demanding* a vacation request form "immediately," M asked her: "Would you have left this note on Jordan's, James's, or Tim's [who all held the same title as M] desk the first day back from *their* honeymoons? Or would you have just brought up the form, asked if they had a good trip, and asked them to fill it out when they get a chance?"

To her credit, the office manager 'fessed up and said no, she wouldn't have left such a raggy note. She apologized to M, and we're guessing she thought twice before being thoughtless with another female colleague. *Warning:* we don't think this move would fly if the Ugly Stepsister is your boss, in which case see the sidebar page 229.

The Moral of the Ugly Story

In the end, we learned to try to love our Ugly Stepsisters, warts and all. After all, in dealing with some intensely difficult women, we learned how to manage intensely difficult people in general, an invaluable skill no matter what you do for a living.

We learned that no one, no matter what her rank, has the power to truly hurt us more than we do ourselves when we give them power over our emotions. Thanks to our Ugly Stepsisters—OK, and a couple of guys who were real jerks—we learned how to avoid taking things so personally and, equally important, how to stand up for ourselves and confront people directly without emotion and without accusation. We are currently living happily ever after, and you can too, Cindy.

I'LL GET YOU, MY PRETTY, AND YOUR LITTLE DOG TOO

Many of The Girls Who Call Us ask about what they should do when the Ugly Stepsister is either a direct supervisor or someone highly influential in the company.

We refer to these women as Wicked Stepmothers because they are in the *best* position to help other women coming up through the ranks, but don't. They are also in the best position to do the most serious career damage to a young woman, and do.

If you work for or with a micromanaging, manipulative Wicked Stepmother who you feel is out to get you or just to squash your will to live, you must proceed with great caution because she has evil magic powers. If the Wicked Stepmother is your boss, complaining about her to *her* boss will probably get you banished to the dark forest. The exec will most likely support the Wicked Stepmother and become suspicious of you. Remember that her boss probably made the choice to hire her in the first place.

If the Wicked Stepmother is not your boss but someone who is in tight with the CEO and is making trouble for you, no one will come to your rescue because *she* has the ear—and presumably the approval—of the Big Cheese.

If it sounds grim, that's because it is. Frankly, there's not a hell of a lot you can do if a Wicked Stepmother has it in for you; 99.9 percent of the time you're screwed and will need to start looking for a new jobbie. But there are some countermoves that, while they won't turn the beast into a beauty, might civilize her a bit.

- **Find a champion.** See if you know someone outside your company who will talk you up to the president of the company. As in: "Oh, I hear you have Jocelyn on your staff. She's amaazing. Hang on to that one!" If, and *only* if, that outside person is impressive enough and has enough influence with the Most Uppity Upper, then the Uppity will make it a point to know who you are and what you do for his company, which *could* force the Stepmother to cease and desist all overt wicked behavior aimed in your general direction.

(continued)

- **Toe the line.** Do your very best work. Show up on time. Don't take long lunches or spend time on personal calls. Do *exactly* what she says, without complaint or argument. Demonstrate real effort on the job and a desire to please her. She *might* just come around.

- **Get Visible.** Do what you can to make yourself Visible to other department heads. Go express interest. Offer to help. Find an influential person in the company and ask her to become your mentor. Focus your priorities on the items in your inbox that will most likely be brought to the attention of other execs, like a way to save or make a ton of money, and make sure your name is on *everything* you do.

- **Suck it up.** We don't really advocate this for most people, but for those who want to do their job, are not promotion-minded, and just want to get home to have a life, this is a viable option. But only if you can meet these three criteria: (1) if you can keep your focus on your personal plan and priorities, (2) if you can avoid taking the Wicked Stepmother's bullying personally, and (3) if your job performance isn't suffering in any way.

Chapter 14

Held
in Contempt

If you always plead the Fifth, you'll never be first

Useful Terms: What We Mean When We Say . . .
Win-Win We all win
Win-Lose Nah-nah-nah-nah-goo-goo
Lose-Lose So what was the point of all *that*?

Ah, what would life be without conflict? There would be no drama. Therefore no movies. No theater. No "he said, she said" sagas from our friends. How boring life would be if we were all just perfect little conflict-free worker bees.

Conflict in the workplace is as inevitable as cellulite. That's the fact, Jackie. And like cottage-cheesy, flubba-lubba fat, you can either deal with it or live with the lumpy, ugly consequences.

Unfortunately, by either avoiding confrontational situations or handling them poorly, you can trash your Reputation. Common postconflict epithets reported by The Girls Who Call Us include: Emotional, Wimp, Manipulative, Backstabber, Insecure, and Hysterical. J worked with a woman whose infamous hissy-fit confrontation technique, which featured screeching, yelling, stomping, and wild arm gesticulations, got her branded as a "Raving Lunatic Bitch."

Waltzing Miranda

If confrontational situations make you queasy, or if you think you might have a *teensy* problem in the Raving-Lunatic-Bitch department, here are just a few reasons to consider why you might want to get a grip on some more effective ways to deal with all those nice people called colleagues when the atmosphere becomes less than collegial:

- **When people know you are unwilling to defend yourself, they will push you beyond your limits,** asking more and more of you. Doormats don't get promoted, they get stepped on.

- **If you don't seek resolution, interpersonal problems can fester into some incredibly unfortunate self-destructive behavior,** like passive-aggression, revenge-seeking, sabotage, and paranoia, to name a few that could flatten your Reputation and/or blow a hole in your job security.

- **If your answer to *every* conflict appears to be explosive,** you may intimidate your way into a few wins, but overall, you'll lose: coworkers and execs will likely judge you as irrational, avoid you, and probably have a good laugh at your emotional expense to boot.

Here's the good news, girlfriend: you are probably better equipped than you think to be a kick-ass diplomat. All you need to do is the same thing you would if some reckless uninsured idiot plowed through a stop sign right into the driver's-side door of your new Honda Civic: call a damn lawyer.

Although Miranda rights don't exist at work—um, no lawyer will be appointed to you, honey—you can and should put yourself on retainer as your own lawyer. Y-O-U are the *only* person who can represent you, your ideas, and your side of things at work.

The old expression goes that only a fool would have himself for a lawyer. Well, in corporate America, only a fool would not act as her own.

Presumed Ignorant

Just because you've never been to law school doesn't mean that you can't quickly get the hang of what we're talking about here. How many zillions of hours of litigation have you witnessed on TV? What about all those revealing Scott Turow and John Grisham legal thrillers? Honestly, you already know how to act like a lawyer, and that's the whole truth and nothing but it.

Our friend Caroline was a brilliant pretend lawyer. A major movie buff and retail marketing VP, Caroline is a cheerful, chatty pussycat of a gal most of the time.

But when confronted, Caroline morphs into Marcia Clark: killer calm, precise, objective, strategy-minded, fearless, and armed with unassailable logic. More than once Caroline has had coworkers scurry away with their tails between their legs because they underestimated how fiercely rational and intractable she could be when she knew she was in the right. Poor little monkeys.

Caroline never lost any friends for being lawyerly in confrontational situations. In fact, she gained coworkers' respect by representing herself objectively and never bothering to waste time feeling bad for the loser of the argument. This is exactly how great lawyers—and great executives—conduct themselves: they do what they have to do, don't take anything personally, and move on to consider the next case.

It's their job, as it is yours.

The Persecution Never Rests

Watch any crime show and you'll see that the very first thing the lawyer will tell the client to do is to stop speaking. No matter what kind of conflict arises at work, the first thing you need to do is seal those lips. Silence is powerfully ambiguous; people just don't know what it means, and it drives them crazy.

The faster you react verbally when challenged or offended, the more likely you will be to say something incriminating. Think. Don't speak. Before you say a word beyond "Please give me a minute to process this," conduct a quickie due diligence—an evaluation of whether this problem is *worthy* of your attention. Cross-examine these factors:

- **Crime.** Is this a minor offense that you can ignore, or is it something that has truly impinged on your rights and/or your ability to get work done?

- **Time.** Is this issue *really* worth one moment of your precious time? Is it important to *your* agenda—or someone else's?

- **Repercussions pro & con.** What are the possible ramifications of engaging in this discussion—whether you win or lose—and do you care?

- **Reputation.** What happens if you choose *not* to confront? Will you be labeled Pushy or a Pushover? What happens if you do? Will you be labeled Confrontational, Oversensitive, or Formidable?

No Contests

If you decide the issue is *not* worthy of your time, you are not *avoiding* the problem out of fear; it's simply not in your best interest to deal with it. Do *not* explain yourself to anyone, especially that nosy coworker.

However, if you have chosen not to confront the offending party directly, never go and blab about the incident to any third party in your office—even if you feel the need to vent and have others validate your inalienable right to be livid.

What you say to others *will* get back to the unconfronted coworker, and she will *slam* you for backstabbing and not bringing the matter to her directly. Gossiping with a third party could lead the coworker to believe that you are manipulative (sabotaging her Reputation), inefficient (wasting everybody's time), and indiscreet (duh), and that you have approximately zero confidence in your own judgment, 'cause otherwise you would shut up or do something about it already.

Deposing & Disposing

If you *do* decide to confront the offending coworker, you need to prepare your argument. Build your case through full disclosure and deposition with yourself:

- **Verdict.** You must know *exactly* what you want out of the exchange. What is your ideal outcome? What are you willing to settle for?

- **The facts.** Write them down. We mean facts, not opinions, not judgments, but your *observations* of the offending behavior and your conclusions on why the behavior was objectionable. So it's not "I need you to be nicer to me because I'm sensitive" but "I need you to stop harassing me every day so I can finish this proposal by the deadline."

- **The evidence.** Always keep your own project Pelican Brief containing copies of everything, including: your notes; dates that decisions and changes in direction were made in meetings; sales projections; correspondence; etc. Thorough, well-organized documentation always speaks way louder than she said, he said, we say hearsay—say what?

This whole due diligence process could take you twenty minutes or less—whereas an inappropriate or mishandled conflict or avoidance of one could cost you your J-O-B. Take the time to give yourself your due!

If you are on the receiving end and someone is in *your* face demanding that you hear him out or explain yourself, you still should go through the same due process. You *can* take control of the situation and put the confronter off so you have time to diligently doodly-due. *Calmly* say: "Judas, I'd be happy to schedule a meeting with you to discuss this problem and how we can solve it. I cannot, however, have the discussion this minute." Caveat: if Judas is your boss, don't give him the kiss-off—you are *sooo* available to discuss it then and there.

Time and Punishment

A debate takes two. Just because you've chosen to confront someone does not mean she'll come along quietly. Your job is to dig in those heels and assert your sincere desire to have the matter addressed and resolved—like pronto. If the confronted *insists* on putting you off, don't leave her side until you have established the date for the big showdown at the not-so-OK coral.

Once you've set that time and place, show up, no matter *what*. If you don't, you forfeit your right to pursue the issue further. If the other party doesn't put in an appearance at the agreed-upon venue, don't bother with her sorry ass again—take it to a higher court, her boss. She had her chance, and she flubbed it.

Likewise, if you approach a coworker and have calmly stated your concern but cannot get him to engage or commit to a discussion date, *or* if he blasts you out of your peds, changes the subject, or otherwise makes it apparent that he will not even *consider* the legitimacy of your position, you are *sooo* D-O-N-E with him. Don't react to his belligerence; just close the mouth, move the feet, and *calmly* stroll right into a friendly HR or boss's office near you.

As long as you first take your grievance directly to the offender, the incident is strictly between you two, but once he denies you your rights in the relationship by bullying you or blowing you off, he surrenders his own. You now have 100 percent justification to spill all to the boss—not just the original issue, but also his unwillingness to work with you in that happy, productive manner called Teamwork.

Our friend Leslie, a social worker, was being badgered by her coworker Sarah. Leslie confronted her in quiet but firm tones, saying that she needed her to back off so she could finish her work. Before Leslie could finish making her point, Sarah started *scah-reeaming,* insisting on her *right* to voice her opinion "however the hell she felt like it." Leslie stopped speaking and marched into their supervisor's office. Sarah, beeee-yond pissed, condescendingly told Leslie how "not cool" it was to complain to the boss. Leslie said: "I *did* try to discuss it with you, but you were irrational, and I *refuse* to deal with that. You've got no one to blame but yourself, Sarah." As far as we know, Sarah is still trying to prove she was Right. Meantime, Leslie has moved on.

Contraptions of Entrapment

In courtroom dramas, you don't ever see the lawyers calling the accused on the phone. They go in person or send the cops to haul the defendant in. You should always do the same.

Don't confront significant matters on the phone unless you have no other option. It's too easy for the other party to hang up on you, and God knows what kind of havoc he'll wreak when you get off the line. Also, you just don't know who might be standing there listening to *his* side of the call. Finally, calling or firing off an email (which might get forwarded) is not a respectable approach. It makes you look fearful and suggests that you don't have enough respect for the person to address the issue face-to-face.

And honey, no matter how angry you are or how justified you think you might be, *never* confront the defendant in a public forum. You will almost always lose by default: eyewitnesses to a public flogging will probably never trust you again because they'll assume you will eventually blast *them* in public too.

What Pleases the Court

Like a lawyer, once actually engaged in the debate you must build your case point by point and present it in a *rational* manner. Think about those courtroom TV dramas—those lawyers are the picture of composure. Their voices, bodies, and faces are neutral and in complete control. They use volume and flashes of emotion strategically, sometimes theatrically, but never randomly. Watch *Law and Order* to rip off mannerisms, attitudes, and techniques (see the list below) that will help you keep order in the court.

☖ **Assertiveness.** It means you stand tall, speak with some volume, keep your chin up, and make your points crisply (see Chapter 9, "Speaking of Talking"). It does not mean you scream or become shrill. Look directly into the eyes of the defendant.

☖ **Dialogue reflection.** Repeat back what the other person says so he knows that you heard him: "Let me make sure I'm understanding your position, John. You say someone in accounting told you it's OK to expense condoms as long as you use them *while* on a business trip?" Reflect, don't interpret.

☖ **Charm.** Charm shows control. A well-placed smile or a joke to lighten the mood is a great tactic to disarm someone who expects you to explode. No Dwarfish self-deprecating humor, though. Also, no inappropriate mixed-message smiling, and no sarcastic humor that you will only need to retract later: "John, judging by this expense report, you must have had one helluva fact-finding mission in Topeka! Whoo-hoo, ladies and gentlemen of the jury, may I present Mr. Stud Muffin."

☖ **Relevancy.** Keep the focus on the main problemo. Don't be pointing out all the *other* things this person does that also annoy the crap out of you but are not material to the issue at hand. Your personal opinions and judgments are also irrelevant. Say: "John, company expense policies do not cover prophylactics," *not* "John, you are an out-of-control sack of shaving cream."

♟ **Resolution.** Keep your questions and comments centered around reaching a resolution. Any behavior that suggests that you are not actively seeking a *solution* means that *you* are a problem. Avoid doing *anything* that would show your motive to be humiliating the person rather than seeking a constructive end to the conflict. Say: "John, I recommend that you don't charge prophylactics to the company in the future," *not* "John, you ignorant slut."

♟ **Court reporting.** Everything you say, particularly during some type of confrontation, might be recorded on paper the second you step out of the room—they might even be pulling a Linda Tripp while you are in it. Be sure to document your side—what you said, what you heard, the tenor of it all—just in case the issue comes up later on appeal. Email yourself a summary of the exchange on the day it happened.

Out of Order

A lawyer is required to listen to all of the other party's evidence while keeping her objections only to items immaterial to the current debate. It is the respectful thing to do, and you might just learn something important, like you were wrong and have some behavior to correct on your end. If you don't do that respectful listening part (i.e., no huffing or eye rolling), then you are not defending your position; you are just defensive and will assuredly be held in contempt yourself.

Other out-of-order behaviors that won't help you in the Case of the Challenging Coworker include:

♟ **Apologizing.** You *can't* start your case with "I'm sorry I have to bring this up. . . ." You are not sorry; chances are *you* did nothing wrong.

♟ **Beating around the bush.** This is a Girlogic tactic for trying to soften the blow. It's talking round and round the mulberry bush instead of about it. If you do the runaround, you are wasting the People's time.

Grandstanding. Have a point, make it once, and move on to the next point. Do *not* try to get your opponent to agree with point number one before you move on to point number two. You are not trying to win on each fact or piece of evidence, only score.

Name-calling. This falls into the realm of personal attack and irrelevant testimony. While it might be tempting (and fun), it will make you look incompetent, defensive, and out-of-control.

Outbursts. Emotions impair your ability to think. Be objective and detached from your wonderful emotional capacity by visualizing yourself as a high-powered attorney. Unchecked emotional content can lead you to say damning things that you can't take back once you let them fly. Steady, girl, steady.

Overgeneralizing. Using words like *always* and *never* creates a digression from the land of fact into friction. Overgeneralizations are emotional, nearly impossible to substantiate, and tend to be perceived as personal attacks: "You *never* hold up your end . . . I'm *always* the one who has to coil up your *endless* slack."

Asked and Answered. Don't repeat the same question or the same point in fifty thousand different ways. In a real court, it's not tolerated except by permission, as in "May I rephrase the question?" Repeating yourself—or allowing the other guy to—leads to circular discussions. The verdict: a big fat waste of time.

Whining. One man's passionate plea is another man's whining. Make sure that you don't give the slightest hint of whining, which is basically an infantile manipulation tactic. Never utter the word *but* twice in a row, as in: "But, but, last month you saaaaid . . ." It will trip the whinometer for sure and you'll be dismissed.

Last word. Contrary to popular belief, having the last word does NOT mean you won. Think courtroom drama—does the one who presents the closing argument *always* win? No. Don't let having the last word be your goal. State your case, and if the other party doesn't agree, particularly if she's your superior, don't feel like you need to keep saying it and saying it until she capitulates. She won't. It's power struggle territory.

THE TRUTH? YOU CAN'T HANDLE THE TRUTH

When you watch those court scenes, don't you just want to throttle the guy on the witness stand who is so *obviously* lying? Every lawyer knows that despite all that swearing on the Bible, people *will* lie to protect themselves.

Don't let lies throw you off course, and whatever you do, do not directly accuse someone of lying when you're engaged in a confrontation because it will change the nature of the dialogue. If you *call* a liar a liar, you'll get the big old "How dare you?" attack for accusing her. If someone lies *to* you during a conflict, take mental note, but make no comment—it's not productive.

Console yourself with the thought that chronic liars usually bury themselves alive at some point anyway. Liars keep lying and invariably contradict themselves, giving them Reputations as either Complete Idiots or Dishonest Creeps. While all that duplicity might not burn them at their jobs, it undoubtedly strangles their personal relationships one by one. No trust = no loyalty = no friendship = the lonely life of a liar.

If someone lies *about* you in front of others, you *must* not let it pass without comment. But don't let it spiral down into name-calling. Brush off the slander like so: "Sheila, that is an absolutely false statement. I did indeed deliver the report on Tuesday," the implication being that Sheila is seriously misinformed. That said, immediately return your focus to the conflict at hand and your goal with regard to it.

Your Honor, This Is a Hostile Witness

When you are engaged in a conflict, expect that most people will be feeling rather, well, defensive. Prepare yourself to encounter obnoxiously overt tactics to derail your train of thought and mangle your argument as well as subtle tactics to divert attention away from the original issue. Here's the lineup of all the usual suspects:

Aggression. This is the tactic most people associate with confrontation and the one women have the biggest problem dealing with. It is a stridency of tone and force that the confronter—or confronted—may use as her usual debate mode. But just because someone is aggressive in her assertions doesn't necessarily mean it's a *personal* attack on your good person.

Don't confuse another woman's directness (i.e., not beating around the bush) with an act of aggression or an attack. If accused of being aggressive (aka a *bitch*) yourself, calmly say to the other party, "I am merely being direct, and I would like to get back to the original issue." Do *not* apologize or soften your approach! On the other side of the bench, if a coworker is truly aggressively hostile (shouting, swearing, or slandering), say: "I am *not* the enemy, and if you can't chill out, we can reschedule this discussion."

Deflection. This might be the first tactic someone will try when you confront him. He deflects *your* issue by changing the subject ever so subtly. Let's say you confront Kevin about refusing to cooperate on a cross-functional initiative. He replies, "Well, you don't usually work in this division." The to-do for you is to recognize the deflection tactic and say: "That may be true, but that is not the point of *this* discussion. The point is . . ."

Escalation. Escalators want a quick win. You confront, but they don't hear you out and instead jump ugly on you after your first sentence, snapping something along the lines of "How can you *say* that?" They then turn and attack you like an automatic pitching machine gone haywire. You will be so busy batting away the 95 MPH spitballs that you are supposed to forget your original issue and back down, cowering with your hands over your head. Don't. Keep your tone level. Do *not* respond to spitballs. Repeat your issue calmly. If the Escalator won't stop hurling curves at you, walk away and take it to the next highest level. Oh, and watch out for escalation in yourself—it's contagious.

Insults. The other party assaults either your logic, your intelligence, your personality, or (our favorite) your gender: "Oh, *all* girls say that . . ." Show them just how smart you are, lady lawyer, by ignoring the bait and repeating your mantra: "Let's stick to the point here, which is . . ."

If you can successfully spot diversionary tactics, not be intimidated by them, and refuse to sink to their level by returning fire with fire, you will become one of the most respected people in your office: a cool-headed diplomat whom all seek out for wisdom and advice—just like Oprah.

Triple Jeopardy Threats

Most cases never actually get to a big fancy trial by a jury of peers. Things are usually settled out of court or only make it as far as small claims. But there are certain times when you *have* to know that you can't reconcile a volatile situation on your own.

If you have any doubt about the integrity of the other person, if you are afraid that what you say will later be misrepresented, do not be alone with her. Get a third-party mediator who is senior to both parties.

If the argument has become circular in nature, seek a senior third party for assistance; otherwise you are just wasting time, causing frustration, and setting up the perfect scenario for an escalation on both sides.

If a conflict ever gets physically abusive, leave the premises immediately and report it to the police—the *real* police and a *real* lawyer. Workplace violence is real, don't mess with it.

Have You Reached a Verdict?

If to you winning is about getting an admission of guilt, you can forget about ever winning. Guilty parties seldom own up to their wrongdoing. When it's over, if you got anything near to what you wanted, consider yourself as having won.

Be aware that sometimes you may lose the argument but still win. J once wanted to get her vacation days rolled over to the following year. J's boss told her it was her own fault for not taking them, and barked at her for even asking for something that was against company policy. Rather than biting back and pinning the blame on him for vetoing her every vacation request, J said, "I won't let it happen again. So can I roll 'em?" J's boss signed off on her request. J rolled over and let her boss win the battle, but she won *her* war.

And honey, if you do win, say thank you and then button up those liperinskis—don't keep repeating why you deserved to win. Yes *always* means yes. Don't push it.

Sometimes a resolution is win-win—these are our favorites. A win-win is always the result of a collaboration, where the two parties come together in a spirit of creatively solving a mutual problem, leave their egos at the door, and come up with a solution that makes *everyone* happy. To us, this is the point of conflict—to scrape through the dirt and make room for everyone's roots to grow deeper and stronger.

Do not confuse *collaboration* with *compromise,* though. These terms do *not* mean the same thing. Compromise is the way most of us girls were taught to deal with conflict. Rather than stand up and fight for

100 percent of what we want, we were taught to make nice and split it all down the middle. The problem here is that usually *no one* is happy with what they get and no one walks away completely satisfied. It's a lose-lose proposition: resentment builds anyway, and those roots start to rot. In a deal-breaker situation, where half is better than none, compromise might be your only alternative—but know that when you choose to compromise, you are only getting half of what you *could* be getting if you were willing to stand your ground or work harder toward a creative solution that fully satisfies the interests of both parties.

The Spoils of Victory

Win or lose, when it's over, think these two words: *Case Closed*.

If you had a clear win, never say: "I told you so." We *know* it's *fabulous* to feel vindicated, particularly if you have been vilified, but no dances in the end zone, please. The world loves (but more importantly, remembers) a gracious winner. Be one.

If you lose, don't look for ways to extract alternative revenge for this same crime. The ability to move forward, to not have any hard feelings—or pretend not to, anyway—is one of the greatest strengths you can cultivate in yourself to prepare for life's inevitable conflicts. When it's over, it's D-O-N-E. Make *no* reference to it again. Move on, move on, move on. Tomorrow is indeed another day.

1

Duhs &
Don'ts

No one likes to admit that they don't know something. 'Fess up: how many times have you stood there nodding when the boss said, "Oh, of course you know about the Schlanger survey," but you really had *no* clue what she was talking about? Now, we're big fans of the fake–it–till–you–make–it school of career advancement, but there are some things you *really* gotta know, because there just ain't no excuse for not knowing them.

Unfortunately, unless you've had a been–there–done–that career mentor, most of us discover the unwritten rules by first posing as the village idiot in front of our colleagues.

Here is a quick roundup of some of the most spectacularly stupid maneuvers we've pulled or that we've seen others perpetrate—when we *all* really should have known better. At the end, you'll find our exclusive Penguin List of excuses that will never fly.

Waaay Too Damn Much Information

Carrie was late for a meeting. Her excuse? Yeast infection. OK, OK. Her boss, Samantha, was sympathetic and let it go. Two weeks later, Carrie comes in *very* late for work and tells Samantha it was because of her period. Buh-bye, Carrie.

DUH: Nobody but your doctor and yer mama wants to hear about your bodily functions or malfunctions.

DON'T ever use the words: *cramp, diarrhea, bowel(s), hemorrhoid(s), vaginal, yeast, incontinence, bloated, gas, discharge, bladder, constipation, (anal) warts.* While we're at it, skip: *phlegm, mucus, vomit, saliva, snot,* and *booger.* Caveat: if you work in the medical field, feel free to use all of the above except *booger.*

Instant Massacring

Gail had a fight with her boss and immediately ran to her office to fire off an IM to her friend about what a jerk-off her boss was. In her irate haste, however, Gail picked the wrong buddy—and accidentally sent the jerk message *to her boss,* who thereafter referred to her as his ASS-istant.

DUH: You can't take back an IM.

DON'T hit send until you double-check the recipient, and don't leave IM messages open on your screen for all the world to read when you walk away from your computer. Log out, lady.

Reading Is Fun-duh-mental

Maris had an epic email volley over the course of several days between three members of the executive team, in which she wrote terrifically snotty comments about a coworker, Daphne. Eventually the email morphed into a question that only Daphne could answer. Rather than sending a *new* email to Daphne—cutting and pasting in the last few relevant emails—Maris, forgetting the original nature of the email, forwarded the whole chain to Daphne—who read it all the way down to the bottom. An U-G-L-Y fight ensued.

DUH: People know how to read.

DON'T just use an old email to send a note to someone, particularly if you will be sending copies to other people. Either read the email all the way to the *bottom* to make sure it's OK for public consumption or create a new email.

The Intercom Before the Storm

Deb and Marie had a huge fight. Deb ran into her office, slammed the door, picked up the phone to call her friend, and started the conversation with "You won't believe what that stupid bitch Marie just had the nerve to . . ." Unfortunately, Deb had inadvertently hit the intercom button, and her conversation was being broadcast through every other phone in the office (Deb couldn't hear it, because she was on her phone). Before anyone could save Deb from herself, it was too late: the damage was done. Deb and Marie never spoke again.

DUH: Know what all those buttons on your phone do.

DON'T slam any coworker while in your office. You just never know.

My First Computer

Bridget was responsible for managing copy for an online catalogue. She was reprimanded regularly for posting unedited copy on the site and missing deadlines. Eventually Bridget was canned, and her boss discovered thousands of randomly named Word docs on her computer, all filed only under My Documents—with absolutely no subfolders or other trace of an attempt at an organizational system.

DUH: You can and will get fired for incompetence.

DON'T skimp on taking the time to set up systems for managing the information of your job; gross inefficiency is hard to hide for long.

Your Cheatin' Art

Claire interviewed for a new position within her company but never thought to mention to her boss that she was considering changing jobs. The boss found out about Claire's interview through a third party and assumed that it was a blatant act of betrayal. He looked like an idiot for not knowing that a member of his staff had applied for another job within the company. He put the kibosh on the new position *and* demoted her.

DUH: If you are interviewing for a job internally, your boss will find out about it.

DON'T forget to request your boss's blessing. The most valuable references you will ever get will be from people who have directly managed you.

Expense Suspense

Trixie claimed $20 on her expense report for a lunch with coworker Alice. The nice guy from accounting asks Alice, "Hey, when did you have lunch with Trixie?" Alice replies: "Um, never."

DUH: Expense reports are subject to scrutiny.

DON'T misrepresent or otherwise fudge expense reports; it's called theft.

I Owe Black and Blue

Wilma borrowed $400 from Betty, a friend/coworker. Wilma paid Betty back in cash. A few weeks later, Betty demanded that the debt be settled. Wilma said, "I *did* pay you." Betty said, "No, you *di'int*!" Wilma had no signed agreement, no canceled check, no receipt, no proof. The disagreement ended in court, and Wilma had to pay Betty $400—again.

DUH: People can be psycho when it comes to money.

DON'T borrow more than ten bucks from anyone at work.

Loose Lips Get Ripped

Gloria got an amazing performance evaluation—all "ones." Pleased with herself, Gloria ran out and told her friend/coworker Edith all about her many ones. Edith then received *her* review—all "threes." Edith complained to HR, which told her: "No one in the company received any ones." "Oh yeah?" said Edith, who then repeated what Gloria had said. One year later, Gloria got a "four" (out of five) in the "trustworthy" category on her annual review.

DUH: Salary and performance info is confidential.

DON'T spill the specifics (good or bad) about your private dealings with the company; there is *nothing* to be gained by doing so.

Forgotten, but Not Gone

Michelle left the original copy of her prenup agreement on the Xerox machine in her office. Later, she found out that word had spread about how her fiancé insisted on having the agreement before he would say "I do."

DUH: Most people are *dying* to know—and talk about—everyone else's secrets.

DON'T use office equipment for personal business; it can only lead to trouble. Kinko's, anyone?

Sexposé City

Blanche was trying to impress some of her male officemates by telling *Playboy*-worthy stories about her wild weekend of nonstop sex. Two days later, every single man in the office was either gawking at her or whispering, "Can you really do *that?*"

DUH: Guys would *kill* to hear your sexcapades so they can fantasize about you during boring budget meetings.

DON'T tell *anyone* a personal story too good not to repeat.

Chew Damn Much

Roseanne liked to eat. Problem was, her job was in telephone sales. All day long, Roseanne was munchin' Fritos *while* she was on the phone with clients. In between snacks, she crunched on the ice cubes in her diet Coke. She was chewed out and let go.

DUH: No one ever wants to hear chewing.

DON'T eat all day long—it's nasty.

Insensitivity Training

On the morning of the funeral of a family member of M's, a coworker called M at home to ask an inane question about a minor work issue. He *knew* that there was a tragedy in the family, yet didn't ask how she was or express any sympathy whatsoever.

DUH: When someone is dealing with a death in their family, they don't *care* about what's going on in the office.

DON'T avoid expressions of sympathy. Say you are sorry, send the note. P.S.: Don't try to be *too* original. M's seventy-six-year-old dad got a try-too-hard card after M's mom died that read: "Don't worry, Bill, you'll be with her soon enough." And don't call the day of a family funeral.

Fun-DUH-Raiser

We had a colleague with five children. The *only* time we ever saw her was when she was waving the latest school fund-raiser sign-up sheet for Girl Scout cookies, walk-a-thons, and all those raffle tickets for stuff we didn't even *want* to win.

DUH: People hate solicitors.

DON'T assault your colleagues more than once a year for fund-raising activities.

Rolling the Sick-Day Dice

Janet planned a trip to Reno but had no vacation time left. She decided to call in sick so she could tack on an extra day to a long weekend. Problem was, Jan told all her office buddies she was going to Reno for three days. So when her supervisor asked, "Where's Janet?" because he hadn't yet picked up the "cough-cough, can't-come-in-I'm-sick" voicemail from Janet, her coworkers said, "Oh, she's in Reno."

DUH: Sick people stay home in bed.

DON'T tell your coworkers your *actual* plans if you are "planning" on calling in sick.

Party Stupor

Melanie was invited to an exec's house for a dinner party but called at the last moment with regrets because she was ill. Melanie was invited a second time but declined because she "had too much work to do." The Uppity Upper took umbrage and never invited Melanie again.

DUH: People have egos.

DON'T turn down invitations from Uppity Uppers who extend themselves to you.

Snoop Doggy Dogs

We have both returned to our offices to find coworkers rifling through whatever files were on our desks; occasionally we've even caught people in a drawer, mumbling something about a Band-Aid.

DUH: People in offices are paranoid.

DON'T touch anything on anyone else's desk without permission—and don't you be walking off with that stapler either.

THE BIG SISTER'S PENGUIN LIST OF EXCUSES THAT WILL NEVER FLY

"I didn't know."

"I forgot."

"Who knew she was the CEO?"

"I left early that day."

"It was just a joke."

"I wasn't thinking."

"I got lost."

"I had too much else to do."

"Because I don't like her."

"Because it's not in my job description."

"I wasn't listening."

"I ran out of gas."

"Shit happens."

Adden-Duh 2

Stuff
you should Read
someday

Memoirs of a Geisha
Arthur Golden
**Odd Girl Out: The Hidden Culture
of Aggression in Girls**
Rachel Simmons

Overworked American
Juliet B. Schor
Virtue of Selfishness
Ayn Rand

I Don't Know How She Does It
Allison Pearson
The Nanny Diaries
Emma McLaughlin, Nicola Kraus

**Something More: Excavating Your
Authentic Self**
Sarah Ban Breathnach
Julie of the Wolves
Jean Craighead George

The 48 Laws of Power
Robert Greene
Don't Sweat the Small Stuff
Richard Carlson

What Color Is Your Parachute?
Richard Nelson Bolles
The Red Tent
Anita Diamant

**Covered Wagon Women: Diaries
and Letters from the Western
Trails, 1850**
Kenneth Holmes, ed.
Bridget Jones's Diary
Helen Fielding

**Cool Dead People:
Obituaries of Real Folks We
Wish We'd Met a Little Sooner**
Jane O'Boyle
Tuesdays with Morrie
Mitch Albom

The Courage to Create
Rollo May
Knitting for Dummies
Pam Allen, Trisha Malcolm

Marcelle Langan DiFalco is an award-winning writer and ex-urban career girl. Prior to writing *The Big Sister's Guide to the World of Work,* DiFalco spent fourteen years learning to navigate the ins, outs, and upside downs of corporate America. DiFalco first cut her teeth as a writer at *Food Arts* magazine, where she was managing editor for seven years. DiFalco is also the former editor in chief of *Eating Well* magazine and one-time vice president/editorial director of Tavolo.com. DiFalco has been a W-2er since she was fourteen and a Big Sister since she was two and a half. DiFalco lives in Vermont with her family.

Jocelyn Greenky Herz is a media consultant and writer. Herz enjoyed a successful twenty-year career as a media executive that spanned stops at Philip Morris, Wenner Media, and Hachette Filipacchi. Most recently, she launched Sider Road Media, which assists international entertainment companies in all aspects of growth including business development, marketing, and broadcast production. She is a graduate of Syracuse University. Ms. Herz lives in New York City with her husband and son.